European Transport Policy and
Sustainable Mobility

David Banister
Dominic Stead
Peter Steen
Jonas Åkerman
Karl Dreborg
Peter Nijkamp
Ruggero Schleicher-Tappeser

European Transport Policy and Sustainable Mobility

Routledge
Taylor & Francis Group

LONDON AND NEW YORK

First published 2000 by Routledge
2 Park Square, Milton Park, Abingdon, Oxon, OX14 4RN

Simultaneously published in the USA and Canada by Routledge
711 Third Avenue, New York, NY 10017

Routledge is an imprint of the Taylor & Francis Group

Transferred to Digital Printing 2009

Typeset in Sabon and Imago by NP Design & Print, Wallingford

British Library Cataloguing in Publication Data
A catalogue record for this book is available from the British Library

Library of Congress Cataloguing in Publication Data

A catalog record for this book has been requested

ISBN 0–415–231892 (hb)   0–415–23409–3 (pb)

Publisher's Note

The publisher has gone to great lengths to ensure the quality of this reprint
but points out that some imperfections in the original may be apparent.

Contents

David Banister is Professor of Transport Planning at University College London and the author/editor of sixteen books on transport policy and planning analysis, the environment and sustainable development.

Dominic Stead is Research Fellow at University College London and Visiting Lecturer at the University of the West of England. His research focuses on transport policy, spatial planning and the environment.

Peter Steen, who died in May 2000, was Professor of Natural Resources Management at Stockholm University, Director of Research at the Defence Research Establishment (FOA) and Head of the Environmental Strategies Research Group (fms), which is affiliated to both FOA and Stockholm University's Institute of Systems Ecology.

Jonas Åkerman is Senior Transport Analyst at FOA/fms and a Doctoral Student at Stockholm University.

Karl Dreborg is Research Leader and Principal Transport Analyst at FOA and Acting Head of fms.

Peter Nijkamp holds a Chair in Regional Economics at the Free University, Amsterdam. His research interests are quantitative approaches to issues related to economic development, mobility and sustainability.

Ruggero Schleicher-Tappeser is Director of EURES – Institute for Regional Studies in Europe – in Freiburg. He is involved in research and consulting concerning transport and regional development policy for a range of clients, including the European Commission, businesses, national and local governments and NGOs.

Acknowledgements

The inspiration for this research arose from Task 13 in the DGVII's 4th Framework Strategic Research programme in 1995. On a cold spring day, a group assembled in the Tinbergen Institute in central Amsterdam to discuss the possibility of putting forward a collaborative bid. Even at that early stage, it was realized that something special was being created, in terms of the different perspectives of the researchers and the potential for innovative thinking on policy scenario building. From that starting point, the Consortium emerged, and in true EU fashion decided on the POSSUM acronym – **PO**licy **S**cenarios for **SU**stainable **M**obility.

Over the next two and a half years, a tremendous amount of work was carried out on the conceptual framework, the modified backcasting methodology, the setting of the policy targets, and the building of the Images of the Future, together with the lengthy process of discussion with the expert groups. The development of the Policy Packages and the Paths took quite sometime (longer than expected), and provided an unexpected challenge to the Consortium, as this was the crucial link between the theoretical framework developed and the actual policy process. The project has provided the most interesting experience in international collaborative work in which many of the members have participated.

In addition to the authors of the book, we would like to thank the following individuals who also participated in the project – Christian Hey, Alan McLellan, Anu Touminen, Veli Himanen, Maria Giaoutzi, Zenia Dimitrakopoulou, Sytze Rienstra, Hadewijch van Delft, Leif Hedberg, Sven Hunhammar, Viacheslav Arsenov and Wojciech Suchorewski. To this list we also add Keith Keen, our project officer from DGVII, who took enormous interest in our work and participated in many of the debates. Although the book has been authored by seven individuals, important contributions have been made by each of the individuals mentioned above. We trust that this book is a fair reflection of the innovative research and wonderful collaboration carried out by the POSSUMs.

Peter Steen died in May 2000 after the completion of this book. All the fellow contributors and researchers in the POSSUM Consortium would like to recognize Peter's work in transport research – he was one of the few individuals willing and able to challenge conventional wisdom. We remember him also as a colleague and a friend. This book is dedicated to him.

'Rail travel at high speed is not possible, because passengers, unable to breathe, would die of asphyxia' Dr Dionysys Lardner (1793-1859) – Professor of Natural Philosophy and Astronomy, University College London.

Lardner also contended that no large steamship would ever be able to cross the Atlantic, since it would require more coal than it could carry. Two years later, in 1837, the *Great Western* crossed the Atlantic.

Chapter 1

Introduction

1.1 Challenging conventional wisdom

One of the great challenges facing policy-makers at the start of the 21st century is to reconcile the different priorities between economic development and environment, whilst at the same time recognizing the different social priorities and the distributional consequences of decisions. Transport offers us the best example of the complexity of these choices. In the past, a high-quality transport system has been seen as an essential prerequisite for economic development and many major investments in transport have been justified on non-transport criteria. This established wisdom has now been questioned, particularly where high-quality well-connected networks already exist (Banister and Berechman, 2000).

Additional links in these networks will result in changes in accessibility, and bring some transport benefits, at least in the short term, through travel time savings. But the additional benefits of inward investment and new employment are not proven. As the transport benefits make up a smaller part of the total economic benefits, it becomes increasingly important to examine the non-transport factors. However, even where there are well-connected established networks, there may still be substantial transport benefits in particular situations, where, for example, missing links are opened or where substantial bottlenecks are eased. But analysis must address more than just the physical aspects of the network. The real value added is reflected in making the existing transport systems and the complementary communications networks compatible, through common organizational and operating systems, and through high-quality monitoring and information systems. It is the integration of networks in this wider sense that true value added is obtained.

In addition to the debate over the economic impacts of new transport investments, policy is equally concerned with the environmental and social costs of transport. It is now widely recognized and accepted that transport in Europe is unsustainable, and that the trend-based path of continuous and continuing growth is unacceptable. This understanding is crucial to the development of transport policy at both the national and European levels. Although there is common agreement on the nature and scale of the problem, little is being done to change the direction of policy in a fundamental way. It is argued (CEC, 1998*a*) that the economic growth objectives of policy are crucial to the competitiveness of Europe and that an explicit realignment of policy objectives towards environmental and social measures will weaken this position – so little real change has taken place.

The view taken in this book fundamentally differs from this conventional wisdom. It is strongly argued here that longer term economic objectives of transport policy are compatible with the wider environmental and social objectives. A sustainable transport policy for Europe is achievable. More important, it is not a costly policy, nor will it result in a major reorganization of lifestyles and businesses, as it can be achieved through a mixture of technologically oriented policies, complemented by actions to reduce the transport intensity of people's and firms' activity patterns. However, it is not easy to achieve change in the transport sector as it will require people to accept that change is necessary. It requires the involvement of all actors and the process and the acceptance of responsibility for change. More important at this stage is the necessity for leadership and the implementation of measures to bring about change. We suggest such leadership can either come from the European Union (top-down) or from the people as a whole (bottom-up) or through a combination of actions at both levels.

The European Union (EU) is in a unique position, as it is the largest population centre in the developed world and as it has one of the highest GDP per capita figures. It is a powerful global player and it can take the lead in promoting sustainable transport policies. In addition, it has the advantage of relatively high densities, strong city centres, and a tradition of using public transport and other green modes of travel. There is an opportunity for Europe to develop a truly sustainable transport system, to demonstrate the 'art of the possible', and as a consequence to take a leadership role within the world (Figure 1.1).

The rhetoric here may all seem wishful thinking to the true sceptics. Some may say let Europe take the lead. We all watch, wait and see. If a serious attempt is to be made to achieve sustainable transport, then a group of nations has to take the lead and demonstrate the art of the impossible. This is the challenge that has been taken up by the EU, and by the end of this book, we hope that considerable reassurance will have been given to the sceptics, and that a strong push will have been given towards policies to promote sustainable mobility at the EU level. The consequences of not taking positive actions are well known, as the environmental and social costs of transport increase. Even within Europe, there are tremendous variations between nations, as some countries have much higher levels of mobility, of car ownership and of energy intensive lifestyles. Other countries have much lower levels of transport consumption, but are rapidly increasing their use of transport. The same patterns are reflected at the sub-national and the local levels within each country (SACTRA, 1999).

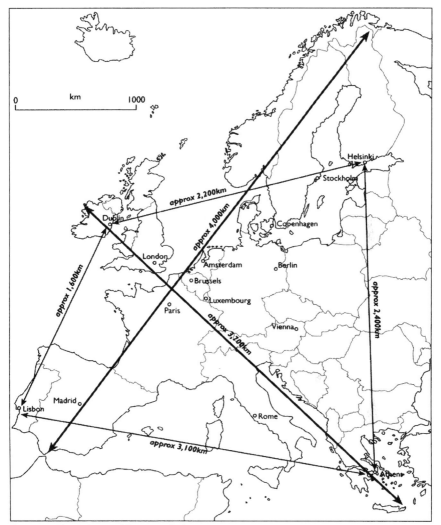

Figure 1.1 Physical map of Europe with distances

Our intention is not be prescriptive, but to describe what is happening in Europe at the international level, and to explore through a scenario building exercise the options for change. The approach adopted is a discursive one, based on the development of policy scenarios, through a visioning process, the setting of targets, and the imaginative packaging of policy measures to achieve the scale of change required. At all stages in the process, expert groups have been used to sound out the visions of the future, the targets, and the policy measures and packages. This essential feedback has helped clarify all stages of the research, and it has also helped to highlight cultural differences, omissions, and some of the difficulties in the implementation of effective action. It has also helped to emphasize the need for action and the general support for new approaches to achieve sustainable mobility.

In this book we have taken a necessarily precise definition of sustainable mobility, set within the broader concept of sustainable development. Sustainable development is a global concept and it requires all sectors in society to stay within the total global sustainability levels. Transport and sustainable mobility is one important sector. We have argued that in our future year (taken as 2020), there should be a substantial reduction of non-renewable energy used in transport from the levels in our base year (1995). In this calculation, we have not included the energy costs tied up in the construction of the infrastructure (and its maintenance), nor in the production (recycling and maintenance) of vehicles using the system. We have only included the energy costs in the use of the transport system. This in itself is a challenging target, as there is a strong expectation that travel will increase by at least 63 per cent over this 25-year period (1995-2020), if current trends and economic growth expectations are continued (Table 1.1). It can be argued that this trend figure is rather modest as the growth over the previous 25 years (1970-1995) was much higher (107 per cent) than the expected increase (63 per cent) over the next two and a half decades.

Table 1.1 Expected transport volume development between 1995 and 2020 in EU15 and Norway, Switzerland and Turkey

	Mode	Volume (billion passenger-km/ billion tonne-km) 1995	Reference case 1995-2020	Expected percentage increase reference case 1995-2020	Actual percentage increase 1970-1995
Passenger	Car	3590	5380	50	125
	Aeroplane	400	1200	200	250
	Bus	370	480	30	50
	Train	290	350	20	40
Freight	Lorry	1130	2260	100	160
	Train	240	240	0	-5
	Inland water	120	130	10	10
Total		6140	10040	63	107

Note: The reference case is built upon fairly conservative assumptions that growth rates will decrease over time.
Source: ECMT (1997), EUROSTAT (1997).

The imperative to achieve more difficult targets has been set by two landmark global agreements – the Rio Stabilization targets for carbon dioxide (CO_2) emissions (1992) and the Kyoto Protocol (1997), where allowable greenhouse gas emission[1] levels have been assigned for 2008-2012. The total commitment is for the industrialized countries to reduce their greenhouse gas emissions by 5.2 per cent on the 1990 levels. Within the EU there is an overall target of an 8 per cent reduction and this has been redistributed according to the internal 'bubble' agreement (Table 1.2). Demonstrable progress in achieving the overall target should be clear by 2005. All the EU15 countries have now ratified the Kyoto Protocol and have the responsibility to achieve their individual mandatory targets. Even though the agreements reached at Rio (1992) and Kyoto (1997) mark a significant change in global policy on the environment and are a considerable achievement in their own right, the real actions need to be taken so that the substantial reductions in CO_2 emissions are realized. This is the new challenge and one that this book directly addresses through the scenario building process within the EU15 context.

Table 1.2 The internal distribution of the EU15 'bubble'

Country	Internal Commitment (% change from 1990 levels)
Austria	−13
Belgium	−7.5
Denmark	−21.0
Finland	0
France	0
Germany	−21.0
Greece	+25.0
Ireland	+13.0
Italy	−6.5
Luxembourg	−28.0
Netherlands	−6.0
Portugal	+27.0
Spain	+15.0
Sweden	+4.0
United Kingdom	−12.5

Source: Grubb, Vrolijk and Brack (1999)

1.2 Rationale and structure of the book

The basic thinking behind the book is that we need to have a fundamental rethink about EU transport policies and priorities so that real progress can be made towards sustainable mobility. Trend-based analysis does not lead in the appropriate direction as it is predicated on trying to mitigate the steady and relentless increase in travel, rather than attempting to stand back and take a longer (and wider) perspective on the problem. Scenario building approaches permit the perspective to be more holistic, trend breaking, and to view transport within its wider economic and social development context. It is the first time that such an exercise has been undertaken, with a range and depth of ideas and experiences, that none of the participants[2] in the research could have anticipated. This is the rationale for the book. It is intended to present both the scenario building methodologies and the substantive research results. We feel that both the method and the empirical findings offer new perspectives on the understanding of and investigation of transport problems at the EU level.

The book is split into three main parts. In Part 1, the context is set as the recent changes in European transport policy are presented. First, the more general forces of change in the transport sector are outlined, covering the globalization trends in the economy, the new service and knowledge-based growth sectors, the changing demographic structure of the population, the decentralization of cities, the growth in affluence and leisure activities, and the fundamental institutional and organizational changes taking place in transport (caused by technology, privatization and deregulation, for example). Economies (and societies more generally) are in a state of transition and rapid change. In one sense, this may give rise to even greater pressures on the transport system, but in another it suggests there are new opportunities to change the way in which many transactions take place.

In the following two Chapters, Chapters 3 and 4, the more specific trends in European transport are covered, together with the policy responses. It is here that unsustainable growth patterns are described and it is shown that many of the indicators of travel are increasing rapidly (such as the number of vehicles, the volume of traffic, trip lengths), together with the growth in congestion and transport intensity (defined here as a measure of the economic activity – or of the energy consumption – as a ratio of passenger movements or freight movements or a combination of both).

This analysis of trends is complemented by a presentation of the European Common Transport Policy (CTP) since its genesis as part of the Treaty of Rome (1957), which set up the EU, to the latest priorities outlined in the Communication to the Commission on the CTP – Sustainable Mobility: Perspectives for the Future (CEC, 1998a). The final two Chapters in Part 1 of the book present the means by which we can measure sustainable mobility through indicators and targets, together with an assessment of the potential for actually achieving the targets set. One underlying common element is the realization that policy measures have to be carefully packaged together for effective action. Individual policy measures can help, but it is only when individual measures are put together in combination that real progress can be made. This makes the measurement and the monitoring of change important in assessing the effectiveness of the policy packages, and single indicators are likely to be replaced by more sophisticated composite measures. It also means that there must be a continuous process of monitoring so that policy adjustments can be made as and when needed. The process of policy implementation is a continuous and flexible one.

In Part 2 of the book, we outline the scenario building methodology. This central group of four Chapters brings together the major methodological contributions that this book makes to the analysis of sustainable mobility. First, in Chapter 7, the scenario building process is outlined in terms of its structure, organization and purpose. Included here are a review of past applications, the background literature review, and the use of the backcasting methodology. This Chapter is followed by the two major components of the scenario building process.

Firstly, in Chapter 8, targets for sustainable mobility in 2020 are set. As mentioned earlier, we take as a starting point the assumption that there should be a substantial reduction in the use of non-renewable energy sources in the transport sector (about 20-25 per cent) in our target year (2020) from the level in our base year (1995). From that we calculate the environmental targets that would have to be achieved, and in addition we establish two other sets of targets, one set relating to the economy (cost recovery and subsidy) and the other to the cohesion objectives of the peripheral regions (through accessibility). These targets are central to the estimates of the changes in the amount of travel that can occur in the 25-year period between 1995 and 2020, in both the freight and passenger sectors. As we will see in those Chapters, the actual amount of travel will vary according to the amount of technology push within each of the scenarios.

In Chapter 9, we use these targets for sustainable mobility to help formulate the Images of the Future. These Images are predicated on the assumption of different types of development within the EU, whether there is a cohesive emphasis in policy with strong central direction, or whether decision-making is much more devolved to the regions. In addition to these two fundamental assumptions, we also put a different emphasis on the technological push that will take place and the complementary decoupling policies necessary to reduce transport intensity. It should be noted that these Images of the Future are not prescriptive but indicative of the types of changes that we might expect, and the levels of change that will need to be achieved if the objective of sustainable mobility in transport is to become a reality, given the different policy assumptions. It is not likely that any of these visions will actually be realized: the future is likely to be a compromise between several of these visions.

In the final Chapter of this Part, we put together appropriate policy measures that will help achieve the targets set in the scenario building process. These policy measures must be packaged to promote the interaction between them and to ensure there is complementarity and value added between them. This is where the backcasting procedures are important, because this process allows us to mix packages together, to emphasize the importance of phasing so that new elements can be introduced, and to give some indication of when action needs to be taken by the policy-makers. All these stages of the scenario building process have gone through an extensive validation process with different groups of experts being asked to comment on the targets, the visions and the policy packages. This process is a lengthy one and requires clear objectives to ensure that these three stages of the scenario building process are fully understood, and that the experts can and are contributing fully to the process of modification of targets, visions and policy packages.

The surprising conclusion from this part of the analysis is that there are many ways in which challenging targets for sustainable mobility can be achieved. This achievement can be facilitated through a greater emphasis on the technological improvement on reducing the transport intensity of movement, or through a combination of both. We started out by thinking that our targets for sustainable mobility would be extremely difficult to achieve over this time period (25 years). In practice, we have found that there are several different ways in which these targets for sustainable mobility can be achieved, but in each case strong intervention and action are required beginning in the near future (3-5 years), otherwise the targets will not be achievable by 2020.

Part 3 of the book brings together the policy actions and the conclusions from the scenario building process. In Chapter 11 the different Policy Packages are presented and elaborated. In each case, the policy measures are put together under headings such as the role of the electric vehicle in cities, fair and efficient distribution of mobility (tradable mobility credits), liveable cities, ecological tax reform, promoting dematerialization in the economy, and promoting subsidiarity. We also consider the means by which these packages can be presented to policy-makers and the public. In many cases the basic measures are well known, but the innovative aspect presented here involves the putting together of the measures, so that they are not all seen as being negative, but that there are also strong positive elements within each of the packages.

In the final Chapter we return to the broader issue related to the limits of technology and decoupling. Our conclusions here are that there must be a strong push on both dimensions, if sustainable mobility is to be achieved. In addition, we discuss the important role that the different actors have to play in the process, and the means by which strong support can be obtained both from politicians and business, but more importantly from the general public. It is here that the implementation issues must be debated and discussed in an open forum. Unless there is support for the types of changes discussed in this book, together with the implementation of policy packages, there is little chance that sustainable mobility will be achieved over the next 25 years.

However, as with all such analysis there are still many questions that need to be addressed. In particular, we have concerns over the huge growth in long-distance travel, particularly by air and for leisure activities. This potentially large growth market has not been extensively examined within this research, but should be given far greater emphasis in future.

Within the freight sector, there are many potentially useful measures and packages that could be introduced to increase both the dematerialization of distribution processes, which is already taking place in many sectors, and in the regionalization of distribution networks so that the transport components of many products can be minimized (glocalization). There are many possibilities for reducing the transport intensity of distribution and production processes in the freight sector. The question here is whether this is something that the market can accommodate itself, or should there be strong intervention from the EU and other levels of government. In the passenger sector, it is much harder to achieve the objective of sustainable mobility, critically in the leisure market.

We started out by thinking that it would be extremely difficult to achieve sustainable mobility in the EU through strong policy action, directed either from the centre or through more devolved decision-making. In retrospect, we have come to the conclusion that sustainable mobility in the transport sector is achievable within Europe, provided that strong action is taken at various levels of government and provided that it has the support of the many actors within the process. Furthermore, it may be possible to have strong action on both the technological and the decoupling dimensions of policy. We have found that the necessary policy actions are perhaps not as costly as we first anticipated. So, rather than trading the higher levels of technology with lower levels of decoupling, or higher levels of decoupling with lower levels of technology, it could be possible to push hard on both the dimensions to achieve large reductions in the use of non-renewable energy in transport and the transport sector over the next two or three decades.

Notes

1 Greenhouse gases – there are six greenhouse gases that are included in the Kyoto Protocol. The most important in the context of this book is carbon dioxide which accounts for 80 per cent of all greenhouse gas emissions from the industrialized world. Transport is a major contributor to CO_2 emissions, accounting for 25 per cent of the total. Emissions of methane (CH_4) and nitrous oxide (N_2O) have declined in the 1990s, but the other three are also important – chlorofluorocarbons (CFCs), Tropospheric Ozone (O_3) and Stratospheric Water (H_2O).

2 The POSSUM Consortium has members from University College London; Free University of Amsterdam; National Technical University of Athens; the Environmental Strategies Research Group in Stockholm; EURES – Institute for Regional Studies in Europe in Freiburg; VTT – Technical Research Centre of Finland in Helsinki; Warsaw University of Technology; and the Ministry of Transportation of the Russian Federation in Moscow.

Part One

The background context to European transport policy

Chapter 2

Forces of change in transport

2.1 Introduction – the drive for mobility

Spatial mobility is at the heart of human activity. It is reflected in nomadic behaviour in historic times, and as long distance commuting in modern times. The Greek philosopher Heraclitus once summarized his view on the world concisely in two words, *panta rei*, meaning 'everything is in motion'. This statement seems to fit our modern world very well, where mobility, interaction and communication have become a leading characteristic: motion is the driving force of progress. The increasing mobility of persons and goods is also a worldwide source of concern. Clearly mobility is a 'normal' and even positive phenomenon in a growing economy. It may increase economic efficiency through gains of trade and labour mobility and it also offers more social opportunities to all members of society through better access to a wide variety of amenities. But there is a growing awareness that the positive effects of mobility are offset by negative externalities such as environmental pollution, congestion or lack of accessibility, and high accident rates. There have been numerous studies on the impacts of transport on the development of regions and cities (Banister and Berechman, 2000; Bruinsma and Rietveld, 1998) and the social costs of mobility (Verhoef, 1996).

Current trends in transport indicate that the system is moving away from sustainability and that major changes are necessary to make the transport system more compatible with environmental sustainability. The industrialized world has the highest transport mobility rates. In particular, the economic heartlands of the developed world have to cope with unprecedented volumes of traffic, and traffic in urban areas is a major problem causing high social costs. Clearly, transport is a necessary part of economic development, but also causes a wide range of negative externalities in the form of congestion, safety, environmental pollution, landscape destruction and solid waste (discussed in more detail in Chapter 3). According to recent estimates, the external costs of transport (excluding congestion) amount to 7.8 per cent of Europe's GDP (International Union of Railways, 2000), and this figure is gradually rising in all countries. In the light of recent policy targets to reduce not only the growth of pollution emissions, but also their absolute levels, it is clear that transport activities contribute to unsustainable development, especially in urban areas (OECD/ECMT, 1995; Stead, 2000).

A wide range of policy measures has recently been proposed to cope with the high social costs of geographical mobility, such as information campaigns, user charges, emission standards, mobility constraints, new forms of land-use and physical planning, and new transport technologies. The main objective in most urban areas is also to stimulate public transport and to reduce car use (Pharoah and Apel, 1996; Banister and Marshall, 2000). Experiences from different countries and cities, however, have shown that there is no single unambiguous and effective remedy. One observation is clear: at both a global and local scale, modern societies appear to be characterized by an unprecedented increase in spatial mobility. The dynamic behaviour of all actors involved (the demand side) and the rapid change in modern transport modes (the supply side) have led to a dramatic rise in the 'mobility radius' of individuals and businesses.

Clearly, transport and communications systems have never been static, but always in a state of flux. In general, transport modes appear to exhibit a product lifecycle marked by phases of take-off, adoption, market penetration, large-scale use, saturation and declining market shares. They then tend to be overtaken by more adequate transport systems. Parallel to transport technologies, transport management styles also exhibit similar lifecycle phenomena. Technical change may intervene here by providing new hardware to facilitate better control or enhance the quality of information, but even if no new technologies or management styles become available in the near future, drastic change in the flows of persons, goods and information might still emerge, notably for two reasons.

In the first place, we increasingly witness a shift in emphasis from isolated transport modes towards integrated systems technology. This implies a more efficient use and management of (sometimes competing) transport infrastructure. It should be noted that an open European market will supposedly generate a high degree of internationalization of all national economies, thus including an increase in international freight transport, commuting and telecommunications. In short then, we notice that transport cannot be conceived of as a self-regulatory system.

Secondly, in the long run, different transport modes may change fundamentally, since various current modes of transport seem to be in the final phase of their lifecycle. In addition, completely different modes of transport may appear. The current revolutionary changes in the field of superconductivity may induce a new generation of rapid, environmentally friendly and energy saving vehicles. In the field of passenger transport, new developments causing changes on the demand side may be distinguished, such as demographic ageing processes, new forms of lifestyle, increased labour force participation, urban sprawl, increased use of telecommunications, flexibility of economic activities, and so on.

In this Chapter, we present a broad perspective of the changes that are taking place globally and in Europe, as they impact upon transport. It is not a deterministic view that all futures are known and that the continued growth in mobility is inevitable. This Chapter recognizes the recent periods of unprecedented change with new driving forces appearing in the economy. The general perspective is one of optimism and opportunity, as technology and new forms of production allow us to be even more efficient and competitive (Sections 2.2 and 2.3). These fundamental economic forces are then set against the new challenges taking place in Europe (Section 2.4), particularly in terms of expansion and integration of the EU and the implications for transport (Section 2.5). The difficulty and scale of the changes required in the transport sector, if we are to develop policies based on sustainable mobility, are also recognized (Section 2.6). This Chapter throws down the challenge which is taken up in the substantive scenario building analysis in Part 2. It sets the scene on the nature and scale of change taking place globally, and as it affects Europe. Indirectly, it also accepts the uncertainty of the future, but it equally accepts the need for new approaches to analysing that uncertainty.

2.2 Recent developments in transport, communications and mobility

At the outset, it should be noted that transport, communications and mobility are rarely (if ever) used or provided for their own sake. They are usually regarded as 'derived demand'. In other words, they are a means to achieving objectives associated with everyday life in our society, such as getting to and from work, and they reflect a basic division which has come to characterize industrial societies – the increasing spatial separation and fragmentation of activities. The demise of the local shop is one such example. The concentration of major public sector investments in, for example, health care or educational facilities in the form of very large all purpose hospitals or schools, is another (see, for example, Stead, 2000). These trends, combined with the increasing tendency for people's homes to be located in suburban and peri-urban areas, create spillovers and consequences for transport policy, not only at a local scale, but also at a national level, while at the same time the importance of the information sector for reinforcing the dynamics of spatial communication is increasing. Some recent developments in this field will briefly be described here in order to sketch a background for this book. The main emphasis in this Section will be on freight transport, passenger transport and information/communication transfer.

2.2.1 Freight

In the area of freight transport we observe the following developments in many European countries:

1   The production of more and more high value, low weight commodities. A decreasing amount of material is needed per unit of national product (dematerialization). This is partly due to the growing share of the service sector, such as the information society in the economy. On the other hand, more sophisticated products are made, while at the same time savings in the use of raw materials have been achieved.

2   Due to a growing segmentation in lifestyles and in product technologies, a more market oriented approach has come to the fore. More diverse, smaller products play an important role, with direct consequences for the geographical distribution of resources and products. Given this shift in product types, road and air transport carry an increasing share of total transport at the expense of modes that used to be more efficient for bulk products (such as water transport and pipeline transport).

3   At the same time, combined transport of previously competitive modes, especially road-rail transport (container traffic) and road-air transport, is becoming more important, in order to increase efficiency and to avoid congestion.

4   The development of transport informatics and logistics as key factors for more transport efficiency and integration is also important. The JIT (just-in-time) principle is one such an example. These trends will affect the spatial configuration of European economies substantially (in terms of mobility patterns and location patterns for example). A further shift in the emphasis of activities of large worldwide transport operators from physical exporter to the role of co-ordinator may be expected. Concepts like door-to-door transport and, increasingly, person-to-person transport (for reasons of security), demand a refinement of the distribution pattern and at the same time greater flexibility. However they also imply fewer degrees of freedom due to these integrated transport concepts.

5   An important element in a European economic context is the globalization of the economy in general. This global shift goes hand in hand with an economic reorientation. Products are increasingly being made by transnational companies for worldwide markets. Energy, raw materials and intermediate goods are obtained at great distances. Within Europe this trend will result in large flows of products between countries. These dynamics constantly call for adaptation and, more importantly, for anticipation of changing economic conditions. It is also clear that this globalization needs full exploitation of telematics possibilities, although the spatial, organizational and socio-economic effects of telecommunications are in general difficult to predict (see Nijkamp et al., 1996).

2.2.2 Passenger transport

In addition to changes in freight transport, there are also significant changes in passenger transport which are related *inter alia* to demographic, socio-economic and technological developments. Some important developments in the field are:

1 Changing population growth. In most Western European countries, birth rates are decreasing and the number of older people is growing, although migration rates and spatial mobility still cause a considerable degree of spatial dynamics. This demographic trend will have serious impacts on the quantity and composition of the working population in the next century, in terms of labour shortages for example.

2 The trend towards smaller and alternative types of households, which affects the need for housing (higher space consumption per head, a disturbed housing market and higher car ownership).

3 After the economic crisis in the 1980s, most countries have experienced stable or slowly increasing income levels which have affected mobility. We now see a dramatic increase in the number of first and second private car owners, partly due to an increase in female labour force participation, partly due to an increase in part-time employment, and partly due to the second generation of suburbanized households. In many cases recent European statistics indicate that motorization has resumed its growth after the economic crisis of the 1980s, resulting in an ever increasing private car use at the cost of public transport modes.

4 Another geographical development in almost all European countries concerns increased commuting and urban sprawl (suburbanization). Generally speaking, rising incomes have contributed to higher car ownership and an increased separation between home and work. Furthermore, the distance between activities has grown considerably. These changes took place at the expense not only of public transport but also at the expense of the environment, particularly in and around large cities.

2.2.3 Information and communication

In the field of information and communication transfer we have witnessed various important changes. Examples are:

1 Production systems going through a phase of structural transition, in which information plays an important role in improving the effectiveness and efficiency of logistic organizations. These future production systems may be expected to exhibit closely interwoven interactions in which communications and transport play a key role. The

just in time (JIT) concept, for example, causes an increase of delivery frequencies, and with it an increase of road haulage.

2   Although from a technical viewpoint the modern telecommunications sector can be seen as a substitute for many physical interactions, this modern technology will be necessary in order to compensate for the rapid increase in physical and human interactions in modern society. At the moment there is incomplete evidence in this respect, especially because the developments in the field of transport logistics and telecommunications are experiencing rapid growth.

3   High-tech, telecommunications and telematics will have a large impact on the development of new rapid modes such as high-speed trains and larger aeroplanes. Modern electronics and informatics have the potential to provide more environmentally friendly solutions. New transport technology, pre-programmed routing and efficient organizational structures and management will make such developments possible.

4   Advanced communications technology may structurally change the demand for passenger and freight transport (telecommuting or teleshopping, for example). On the other hand, the information society may lead to more flexible working arrangements with an increasing number of commuters without a fixed place of work, relying more heavily on the car.

This sketch of important developments in the field of commodities, passengers and information illustrates the importance of the new drive for mobility. Transport provides a clear illustration of the wider changes that are taking place in the global economy. These in turn are resulting in new patterns of mobility and they have strong implications for all aspects of economic life.

2.3   The changing economy

The transformation from stable development to structural dynamics is a marked and noteworthy feature of our modern economy. The external environment of business life has drastically changed in recent years: new markets, new international policy arrangements, new technologies, new tastes of consumers and so on. Business life is faced with a great variety of new challenges and opportunities. In this Section we address four major driving forces impacting on mobility behaviour and their expected consequences for economic activities (see Figure 2.1). These four drivers are: the emergence of global markets, the development of industrial networks reflected in particular in various forms of outsourcing, the rise in flexibility in working arrangements leading to a 24-hour economy, and the trend towards economic and political power concentration in large-scale agglomerations.

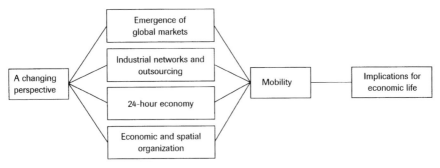

Figure 2.1 Driving forces of mobility

2.3.1 The emergence of global markets

Although it is an exaggeration to call the world a global village, it cannot be denied that the action radius of economic activities has increased to an unprecedented degree. The rise of global markets and global players is particularly noteworthy. The globalization trend not only leads to the flow of more goods, services, people and information, but is also accompanied by new foreign investments, not only in the industrialized heartland of the world, but in all regions where new opportunities are likely to emerge. This means that there is a trend towards a Schumpeterian1 economy with a strict competition for new market opportunities.

In the same vein we also observe the development towards globally operating commercial companies. The globalization trend is also reflected in worldwide integrated product markets, access to global knowledge and technology, and the emergence of global capital markets. The improvement in transport technology and the extension of transport networks also causes a geographical spread of commodity markets.

Business enterprises are shifting their operations towards locations with the most favourable cost-efficiency or productivity. New competitive factors seem to become important drivers of location and investment decisions of entrepreneurs. This holds not only for globally operating, multinational companies but also for firms with a local or regional sales market, which are faced with strong competition from outside.

In a competitive global market we observe monopolistic competition elements with distinct market niches, a phenomenon sometimes called the 'hamburger economy'. This type of economic organization is based on rationalized and standardized products (Coca-Cola, McDonalds and so on), which have a worldwide image, and whose marketing activities have a high penetration rate. Thus, it seems that the trend towards global markets will be accompanied by a trend towards worldwide market niches.

2.3.2 Industrial networks and outsourcing

A phenomenon that is accompanying the current globalization is the trend towards a network economy at all levels: from the local through to the regional, national and global levels. Industrial interdependencies are emerging in an attempt to minimize costs in a mature industrial economy, in particular through outsourcing. The fierce competition in mature markets leads to a trend towards a concentration on core activities, with a strong emphasis on a logistic organization of production. Physical production may then become more fragmented with the loss of integrated chain production within the firm, while assembling and distribution gain in importance. The emerging component industry is based on worldwide trading and transport (Lagendijk, 1994).

The new information and communication technology (ICT) sector allows for a sufficient and efficient co-ordination of dispersed production patterns. Production tends to become also more footloose, due to the integrating potential of the ICT sector. Global networks are supporting this phenomenon, not only in terms of industrial linkages, but also in terms of infrastructure networks. These networks which are based on high mobility are becoming the vehicles for intensive global competition.

2.3.3 Flexible labour organization and the 24-hour economy

From a socio-economic perspective, we are witnessing a clear break with the past. Instead of a standard working week of 40 hours with fixed working hours over 5 days, we observe a tendency to totally different types of labour organization and working arrangements. More labour force participation of traditionally non-active population segments, more part-time jobs, more flexible wage contracts and more shifts towards work at other times of the day are the signs of a rise in flexibility in the labour market. This flexible behaviour is also accompanied by shifts in consumer behaviour (shopping times for example). Thus, the daily time span of economic activities is extending towards a 24-hour operation of the economy. This is also reflected in the industrial sector, which tends to move towards multiple shifts in order to make the most efficient use of the capital stock. In a globalizing economy this flexibility is also important, as it allows for direct worldwide contacts despite the existence of time zones. The emergence of call centres is a good illustration of this phenomenon.

This flexibility in working arrangements leads also to an increase in individual modes of transport. Mass transit may become more problematic, as the mass flows which make public transport profitable are only compatible with the traditional labour model. On the other hand, the existing infrastructure may be used more efficiently as in the case of flexible working arrangements.

2.3.4 Economic and spatial concentration

In a network, nodal centres play a strategic role. Such nodal centres refer to industrial power concentration in the form of global oligopolies controlling a significant part of the world market, and also refer to main ports and gateways in international and infrastructure networks. The proximity effects of these networks, through their intense communication possibilities, give them many advantages. Although the ICT sector may suggest a 'death of distance', geographical agglomeration forces are becoming increasingly important for an industrial network economy. Thus scale economies of all kinds seem to favour concentration and agglomeration, while at the same time the ICT sector allows for a spatial spread of production. Clearly, the economies of density and scale may be affected by congestion and accessibility problems, thus causing an outflow from central city areas (CBDs) to suburban areas and new extra-urban locations (such as the edge city), but the main orientation still remains to the city as the pole of innovation, incubation and communication (Capello *et al.*, 1999). The resulting mobility patterns are diverse and include mass flows between major metropolitan areas and diffuse flows within the metropolitan area.

2.3.5 Implications for the economy

There are clearly changing perspectives for modern business life, which will impact on mobility patterns. There seems to be an overriding trend towards higher mobility rates, although the resulting patterns are not always unambiguous. For example, globalization may be reflected in more trade and transport, but it may also be that globalization leads to more regional outsourcing and concentrated regional foreign investment. In the latter case new systems of regional markets may emerge, which include a lower mobility rate than a uniform globalization development. Thus, the geographical scale at which a phenomenon takes place may be decisive for the changing patterns in mobility rates.

Another phenomenon is the emerging specialization and market niche orientation which prompt logistic and storage capacity challenges. These tendencies are also reflected in changing consumer behaviour (such as home shopping and internet use). This may also have complex mobility consequences, which may however differ by region or economic sector. It seems plausible that the changes in the external environments of modern business life are facilitated by and in turn lead to high mobility transport systems, but the relationship between these two phenomena is not a rectilinear one. As a consequence, it will also be hard to provide unambiguous views on the likely mobility patterns in future and the socio-economic and spatial ramifications for society. Clearly, the predictive power of our analytical apparatus is insufficient to provide unambiguous views about future patterns of mobility. This issue will be taken up again in the context of scenario building in Chapter 7 of the book.

2.4 The European dimension

Our world shows clear signs of socio-political re-orientation and economic-technological restructuring. In recent years the world economy has changed rapidly. Traditional patterns of competition within national borders are increasingly being replaced by vigorous competition on a multinational and even worldwide scale. 'Intra-country' competition is being replaced by 'inter-trade-block' competition as traditional boundaries disappear. Countries within such trade-blocks are becoming part of an economic network. To maximize the competitiveness of such a network and to maximize its socio-economic potential and performance, the quality of infrastructure is of critical importance, as transport has become an important component of modern production structures and processes *inter alia* because of intensified division of tasks between firms (in different countries).

Furthermore, European countries are also increasingly showing signs of an integrated economy, in which trade barriers are being removed and spatial interactions are increasing. The full exploitation of each nation's competitive advantage in an open international economic system has long been recognized as an important key force for maximizing national economic growth. Over the past decades a succession of agreements (such as the General Agreement on Tariffs and Trade, GATT, and the agreements made by the World Trade Organization, WTO) and trading unions (notably the European Community and the Benelux Union) have been introduced. These have attempted to remove (or at least reduce) the effects of various tariff, quota and subsidy systems and other protectionist measures which have been introduced at various times by national governments to further their own economic growth.

Because of this globalization trend and other socio-economic factors (including the need for higher and sustained economic growth), transport in Europe has grown enormously, especially in recent years (Chapter 3). As the supply of infrastructure has, for various reasons, only partially followed this trend, infrastructure bottlenecks have been accentuated. This is a very serious problem, since economic development and infrastructure development have always been strongly interlinked. The full benefits of the foreseen Internal European Market will only be reaped in the case of effective (physical and non-physical) infrastructure adjustments in Europe. What is needed in this context, is European (*not* national) thinking and action in infrastructure policy, based on past successes and failures and the future needs of the economy, the population of Europe and their (increasingly threatened) natural environment (see for example Masser *et al.*, 1992).

Unfortunately, interest in the European scale of networks has not until recently been very significant, as transport policy and planning is seldom performed from this perspective. National frontiers have always provided a clear physical barrier between countries, despite growing transport demand. Intra-European transport infrastructure networks have not followed this rising trend and show nowadays various bottlenecks in terms of missing links and missing networks (Nijkamp *et al.*, 1994). The emerging Internal Market between the EU15 has put the focus on issues of socio-economic harmonization to reduce distortions to free competition between industries in the various member states. Increasing consideration is now given to transport as this has a major role in facilitating the free market in Europe.

The major difference between a (more or less) national and a European approach to infrastructure network planning can best be described in terms of its economic effects. National infrastructure planning means focusing on the way in which national infrastructure building companies, vehicle producers and transport companies are given a competitive advantage at the cost of their foreign counterparts. As other countries will probably use the same tactics, all parties will be losers in this way, since efficient economies of scale are not reached and large sums of public investments are wasted. One of the reasons for this is that external competitors (from Asian or American companies for example) may then outperform European companies and maintain large home markets.

However, if the focus was on the European potential and the 'pooling' of infrastructure investments to develop European infrastructure networks, scale economies could be reached and costs saved, as factors of production would then be available. This would mean developing an innovative European strategy for transport, incorporating strategic long-term issues such as sustainable mass transport systems. This strategy is also necessary, given the urgent transport capacity and environmental needs of our society.

Historically, major transitions in the European economic system were always accompanied (or even induced) by major changes in transport and communications infrastructures. Four main transport and logistic revolutions in the history of Western Europe can be distinguished, each of them characterized by the emergence, adoption and implementation of a new type of international infrastructure. According to Andersson and Strömqvist (1989), these four revolutions are:

1   The Hanseatic period (from the thirteenth to the sixteenth century), in which waterways (inland and coastal transport links) emerged as a new logistics system connecting cites along rivers and coastal areas;

2   The 'Golden' period (from the sixteenth century to the seventeenth century), characterized by a drastic improvement in sailing and sea transport and by the introduction of new banking systems, through which trade to the East Indies and West Indies was stimulated (with Lisbon, Antwerp and Amsterdam as major centres);

3   The Industrial Revolution (from the middle of the nineteenth century onwards), in which the invention of the steam engine generated new transport modes (sea transport, railways) which also created new market areas (such as North America); and

4   The period from the 1970s, which is marked by informatization and flexibilization, in which JIT systems and material requirements planning (MRP) have evolved as new management principles. The rapid developments in the area of new information technology have also led to the emergence of integral logistics. This may mark the beginning of a new era (the 'fourth logistics revolution').

Economic development and infrastructure development are thus mutually dependent driving forces. The European economy will therefore remain critically dependent on well-functioning networks as catalysts for future development. There is a growing awareness that the current European infrastructure network is becoming outdated. If it is not replaced by modern facilities, Europe's competitive edge may disappear. Missing networks emerge, because transport systems are developed in a fragmented way, each country seeking its own solution without keeping an eye on the synergetic effects of co-ordinated design and use of new infrastructure. Another reason for missing networks is the focus on hardware and the neglect of software and organizational aspects as well as financial and ecological implications (Nijkamp and Blaas, 1993). Cabotage, protection of national carriers, segmented European railway companies, and lack of multi-modal transport strategies are but a few examples of the emergence of missing networks. A European orientation of all transport modes is necessary to cope with the current problems of missing and competing networks. At the same time there is a clear need for sustainable transport solutions which are compatible with environmental requirements.

Over the past decade, transport and communications have become more intensive, not only locally and regionally, but also internationally. The potential offered by modern information systems, the need for reliability, flexibility and multi-modality in modern transport systems all require advanced infrastructure networks. The presence of bottlenecks and missing networks in Europe is at odds with a balanced, competitive and sustainable European development after economic integration.

The expected integration benefits will only come into being if Europe becomes an open and flexible network in which transport and communications infrastructure provides efficient connections between all regions and states in Europe. Consequently, the opportunity costs of missing networks are extremely high. There is much evidence from the literature that productive investments and social overhead investments (notably infrastructure investments) need each other to arrive at a balanced economic development of nations and regions (Bruinsma *et al.*, 1991). It therefore seems plausible that the spin-off effects of new infrastructure investments are significant, provided they are tailor-made with respect to local and regional economic needs. Nevertheless they need a careful investigation, as will be shown in the next Section.

Transport and communications provide a stimulus for economic development (exchange of commodities, division of tasks, specialization and so on). According to the Cecchini Report presented to the European Commission, any additional economic growth is critically dependent on the physical exchange capacity of Europe.

Improvements in transport and communications systems are thus a critical success factor in generating highly significant dynamic integration effects. And there is an urgent need for such a strategic improvement. From a geographical viewpoint Europe is changing rapidly. Commuting distances are rising, the volume of commodities transported nationally and internationally is increasing, and airline activities for both passengers and commodities are booming. This mobility drift in Europe has been described as the 'Euro-mobile' phenomenon (Nijkamp *et al.*, 1991).

Transport policy favouring the free movement of persons and commodities in the EC is a *sine qua non* for a single market. The removal of existing barriers is of great importance for obtaining the highest dynamic integration benefits from a network economy. In recent years transport in most European countries has exhibited clear signs of devolution or subsidiarity, leading to less involvement by central government. This devolution appears to be a uniform phenomenon, although in different countries and cities it manifests itself in different forms, in terms of deregulation, decentralization and privatization.

In this context, the first and most notable observation is that there has been a striking parallel movement of transport infrastructure policies in most European countries over recent decades, characterized by a period of expansion in the 1960s, a period of contraction in the 1970s, and an era of selective expansion in the 1980s, in which the direction is strongly governed by either market forces or by decentralization principles. Countries with more liberal policies and/or with severe deficits in the public budget were the first ones to advocate privatization (in combination with deregulation) of transport policy. This was not only in the airline and freight sector, but also in the public transport sector.

A second observation to be made here is that European transport policy should focus not only on an improvement of the intra-European infrastructure network, but also increasingly on external links of this network. An open Europe has the highest benefits for both the Member States and the world economy as a whole. Thus the improvement of cross-frontier routes, such as the Trans-European Network and the Scandinavian links, is extremely important. In the near future, major new links to East European countries are envisaged. There is also a strong case here for co-operation between non-member countries, which provide (transit) links between EC-members, such as Switzerland and the former Yugoslavia. It goes without saying that a balanced transport policy is of critical relevance for regional equilibrium in the Community. The current tendency toward major fast links is not by definition beneficial to all regions. Extensive evaluation research will be necessary here to provide policy-makers with adequate guidelines.

A third major observation is that a major stimulus for new advanced infrastructure policy is given by information and communications technology (information, telecommunications and micro-electronics). Physical distribution is increasingly reliant on informatics-related activities. That holds true for containerization, high-speed trains and airlines. Accessible and internationally co-ordinated information systems are becoming a major vehicle for a further improvement of the transport and logistics network in the Community. A necessary condition for the further penetration and success of such information systems is standardization, and this policy issue is one of the most crucial corner stones of European transport policy. JIT principles and multi-modal logistics chains will never become fully operational without sufficient European standardization. Thus the potentials and the barriers in European infrastructure need thorough scientific analysis, in which various countries would need to participate.

From this review of the challenges and changes taking place in Europe, certain key themes seem to emerge at the European level. The first crucial theme is the political future of the EU and whether it expands or consolidates – this theme forms part of the context within which the Images for the Future are constructed (Chapter 9). The second theme concerns the development of the new network economy and the infrastructure within Europe, and the degree to which competition for access is permitted. The third theme more explicitly explores the new technology and its impacts on the network. Finally, there is an important underlying theme central to this book, namely the links between transport and sustainability. Each of these themes is discussed in more detail in the next Section, and certain questions are posed to stimulate new thinking on the future for Europe. Some of these challenges are taken up later in the book.

2.5   Challenges in European transport policy

2.5.1 Integration and disintegration in Europe

The disappearance of the iron curtain has led to a widening of Europe, which will have far reaching economic, spatial and political consequences into the future. It has led to both re-integration (Germany) and disintegration (USSR, Yugoslavia, Czechoslovakia) at the same time. The completion of the internal market in Europe by 1993 created an 'open arena' for business life in Europe, connecting countries and regions which in former times were isolated. At the same time, when national borders are removed, we observe a strong tendency towards more regional, economic, political and cultural identity and even autonomy (Spain, Italy, Belgium and the UK for example).

The reconstruction and bonding of a greater and more open Europe of more than 500 million people is an enormous task. It will necessitate high levels of investment supported by the European Regional Development Fund (EFDF) and the European Investment Bank (EIB). This will involve consideration of such issues as the direction, size and geographical distribution of infrastructure investment, regional development, and environmental protection. Many questions emerge.

- Should the cities and countries of Central Europe see the West as models to be followed?

- Or does the new concern for sustainable development require them to shape their future economic, regional-urban, and infrastructure trajectory in new ways?

- Will the citizens of Poland or Hungary, for example, accept a future which is not a copy of what they have seen as an ideal model for many years?

- Is it realistic to assume that the rise in spatial mobility will also be reflected in all countries in Central and East Europe?

- Will the view of the new Europe as the homeland of many cities, regions and nations be strong enough to cope with the threats of monopoly power and protectionism?

- What are the critical success factors that will ensure that the new Europe does not lose its momentum during the present difficult transition period?

- And, last but not least, what is the mission of a European-oriented transport planning which aims both to alleviate the transaction costs of European restructuring and to exploit the competitive advantages of European cities, regions and nations?

2.5.2 Competition in European networks

The current European dynamics may be characterized by two complementary forces from a spatial-economic viewpoint: a drive towards an open economic network and a drive towards more competition between regions and/or industries. Recent developments in Europe add a new dimension to the interaction between transport and communications networks and spatial development:

- New, faster transport networks (high-speed rail and air) create new spatial concentrations of accessibility in Europe;
- The difference in accessibility between West and East will remain large despite the re-integration of East European transport networks;
- New telecommunication networks such as ISDN and satellite communications create areas of high informational accessibility at nodal centres.

The combined effect of these developments will be a polarization of accessibility and an increase in the locational advantage of the regions in the European core over those at the periphery (see for example Vickerman *et al.*, 1999). Policies to improve Scandinavian sea crossings or the conversion of the Spanish railways to standard gauge are not likely to offset this polarization tendency. The European Community has realized the risks associated with increasing spatial disparities in Europe and in the Maastricht agreements it calls explicitly for the utilization of Trans-European Networks to promote cohesion in and between the regions in the Community (Chapter 4).

Clearly, the network concept is analytically not an unknown concept, but its functioning and implications in a European economic setting need to be investigated more thoroughly. Concepts like the European 'blue banana' are interesting and creative ideas, but they need to be substantiated with solid research and appropriate policy strategies (Masser *et al.*, 1992). This leads to a series of important research questions:

- Is, for instance, a European network economy beneficial to lagging or peripheral regions?
- Is the European network economy compatible with environmental quality standards?
- To what extent does a network configuration provide a new geo-political structure impacting on national or regional socio-cultural identities in Europe?
- Is a network system determined by the spatial organization of multinational European firms or does the network shape the linkage patterns of such firms?
- Is a European network concept a realistic idea if it is not supported by co-ordinated European policy strategies for sophisticated transnational infrastructures?

- If a European network cannot be built up simultaneously but needs some phasing of activities over a time span of some 20 years, is there a real danger of the emergence of a two-speed Europe?
- What type of transnational infrastructure agencies have to be envisaged for co-ordinating such activities?
- Who decides on the types and models of network infrastructures to be developed?
- Will the emerging European network generate sufficient comparative advantages to be internationally competitive?

2.5.3 New technologies and infrastructure

Transport and new technologies are interwoven in two complementary ways. First, transport and infrastructure shape the geographical form, which determines to a large extent the location patterns of industries and households. More efficient transport systems favour the competitive position of firms in such a network and hence favour the cities of regions linked to such a network. This means that transport infrastructure has a particularly important impact on access and communication. In general this holds true for most high-tech firms, so that communication and transport networks may be regarded as catalysts for high-tech development, an assumption which is supported by empirical evidence.

In the second place, new technologies also have an impact on the degree of sophistication of a network. This does not only hold for the airline or rail transport sector, but also for the road transport sector. The impact of modern logistics and telematics on transport behaviour and the efficiency of transport movement is increasing.

From a policy point of view, the role of transport for spatial development has become central to transport and telecommunications policy in Europe at a time when new high-speed rail, motorway and advanced telecommunication networks are about to fundamentally transform the map of Europe. In addition, the unconstrained trend towards higher levels of mobility causes serious social and environmental imbalances so that the identification of feasible policies to curb this trend is a highly desirable goal.

All such developments lead to intricate future oriented research questions. A few of them will be posed here.

- Is it plausible to assume that high-tech infrastructures favour economies of scale and may therefore induce the emergence of 'hub and spokes' systems?
- Is it possible to develop realistic future scenarios for the impact of telecommunication on the transport sector and the spatial behaviour of people or organizations?

- Will telematics ever have a significant impact on spatial mobility or will it, at the same time, favour further urban sprawl?
- Will the car industry be able to develop new technologies, which will make the car compatible with ecological and spatial constraints?
- Or will the car play an even more important role as an extension of the office and the home (including telephone, fax, personal computer, video and television)?
- Do such new technologies discriminate between different regions in Europe?
- Which are the social implications of teleworking on family life or on female labour force participation?

2.5.4 Transport and environmental sustainability

Environmental costs imposed by the transport sector are high and increasing, despite extensive legislation and regulation at the European and national levels (Chapter 5). Clear policy directions need to be given to the transport industry so that production processes can be cleaned up, and so that more environmentally benign transport modes can be encouraged. The private sector contribution would complement that of the public sector in giving priority to public transport and cycling within cities, and in encouraging energy efficient urban forms. In general, one may claim that private sector contributions have an important role to play in supplementing public sector investment in transport and communications infrastructure. Various forms of partnership must be established between funding agencies, between sources of European capital (such as the European Investment Bank and the European Bank for Reconstruction and Development), and between national governments, as the levels of capital required for investment in Europe are often too a large for a single agency.

It should be noted that economic concepts are clear in that the user and the polluter should pay the full costs of travel including all externalities. However, there are many problems with the implementation of such concepts, as the public acceptability is low and international agreements are difficult. For instance, any such implementation would ideally have to be fiscally neutral, otherwise the policy could be inflationary and could lead to increases in unemployment.

The need for sustainable mobility and compact city design has been identified by the European Commission. However, the necessary (large) investments in transport and communications networks, particularly on a regional and international basis, are likely to increase journey lengths and levels of mobility. These outcomes are inconsistent with the objectives put forward by the Commission.

It goes without saying that the social costs incurred as a result of modern transport systems generate many research questions. Examples are the following:

- Do current European developments open a possibility for finding politically acceptable ways of internalizing transport's external costs?
- Is it possible to charge the wide range of external costs (road casualties, noise, gas emissions, severance of communities, destruction of wildlife and so on) in a meaningful way to the user?
- Which policy strategies can be envisaged to ensure sustainable development (new car technologies, strict regulations, road pricing, parking policy, physical planning and so on)?
- If a system of directly-debited road user charges is canvassed as the best instrument for internalizing congestion (and other) costs, what are their likely side effects?
- How would such a system impact on urban form and (re-)location behaviour of people and firms?
- What are the likely impacts of telematics (such as route guidance or advance booking or parking spaces)?
- Are there sufficiently strong economic arguments for reducing traffic congestion by contriving a shift in urban travel from car to public transport?
- For which target groups will a particular form of public transport service be the most suitable means?
- Is it possible to reconcile the need of low-income people for low fares with the desire of car owners to travel at a standard to which they are accustomed?
- Would it be feasible to have differential segments in public transport – high quality high price services for the affluent and cheaper utilitarian ones for lower income people?
- Should telematics and information technology, rather than public transport, be seen as a high quality alternative to travel?
- And, last but not least, is our way of living, working and moving compatible with the justified desires of developing world people for a higher level of sustainable development in which they wish to have a fair share?

The achievement of a sustainable transport system, which would imply a balance between economic development, broad access to transport facilities and a sufficiently high environmental quality is fraught with many difficulties. There is a variety of factors impacting on the spatial movement pattern of people and goods, and many of these factors are rather autonomous and beyond the control of policy-making bodies.

Three external driving forces seem to be most important.

- *The rate of development.* This comprises a variety of driving forces that influence the transport system, such as population increase, the rise in international trade as a result of the liberalization of world trade under the auspices of the WTO (World Trade Organization), the increase in car dependency and car ownership in large parts of the world (such as India, China, Latin-America and Africa), or the depletion of energy resources.

- *The transition to a knowledge society.* It is sometimes assumed that a knowledge intensive society would require less physical movement, but the facts show a different pattern. More information and knowledge seems to be accompanied by more physical movement. On the other hand, the increased knowledge base may lead to a more efficient operation of a transport system (such as value added logistics) which may also be more environmentally benign. Another element is that knowledge intensive firms are less dependent on a location close to natural resources ('death of distance'). And finally, the transition to an ICT-driven economy may prompt new logistic systems and transport technologies which may lead to a de-linking of movement and environmental decay (the well-known 'factor 4' or 'factor 10' discussion – see, for example, von Weizsäcker *et al.*, 1997).

- *Patterns of social change.* In the past decade, lifestyles have changed in terms of family composition, leisure behaviour, and so on. This has all had severe implications for mobility patterns of people: more people travel more frequently over longer distances. The changes in demographic and socio-economic conditions are another factor contributing to a new mobility culture.

The challenges facing transport policy-makers in the EU are fundamental to the way in which Europe will develop over the next 20 years. We do not have all the answers to these challenges, but we would strongly argue that these issues must be discussed with policy-makers through the scenario building process. External factors such as the integration or disintegration of the EU are fundamental to the development of policies on sustainable mobility. For example, tougher targets on CO_2 will have to be accepted in the core countries so that the peripheral and accession countries can increase their levels of emissions, and the EU as a whole can achieve its target set at Kyoto (Table 1.2). Assumptions about the competitive environment within which Europe operates have clear implications for the policy packages in the scenarios, as do the roles assigned to new technologies and the optimization of the use of the existing infrastructure. The four challenges set out here are at the centre of the effective means to move towards sustainable mobility.

2.6 Transport in Europe and the city

2.6.1 Constraints and changes in transport

The European transport system is the circulation system underlying the European economy. Unfortunately, hardly any coherent view on the functioning of the European transport system has been developed so far. Instead of a systemic view in which the transport sector would be looked at from the viewpoint of coherence and positive synergies, policy-makers and planners have tended to develop fragmented solutions to emerging bottlenecks by looking for specific local or modal solutions, without due regard to the connectivity of the transport system across different regions, sectors and modes. One of the main frictions in European transport policy is the absence of a strategic view of the European transport system as a single entity at all geographic levels.

Despite the increasing trend of JIT systems and related concepts, the actual practice of both commodity and passenger transport is disappointing and often frustrating. A number of examples illustrates the difficult situation faced by the European transport sector:

- severe traffic congestion at the urban or metropolitan level;
- unacceptable delays in medium and long distance transport during peak hours;
- unsatisfactory levels of service in European railway systems and public transport;
- unreliable airline connections due to limited airport capacity;
- the slow technical and institutional renewal of air traffic control in Europe.

And there is no clear expectation for a drastic improvement of this situation. On the contrary, it is increasingly claimed that the situation may worsen in many of the European regions.

Another important factor will be environmental policy. In contrast to the deregulation trend regarding transport, environmental policy is critically dependent on regulations and interventions on both the supply and demand side. In particular, technical restrictions are likely to be imposed, such as limited (or even zero) emission levels for vehicles or maybe even a selective prohibition of the use of certain transport modes. Recently, various pleas for car-free cities have been voiced. Transport policy-makers in most European countries find themselves in extremely complicated situations. Many interest groups, ranging from multinational companies to local environmentalists, are urging them to take action, but often in quite different directions. On the one hand it has become obvious that the environment poses limits on the volume, character and pace of the extension of transport infrastructure. On the other hand, many businesses in Western Europe are concerned about their competitiveness in a global context due to inadequate infrastructure. Inadequate infrastructure affects business in several ways. Firstly, the relatively slow development of sophisticated telecommunication infrastructure in Europe may curtail the ability to offer new services. Secondly, it may limit the possibilities to speed up international trade in an efficient way. And thirdly, the restricted capacity of inland transport networks may cause higher production costs in Europe and affect global competitiveness.

For these reasons, Europe must improve its transport and communications infrastructure to increase its competitive power, while at the same time sufficient care should be given to environmental considerations. This raises an extra difficulty, as due care is usually incompatible with swift action. Short-term solutions, as advocated by some business-oriented interest groups, tend to rely heavily on a further massive extension of the European motorway system. This option may make sense in Southern and Eastern Europe, but for Western Europe this option does not seem viable in the long run. Since supply tends to generate its own demand (the 'Law of Say'), network extensions beyond the level of relieving unacceptable bottlenecks will create a new era of congestion at a higher level. Furthermore, this scenario will also be detrimental to a balanced spatial development of urban areas and the environment in Western Europe.

In conclusion, Europe is facing a major development constraint, in that its infrastructure network is highly fragmented, whilst policy strategies to build a multi-modal European-oriented infrastructure network are just beginning to emerge. European infrastructure development is thus coping with important restrictions, but it also deserves full-scale scientific investigation. The ways in which governments can influence international transport costs are numerous. In most countries it is still the national government, which provides (directly or indirectly) the major components of infrastructure, such as ports, airports, fibre-optic networks, railway tracks, and so on. Despite deregulation, the provision and presence of infrastructure itself gives power, because through its very location or capacity infrastructure can influence the magnitude of a country's trade. The power to charge for the use of the national transport or communications infrastructure offers a further device by which a government may attempt to influence trade. Apart from more direct measures and institutional arrangements which also serve to influence the costs of international transport (and thus violate the principle of *laissez faire*), governments may also intervene, again in numerous different ways, to protect their own domestic transport industries from external competition. For instance, cabotage is often viewed in the same way as the 'dumping' of goods in a market and is the subject of particularly severe restrictions in many European countries.

In other countries, the production of transport products (including the supply of consultancy and civil engineering expertise as well as that of vehicle and aircraft manufacturers) is regarded as very important (often for reasons of domestic economic stability and protection of traditional sectors rather than on the grounds of strict economic efficiency). Government intervention then restricts the working of the free international market. For instance, domestic industries may be protected by design standards, quota systems and tariff regimes.

It is thus no surprise that international transport agencies call for more national deregulation. Although agencies (such as the European Conference of Ministers of Transport, the European Commission, Benelux, and so on) fulfil an important function as a discussion platform in policy preparation, it is still very difficult to get all member countries on the same policy wavelength. European history tells us that it is difficult to harmonize so many different interests and that, after a compromise has been reached about joint policy formulation, the implementation (and the maintenance) is often neglected.

Clearly, the field of international transport and communications is often characterized by *ad hoc* and partial policy measures. Government actions tend sometimes to be taken more in response to crisis situations, rather than as part of a co-ordinated and preventive policy programme that is strategic, holistic and pro-active in nature. An important question is of course whether the current trends in mobility growth will come to a standstill. Governments all over the world witness serious concerns on the impact of CO_2. Many policy documents express a curbing of mobility growth as a major target, but it is questionable whether this reversal of trends is a realistic or plausible option. Experts predict that the chances for a drastic change in mobility behaviour are extremely low (Nijkamp *et al.*, 1998). The 1997 Kyoto Protocol is extremely modest in the light of the expected increase in welfare and population.

2.6.2 Urban transport and spatial organization

There are a number of problems in the field of urban transport (see, for example, Hart, 1994). Large urban areas continue to be productive and innovative and consequently the land area covered by many large metropolises has increased. At the same time, suburbanization has taken place, and car ownership and use has risen dramatically (Nijkamp, 1994). Awareness has grown that the future of cities is largely dependent on transport accessibility, while at the same time transport externalities have eroded the quality of life in cities.

A general phenomenon experienced by almost all cities in the world is the suburbanization of population. Although the first waves of suburbanization occurred many decades ago (partly based on public transport), the extent to which it has developed since the early 1960s has been unprecedented. The private car has brought low-density living within reach of large groups of people. Suburbanization of living was a consequence of various broad changes in society, such as income increases, smaller households, more leisure time and changing housing preferences. Suburbanization is usually also associated with negative socio-economic and environmental impacts, such as longer working and shopping trips, more energy consumption, pollution, accidents and problems of public transport provision in low-density areas (Masser *et al.*, 1992; Stead, 2000).

The suburbanization of living was followed by a second wave of suburbanization of employment in the 1970s and 1980s. Thus, dwellings as well as jobs tended to disperse further from urban centres into a broader metropolitan area, a process which may be called extended suburbanization or counter-urbanization (Breheny, 1996). Such decentralized cities are usually negatively valued, because they contribute to an increase in the length of work trips and prohibit public transport solutions for commuting.

At the same time, however, there are some signs which suggest that suburbanization of living may have passed its peak and that a phase of re-urbanization may start. In this view, there is a strong revitalization trend in inner-city areas, accompanied by the attraction of affluent residents who can afford to pay the increased rents in city centres (gentrification).

In the light of the above trends in suburbanization and urban sprawl, one particular extreme type of future city can be identified, namely the diffuse (decentralized) city. Large cities such as London and Paris, and smaller ones such as Milan and Brussels, seem to conform to this development pattern. In regard to spatial planning however, a contrasting concept has recently gained much popularity: the 'compact city', where housing is provided at a relatively high density and jobs are concentrated in the central city and in a limited number of sub-centres. The compact city has become a leading principle in Dutch physical planning in recent years, and is currently adopted in Europe as a guideline for urban planning (Breheny, 1996).

Such compact urban spatial organization may have a drastic impact on the future of transport, mobility and modal split (Nijkamp and Rienstra, 1996). At the same time, however, it should be noticed that the compact city concept also has some intrinsic limitations in terms of quality of life, land use and prices, and congestion, while many other success factors (for example, level of well-being, telecommunications) also have a huge impact on the role of transport and new technologies (Banister and Marshall, 2000).

2.6.3 Institutional, economic and social factors

In recent years, a marked shift towards emphasis on economic principles for a combined transport, environment and spatial policy can be observed. In spatial planning a trend towards the abolition of rigid planning systems is found, because government intervention is less accepted in society and is perceived to be less effective (Fokkema and Nijkamp, 1994). In transport policy, various user-charge principles are increasingly being discussed and implemented, such as road pricing, toll principles, parking fees and perhaps in the long run even tradable permits. These measures mainly affect car transport and may stimulate the use of public transport.

However, there is also the trend to abolish unjustified and unnecessary protectionist or privileged regulations in order to increase the efficiency of transport operations. In this respect, increased attention is being paid to the efficiency and the profitability of, for example, public urban transit companies. As a result, in many cities of the UK, public bus companies have been privatized, which has had an enormous impact on the way the bus network is being operated. An important factor in this respect is the minimum volume of passengers between given points necessary for public transport to be economically feasible. Barriers to adoption arise when (critical) spatial threshold levels of demand for public transport modes are not reached – for example, due to a low population density (Rienstra *et al.*, 1996).

Another aspect in which public transport systems may be distinguished from individual ones concerns the dependence on supplementary transport systems. Travelling by public transport is intermodal by nature, while individual modes offer door-to-door transport. This makes the functioning of public transport modes dependent on connectivity with other transport systems (including walking and cycling) that offer transport to-and-from nodes. Co-ordination problems between different modes may be an important failure factor in this case.

The private car appears to have a strong psychological appeal, because factors like pleasure, privacy, personal control and individuality largely contribute to the preference for the private car (Vlek and Michon, 1992). The same may hold for residential choice, where living conditions in compact urban areas are often considered less attractive than those in smaller, less dense settlements.

There are many problems with encouraging use of public transport, as it seems to be an inferior mode of transport and individuals' behaviour is difficult to change. Conversely, new infrastructure construction may also prove difficult to implement in cities as space is scarce and public opposition is often substantial. In this respect, it should be added that democratic governments do not favour measures which largely run counter to public opinion (Rietveld, 1997). Therefore, a change in public attitude would first have to occur before many policies could be introduced successfully.

2.7 Conclusions

From this synoptic view of the main forces of change, it seems that the ultimate goal of sustainable mobility is elusive and hard to achieve, given the huge variability in the nature of change. Underlying much of the argument is the assumption that there is a continuing drive for mobility in all sectors of transport and that the advent of new technology is likely to increase that drive as networks expand, as new opportunities arise, and as information becomes more tailored to individual requirements.

To limit the scope of the discussion, the focus has been restricted to developments in the EU. But even here, there is substantial scope for increases in unsustainable transport as we enter the fifth transport revolution – one of personalization and individualization of transport (Andersson and Strömqvist, 1988). Europe has to respond to international pressures relating to the globalization of economies, new industrial networks and outsourcing, the 24-hour economy, and new patterns of economic and spatial organization. The challenges are outlined in this Chapter, together with some of the responses from the EU (Section 2.4 and Chapters 3, 4, 5 and 6). It is here that inconsistencies can be seen within the position of the EU, which on the one hand wants to promote expansion and strong leadership, but on the other is committed to subsidiarity and regional/local development. Similarly, the drive towards maintaining and improving the European economy, its growth and competitiveness within world markets may result in issues relating to sustainable mobility being pushed lower down the agenda. As with all decisions, the new complexity should not be underestimated.

In this Chapter, we have tried to outline the difficult decisions and choices that have to be made, highlighting the drivers of change and the rapidly evolving new economy which has impacts at all scales from global to local levels. Two main conclusions emerge. One suggests that traditional trend-based methods are too narrow and rigid in their construction to give real insights into the new agenda and the complex choices that have to be made. Hence new methods from scenario building and visioning, based on different combinations of the driving forces, have been used in this book. The second suggests that flexibility and responsiveness to change are critical components of any new thinking about transport as change is taking place so rapidly. Adaptability is a key element of the new policy agenda, but this must not be seen as an excuse for weak action or inaction.

Note

1   Schumpeter argued that innovation and adaptation took place during depressions in the economic cycle, so that new industries were generated and growth took place. This resulted in an upturn in the economic cycle until market saturation was reached (Schumpeter, 1934).

Chapter 3

European transport trends

3.1 Introduction

European transport trends have changed dramatically since the creation of the European Community a few decades ago. There has been a mobility explosion, in which the growth in passenger and freight transport has greatly outstripped the increase in population and the increase in economic activity (changes in transport intensity will be examined in more detail in Section 3.12). Over the last 25 years, passenger transport has more than doubled, the number of cars has increased by more than one and a half times and the increase in the length of motorways has more than trebled. These trends still continue in almost all European Member States. Extrapolation of these trends indicates increasing problems of congestion and pollution for the future. In this Chapter, we take a retrospective view over 25 years (1970-1995) which sets the scene for a prospective view of the next 25 years. This more quantitative Chapter matches the broader picture given on changing trends in Chapter 2.

3.2 Economic activity

Economic activity has increased substantially in all European Member States over recent decades. Between 1970 and 1995, the overall GDP per capita of all current European Member States[1] increased by 65 per cent in real terms: an average increase of around 2 per cent per year (Figure 3.1). The largest increases in GDP per capita were in Luxembourg, Ireland and Portugal, where economic activity more than doubled between 1970 and 1995 (an average increase of around 3 per cent per year).

3.3 The costs of travel

At the same time that economic activity and incomes in Europe have been increasing, the costs of private transport have been decreasing in real terms (OECD/ECMT, 1995). By contrast, public transport costs (and usually fares) have been increasing in most countries (*ibid.*). In the UK, the costs of bus and rail fares increased by 48 and 56 per cent respectively between 1989 and 1996: both higher than the 33 per cent real increase in the retail price index

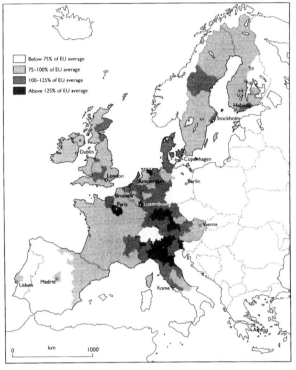

Figure 3.1 GDP in EU15 countries (1995)

(Department of the Environment, Transport and the Regions, 1999). Meanwhile, the cost of motoring, which includes costs such as insurance, servicing, repairs, road tax, fuel and oil, increased by only 38 per cent, even though the real price of fuel and oil increased by 54 per cent between 1989 and 1996 (*ibid.*).

The costs of fuel for transport vary substantially across EU Member States, as do vehicle costs (Figure 3.2). Fuel costs are to some extent related to GDP: countries with a lower than average GDP tend to have lower than average fuel costs. There are exceptions, however. In 1995, Luxembourg had the highest GDP per capita of all EU countries but had lower transport fuel costs than almost all other Member States. The highest fuel prices for transport in 1995 were in the Netherlands. The price of fuel increased much faster than the growth in the economy in most European countries. Between 1990 and 1995, the price of petrol increased most in Finland and least in Ireland and Italy (where the price of unleaded petrol actually fell). The price of diesel increased most in Greece between 1990 and 1995 (by 94 per cent) and least in France (where the price stayed the same). Correlation analysis indicates a possible link between fuel price and transport volume, particularly with freight transport volume.

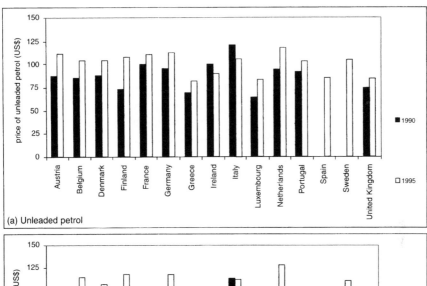

(a) Unleaded petrol

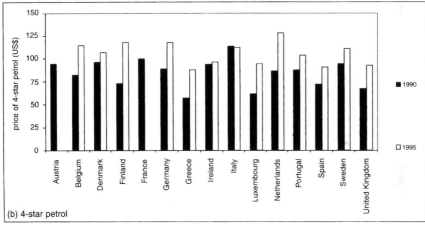

(b) 4-star petrol

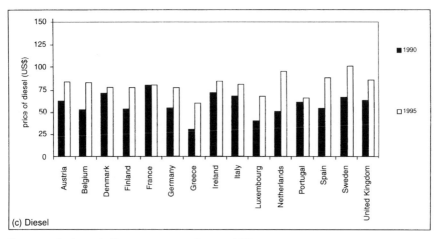

(c) Diesel

Figure 3.2 Fuel costs in Europe, 1990-1995 (Source: OECD, 1997)

3.4 Household composition

Household size is decreasing, with the consequences of increasing the number of dwellings required to accommodate the population and reducing the opportunities for householders to share transport. In 1970, there was an average of 3.1 persons per household in Europe. By 1995, household size was around 2.3 persons (Figure 3.3). One- and two-person households of young adults, single parents and elderly people are increasingly common for a variety of demographic, social and lifestyle reasons.

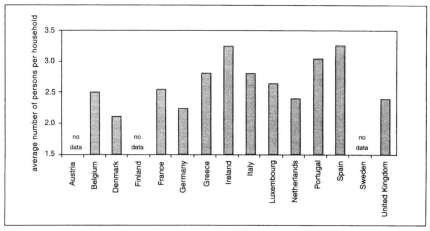

Figure 3.3 Average household size in the EU, 1994 (Source: CEC, 2000)

3.5 Car ownership

Increasing economic activity and changes in transport costs are both stimuli to the growth in car ownership. The total number of cars per capita in Europe increased substantially more rapidly than economic activity between 1970 and 1995. In 1970, average car ownership in all current European Member States was 181 cars per thousand persons. By 1995, average car ownership in Europe was 428 cars per thousand persons: an increase of 137 per cent over 25 years. Car ownership increased at different rates across Member States (Figure 3.4). The fastest rate of growth in car ownership occurred in Greece, Portugal and Spain: the countries with the fewest cars per head in 1970. Car ownership per capita in these three countries increased by 825, 515 and 410 per cent respectively between 1970 and 1995. Although car ownership increased most in the countries with fewest cars per capita, there is little evidence to suggest that the level of car ownership is converging across European Member States. Car ownership in Italy and Germany, where car ownership is now higher than other Member States, increased more rapidly than the European average between 1970 and 1995. On the basis of these trends, car ownership per capita could double in Europe between 1995 and 2014. The effect of increased car ownership on travel patterns is not just the substitution of journeys made by other modes but the increase in the number of journeys *and* the increase in the journey distance (see for example OECD/ECMT, 1995). These impacts of increasing car ownership on travel patterns have important implications for the environmental impacts of transport (see Chapter 5). With the increases in car ownership, travel is becoming more individually based, where people often travel independently rather than with others.[2]

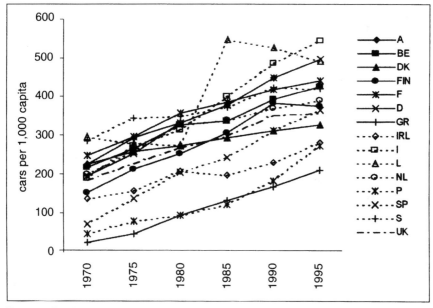

Figure 3.4 Trends in car ownership in the EU, 1970-1995 (Source: EUROSTAT, 1997)

3.6 Lifestyles and employment

Increasing incomes, more leisure time and the diversity of activities all add to the growth in travel. Higher levels of car ownership put more activities within reach and stimulate travel. High car ownership and cheap car travel encourage preferences to live outside urban areas, far from local work, services or facilities, which then adds to the need to travel. Elderly people, who are living longer and more active lives, have a great deal of free time and travel more than ever before. The specialization and centralization of employment is increasing the distances people travel to work.

3.7 Land use

Recent decades have seen the gradual dispersal of population, employment, leisure and retail developments, from central urban areas to outer city locations and to small and medium-sized settlements (Stead, 1999; Stead, 2000). The development of science parks, out-of-town shopping centres and retail parks has added to this dispersal and has contributed to the increased need to travel. Many different types of services and facilities (such as shops, schools and hospitals) have been centralized, where fewer, larger services and facilities have replaced a large number of small-scale ones, making local services and facilities increasingly scarce. Supermarkets have eroded the profitability of smaller shops and forced some out of business. These factors have acted to increase travel distances and to increase reliance on motorized forms of transport. Meanwhile, few new services and facilities have been provided in many new residential developments resulting in less self-containment of development and more travel.

3.8 Transport infrastructure

In 1970, there were 15,935 kilometres of motorway in the fifteen current European Member States. By 1995, this figure had trebled to 49,024 kilometres. The length of the motorway network increased in all Member States but the largest proportional increases took place in Luxembourg, Spain and Greece, where the length of motorway increased more than tenfold (Figure 3.5). Spain and Luxembourg now have the most motorway per capita of all Member States, whilst Ireland and Greece have the least. Investment in transport infrastructure, has been supported by European transport policy (Trans-European Networks – TENs) and European Structural Funds, particularly in the peripheral regions of Europe (see Chapter 4).

According to the OECD (1988), road-building in many northern European countries has been scaled down and/or implemented much more slowly over recent years due to factors such as:

- the reluctance of governments to spend money on roads, especially new construction, in line with general cuts in public expenditure (which has encouraged some highway authorities to explore alternative sources of funding, including greater involvement of the private sector);
- the increased cost of road-building as land, engineering and labour costs have grown, particularly in urban areas, where more complicated construction techniques are sometimes necessary;
- increasing political concerns about the adverse social and environmental impacts of road-building, which have resulted in the introduction of wider public consultation procedures: some schemes have been

abandoned as a result of strong opposition from businesses and/or residents.

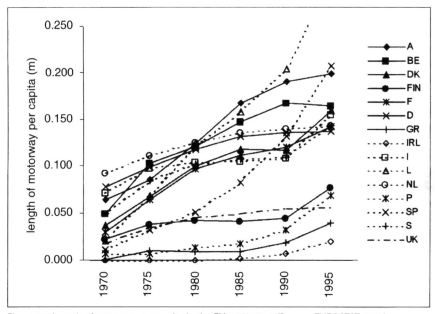

Figure 3.5 Length of motorway per capita in the EU, 1970-1995 (Source: EUROSTAT, 1997)

In contrast, the length of the European railway network decreased in almost all Member States between 1970 and 1995. The length of railway track in Europe fell by 9 per cent between 1970 and 1995, from 170,541 kilometres to 155,836 kilometres (or 50 and 42 centimetres of track per capita in 1970 and 1995 respectively). Only Luxembourg had more railway track in 1995 than in 1970. A few countries have experienced no overall change in the length of the railway network between 1970 and 1995 (Denmark, Finland and Italy). In Portugal and Belgium, the railway network was cut by one-fifth between 1970 and 1995. Sweden and Finland have the most railway track per capita of all Member States, whilst Greece, Italy, Portugal and the UK have the least (Figure 3.6).

3.9 Passenger transport

3.9.1 Distance

The average distance travelled per person per year almost doubled in Europe between 1970 and 1995. This was primarily due to people travelling further

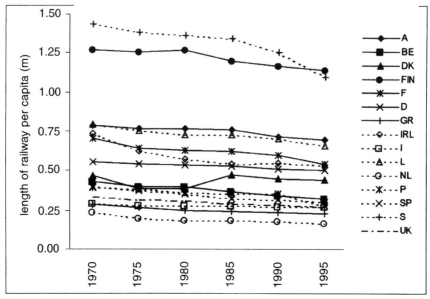

Figure 3.6 Length of railway per capita in the EU, 1970-1995 (Source: EUROSTAT, 1997)

rather than travelling more frequently. In 1970, the average yearly travel distance was 6,292 kilometres per person and by 1995 it was 12,337 kilometres per person. In 1995, the average annual travel distance of a European was approximately 10,000 kilometres by car, 970 kilometres by bus, 730 kilometres by train and 700 kilometres by air. Increases in passenger travel distance in Greece and Portugal were the highest, partly as a consequence of the rapid increase in car ownership, whilst increases in Luxembourg and Sweden were the lowest (Figure 3.7). In 1995, France, Ireland and Italy had the highest average travel distance per person and Greece and Spain had the lowest.

3.9.2 Modal split

The use of the car is growing rapidly and reliance on the car is increasing (Figure 3.8). Travel by car more than doubled between 1970 and 1995 and around 80 per cent of passenger-kilometres were by car in 1995. The reliance on the car varies across European Member States. In Greece, 88 per cent of travel distance is by car, whereas in Austria, only 71 per cent of travel distance is by car. The use of air transport is a small but rapidly growing proportion of passenger transport. Travel by air increased more than six-fold between 1970 and 1995 and now accounts for more than 6 per cent of passenger-kilometres. Travel by bus and rail increased at a much slower rate than by car or air and now accounts for around 14 per cent of passenger-kilometres. Bus and coach travel increased by 39 per cent between 1970 and 1995 in Europe (most of

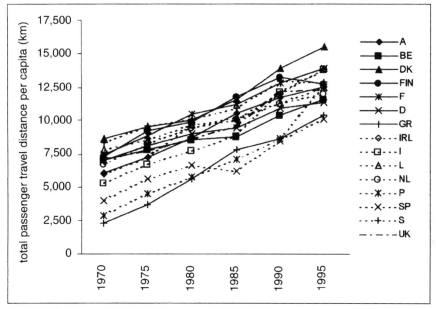

Figure 3.7 Average annual travel distance per capita in the EU, 1970-1995 (Source: EUROSTAT, 1997)

this increase occurred between 1970 and 1980). Travel by rail increased by 25 per cent, with most of this increase taking place between 1970 and 1990. The UK was the only country in Europe to experience a decline in travel by bus or rail over this period: travel by bus fell by 28 per cent in the UK and travel by rail fell by 4 per cent. In Portugal, bus travel increased almost threefold between 1970 and 1995 and in the Netherlands rail travel increased by 75 per cent (EUROSTAT, 1997).

In 1995, the average annual travel distance by *car* was highest in France, Denmark and Ireland (more than 15 per cent above the European average) and lowest in Spain, Austria and Belgium (more than 10 per cent lower than the European average). The average annual travel distance by bus was highest in Austria and Denmark (more than 70 per cent above the European average) and lowest in Greece (more than 40 per cent lower than the European average). The average annual travel distance by train was highest in Austria (more than 65 per cent above the European average) and lowest in Ireland (half of the European average).

3.10 Freight transport

3.10.1 Distance

Freight transport volumes in Europe increased by 71 per cent between 1970 and 1995, primarily due to goods being moved further rather than more

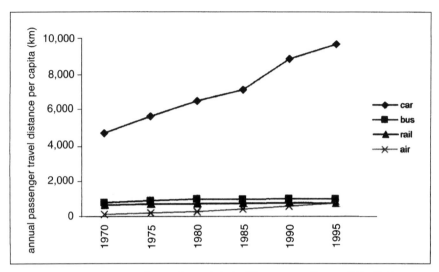

Figure 3.8 Passenger transport distance by mode in the EU, 1970-1995 (Source: EUROSTAT, 1997)

goods being moved (Whitelegg, 1997). In 1995, the average yearly freight transport distance per capita was 2960 tonne-kilometres by road, 590 tonne-kilometres by rail, 310 tonne-kilometres by inland waterway and 230 tonne-kilometres by pipeline. Increases in freight transport were the highest in Italy

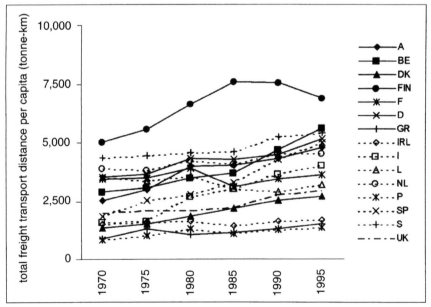

Figure 3.9 Freight transport distance per capita in the EU, 1970-1995 (Source: EUROSTAT, 1997)

and Spain, where freight transport increased by more than 150 per cent, and lowest in Luxembourg, where total freight transport increased by just 8 per cent between 1970 and 1995 (Figure 3.9). In 1995, Finland had the highest freight transport volume per capita in Europe (more than 50 per cent above the European average), whilst Greece, Ireland and Portugal had the lowest volume of freight per capita (less than half the European average).

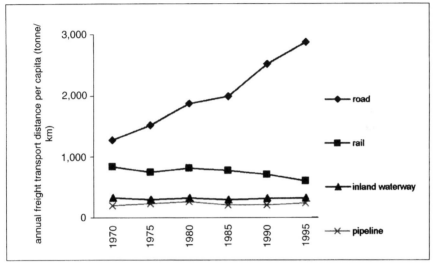

Figure 3.10 Freight transport by mode in the EU, 1970-1995 (Source: EUROSTAT, 1997)

3.10.2 Modal split

The reliance on roads for transporting goods is increasing (Figure 3.10). In 1995, almost three-quarters of freight transport was moved on roads, compared to less than half in 1970. Freight transport by road increased by more than 150 per cent in Europe between 1970 and 1995. The reliance on road freight transport varies across European Member States. In Greece, 98 per cent of freight transport is moved on roads, whereas in Austria, the figure is only 41 per cent of all freight transport. The use of air transport is a small but rapidly growing proportion of freight transport. Freight traffic increased by more than 8 per cent at the major European airports in the space of a year between 1994 and 1995 (EUROSTAT, 1997). Freight transport by inland waterways and pipeline increased at a much slower rate than by road or air and now accounts for around 14 per cent of freight tonne-kilometres. Freight transport by inland waterways increased by 6 per cent in Europe between 1970 and 1995, although there were bigger increases in Germany and freight transport by pipeline increased by 29 per cent across Europe. Goods movement by pipeline increased more than fourfold in Denmark, Spain and the UK between 1970 and 1995. Meanwhile, freight transport by rail fell between 1970 and 1995, accounting for only 14 per cent of freight transport in 1995, compared to almost 32 per cent in 1970. The biggest decreases were in Greece and the UK, where freight transport by rail fell by more than half. In Sweden and Finland, however, freight transport by rail increased over this period. Rail freight still forms a major mode for the movement of goods in both these countries (accounting for 39 and 36 per cent of freight-tonne kilometres in Sweden and Finland respectively).

In 1995, per capita freight transport by road was highest in Belgium, Finland and Spain (more than 40 per cent above the European average) and lowest in Luxembourg and Portugal (less than half the European average). Per capita freight transport by rail was highest in Finland and Sweden (more than three times the European average) and lowest in Greece (less than one-twentieth of the European average). Per capita freight transport by inland waterways was highest in the Netherlands (more than seven times higher than the European average). Very few goods were moved by inland waterways in a number of countries (such as Denmark, Greece, Ireland, Portugal, Spain and Sweden). Per capita freight transport by pipeline was highest in Austria and Denmark (more than double the European average). Very few goods were moved by pipeline in Finland, Greece, Ireland, Luxembourg, Portugal and Sweden.

3.11   Transport energy use

In 1970, the average amount of energy used in the transport sector was 0.40 tonnes of oil equivalent (TOE) per capita in Europe. By 1995, this figure had almost doubled to 0.77 TOE per capita. The fastest increase was in Luxembourg, where transport energy use per capita increased more than fivefold between 1970 and 1990 (Figure 3.11). In 1995, transport energy use per capita in Luxembourg was more than three times higher than in any other European Member State. Transport energy consumption per capita in Portugal was the lowest of all Member States in 1995 (0.50 TOE per capita), partly as a consequence of the low level of car ownership and the low level of freight transport compared to the rest of Europe. There is little evidence from the trends between 1970 and 1995 to suggest that energy consumption per capita is converging across European Member States.

3.12   Energy efficiency and transport intensity

Two distinct types of measures of transport intensity are examined here: measures of *transport energy efficiency* and measures of *economic efficiency* (relative to transport volumes). The first and more commonly encountered category of transport intensity measures is defined according to energy

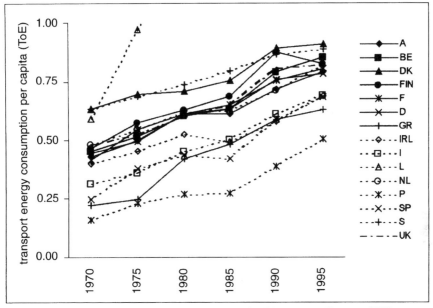

Figure 3.11 Transport Energy Consumption per Capita in the EU, 1970-1995 (Sources: OECD, 1992, 1997)

consumption as a ratio of passenger movements, freight movements or a combination of both (using the concepts of *net mass movement*[3] and *gross mass movement*,[4] discussed in more detail by Peake (1994). Authors such as Scholl *et al.* (1996) and Michaelis and Davidson (1996) use this type of measure when referring to transport intensity. The second category of transport intensity measures is defined according to economic activity as a ratio of passenger movements, freight movements or a combination of both (again using the concepts of *net mass movement* and *gross mass movement*). SACTRA (1999) use this type of measure when referring to transport intensity. One of the commonly used and most widely available measures of economic activity, Gross Domestic Product (GDP), provides a way of comparing economic activity in different countries. However, this measure has a number of limitations when considering issues of welfare or sustainability, since the calculation of GDP includes spending on actions such as pollution clean-up and medical treatment for road accident victims (for more detail, refer to Anderson, 1991 or Jackson and Marks, 1994). Other indicators of economic activity have been proposed to give a more sustainable view of national accounts (such as the Index of Sustainable Economic Welfare, developed in the United States by Daly and Cobb (1990)) but there is at present insufficient data to calculate and compare transport intensity using these indicators across European Member States. In addition to the problems of accounting for externalities, GDP does not take account of unpaid household production (such as caring, catering, education and housework), even though this supplies services to the economy. This makes long-term analysis of GDP trends even more difficult.

Examples of a range of indicators for transport intensity (three indicators of *transport energy efficiency* and four indicators of *economic efficiency*) are presented in Table 3.1. Beside these indicators are data which illustrate trends for the EU as a whole between 1970 and 1995. Some data indicate reductions in transport intensity whilst others indicate little overall change. The ratio of transport energy consumption per passenger-kilometre remained fairly constant between 1970 and 1995, whilst the ratios of transport energy consumption per tonne-kilometre and transport energy consumption per net mass movement increased, indicating that transport energy efficiency decreased.[5] Between 1970 and 1995, the ratios of GDP per tonne-kilometre and GDP per net mass movement remained fairly constant, whilst the ratios of GDP per passenger-kilometre and GDP per unit of transport energy consumption decreased, indicating that transport economic efficiency decreased. Thus, the overall picture of transport intensity using this selection of indicators is one of stability or decline, depending on the choice of indicators.

Table 3.1 Indicators of transport intensity

Type of measure	Indicator of transport intensity	1970 (EU15)[1]	1995 (EU15)	% change 1970-1995
Transport energy efficiency[2]	Transport energy consumption per passenger-kilometre	64.8	63.6	-2%
	Transport energy consumption per tonne-kilometre	153.6	186.8	22%
	Transport energy consumption per net mass movement	159.4	192.5	21%
Economic efficiency[3]	GDP per passenger-kilometre	1.47	1.19	-19%
	GDP per tonne-kilometre	3.74	3.82	2%
	GDP per net mass movement	3.87	3.93	2%
	GDP per unit of transport energy consumption	22.6	19.1	-15%

Notes
1. Only 6 countries were part of the European Community in 1970 but for comparison purposes, the data for 1970 and 1995 relate to the 15 countries that are currently members of the European Union.
2. Note that these figures refer to total transport energy consumption (across both passenger and freight transport sectors) and further disaggregation of the energy consumption data is obviously necessary in order to determine energy efficiency trends in the freight and passenger sectors.
3. The four economic efficiency measures were calculated using data for all countries that are currently members of the European Union with the exception of Germany, where comparable GDP data for 1970 were not available.
Sources: EUROSTAT (1997); OECD (1992); OECD (1997); World Bank (1998).

Transport intensity trends across individual European countries show a substantial amount of diversity from the trends for Europe as a whole (Stead,

2001). Most of the fifteen EU countries have experienced quite individual trends in transport intensity between 1970 and 1995 (Table 3.2) and few common patterns are obvious over this period. SACTRA (1999) observe that 'traffic intensity, however measured, shows very considerable variation from country to country'. Some indicators of transport intensity used here (such as transport energy consumption per passenger-kilometre or GDP per tonne-kilometre) show improvements in the majority of EU Member States between 1970 and 1995, whilst others (such as transport energy consumption per tonne-kilometre or GDP per unit of transport energy consumption) show worsening trends in transport intensity in most EU countries. The trends

Table 3.2 Summary of transport intensity trends in Europe, 1970-1995

	Transport energy efficiency:			Transport economic efficiency:			
	TEC/ pass-km	TEC/ tonne-km	TEC/ net mass movement	GDP/ pass-km	GDP/ tonne-km	GDP/ net mass movement	GDP/ TEC
Austria	✓			✗			
Belgium		✗			✗	✗	✗
Denmark	✓	✓	✓	✗	✗	✗	
Finland		✗	✗		✓	✓	
France		✗	✗	✗	✓	✓	✗
Germany		✗	✗	n.a.	n.a.	n.a.	n.a.
Greece	✓	✗	✗	✗		✗	✗
Ireland	✓	✗	✗		✓	✓	✓
Italy	✓	✓	✓	✗	✗	✗	✗
Luxembourg	✗	✗	✗	✓	✓	✓	✗
Netherlands		✗	✗	✗	✓	✓	✗
Portugal	✓	✗	✗	✗	✓		✗
Spain	✗			✗	✗	✗	✗
Sweden	✓	✗		✗			
UK		✗	✗				
EU		✗	✗	✗			✗

✓   denotes more efficient transport intensity by more than 10 per cent between 1970 and 1995[1]
✗   denotes less inefficient transport intensity by more than 10 per cent between 1970 and 1995[2]
GDP   Gross Domestic Product
TEC   Transport Energy Consumption

Notes
1   More efficient transport intensity means either:
    (i) a decrease in the energy efficiency value (i.e. less energy used per unit of transport movement or per unit of transport energy consumption); or
    (ii) an increase in the economic efficiency value (i.e. more economic activity per unit of transport movement or per unit of transport energy consumption).
2.   Less efficient transport intensity means either:
    (i) an increase in the energy efficiency value (i.e. more energy used per unit of transport movement or per unit of transport energy consumption); or
    (ii) a decrease in the economic efficiency value (i.e. less economic activity per unit of transport movement or per unit of transport energy consumption).

in the seven measures of transport intensity for each country often do not follow the same direction – some indicators suggest that transport intensity is increasing whilst others suggest the reverse. No country in the EU can claim substantial increases in transport intensity between 1970 and 1995 across all seven indicators. On the other hand, none experienced substantial reductions in transport intensity between 1970 and 1995 across all seven indicators. There is a certain amount of evidence for the decoupling of economic activity and transport volumes between 1970 and 1995 in some countries (such as Finland and Ireland) although transport energy efficiency decreased over the same period in these countries, according to at least some indicators. On the other hand, measures of economic efficiency suggest some evidence of worsening trends in countries such as Belgium, Denmark and Spain. Only Italy and Denmark experienced improvements in *transport energy efficiency* according to the three indicators. Luxembourg was the only country to experience a substantial decline in *transport energy efficiency* according to the three indicators used here. Across Europe as a whole, the indicators tend to suggest that transport intensity became less efficient between 1970 and 1995. This corresponds with Peake's observation that transport intensity has become less and less efficient over the last 40 years (Peake, 1994).

Comparing the most recent measures of transport intensity (Table 3.3 shows 1995 values) with the European average, few common patterns are obvious here either. For many countries, some indicators suggest that transport intensity is more efficient whilst others suggest the reverse. No country in the EU can claim to be substantially more efficient than the EU average across all seven indicators of transport intensity but no country is less efficient than the EU average across all seven indicators. This corresponds with SACTRA's observation that 'there is no overwhelming evidence that "efficient" countries are consistently marked by high, low, increasing or decreasing levels of transport intensity' (SACTRA, 1999).

The conclusion from this analysis is variability both over time (between 1970 and 1995) and at a single point in time (1995). Different EU countries have followed different paths and are at different stages in terms of economic and social development. The measures of transport intensity for individual countries are dependent on economic trends as well as travel trends and overall transport demand (influenced by topography, geography, land-use characteristics, socio-economic factors, transport infrastructure and so on). This variability of transport intensity indicators across European Member States also reflects the crudeness of the measures used and the limitations of the available data. The variability is an issue which has been noted elsewhere (for example, SACTRA 1999). Some forecasts assume that transport intensity will reduce over time (even though past trends show continuous increases in transport intensity), believing that vehicle saturation may lead to improvements in transport intensity (see, for example, SACTRA, 1999).

Table 3.3 Summary of transport intensity measures in Europe relative to the EU average (1995 figures)

	Transport energy efficiency:			Transport economic efficiency:			
	TEC/ pass-km	TEC/ tonne-km	TEC/ net mass movement	GDP/ pass-km	GDP/ tonne-km	GDP/ net mass movement	GDP/ TEC
Austria		✓	✓	✓		✗	✓
Belgium	✓	✗	✗	✓	✗	✗	
Denmark	v	✗	✗	✓	✓	✓	✓
Finland		✓	✓	✓	✗	✗	✓
France		v	✓			✓	✓
Germany		✓	✓	n.a.	n.a.	n.a.	n.a.
Greece		✗	✗	✗		✗	✗
Ireland	✓	✗	✗	✗	✓	✓	
Italy	✓		✓			✗	✓
Luxembourg	✗	✗	✗	✓	✓	✓	✗
Netherlands			✓	✓		✗	✓
Portugal	✓	✗		✗		✗	✗
Spain	✗	✓	✓		✗	✗	✗
Sweden		✓	✓	✓		✗	✓
UK		✗	✓		✓	✗	✗

more denotes more efficient than the European average (by more than 10 per cent)[1]
less denotes less efficient than the European average (by more than 10 per cent)[2]
GDP Gross Domestic Product
TEC Transport Energy Consumption

Notes
1 More efficient transport intensity means either:
(i) less energy used per unit of transport movement or per unit of transport energy consumption; or
(ii) more economic activity per unit of transport movement or per unit of transport energy consumption.
2 Less efficient transport intensity means either:
(i) more energy used per unit of transport movement or per unit of transport energy consumption; or
(ii) less economic activity per unit of transport movement or per unit of transport energy consumption.

3.13 Conclusions

At the beginning of this Chapter, we stated that we would present a quantitative retrospective and prospective analysis of trends in the European transport sector. Most of the indicators are in the wrong direction if European transport policy is to reduce the transport and energy intensity of the economy (Chapter 4). Economic activity has continued to grow over the last 25 years, and this is unlikely to change (indeed, economic growth is a key policy objective of practically all governments). The close links between economic activity, transport energy consumption and the increased dependence on the car, need to be addressed. One characteristic of a sustainable transport policy would be to decouple economic activity and transport use. This would ensure increased efficiency in the economy, less use of non-renewable resources and less pollution and waste. The real costs of using the car have declined over the last 25 years, even though in some countries this is now being redressed. The net effect has been decreases in the efficiency in the economy, more use of non-renewable resources and more pollution and waste. In addition to economic factors, there have been social changes in terms of the demographic structure of the population, household composition and lifestyle/employment factors, all of which seem to have encouraged greater car dependence and longer car journeys. These trends may have been influenced by more dispersed land-use patterns and investment in transport infrastructures that have themselves also reinforced the social trends. Consequently, even greater dependence on the car and greater travel distances have resulted. All of the economic, social and physical changes are reflected in the EU statistics with substantial increases in distances travelled, the dominance of the car and the lorry, and in the modal split proportions for both the passenger and freight sectors. The net result is not surprising: the trends in energy efficiency are quickly outweighed by the growth in travel by the less efficient modes of transport, and the indicators of transport intensity generally support this movement towards unsustainable transport futures.

Notes

1   Current European Member States (2000) comprise: Austria; Belgium; Denmark; Finland; France; Germany; Greece; Ireland; Italy; Luxembourg; the Netherlands; Portugal; Spain; Sweden; and the United Kingdom.
2   This may not be the case for children, however. In fact, evidence from the UK suggests that children's travel is less independent than in the past (Hillman et al., 1990)
3   The net mass movement of people and goods is calculated using a method similar to Peake (1994): by dividing total passenger-kilometres by 11.11 (on the assumption that people with luggage weigh 90 kilogrammes on average) and adding this figure to the total volume of freight moved (in tonne-kilometres). Note that the assumption about average weight per passenger here is substantially different to that used by Peake (1994), who assumed an average weight of 50 kilogrammes, which seems quite a low estimate.
4   Calculation of gross mass movement of people and goods is similar to the calculation of net mass movement but also includes the mass of the vehicles used to carry the people and goods and the movements of empty vehicles.
5   Further disaggregation of the energy consumption data is necessary in order to determine energy efficiency trends in the freight and passenger sectors.

Chapter 4

European transport policy responses

4.1   Introduction

As we have seen in Chapter 3, there has been a continuous growth in traffic in Europe, reflecting increased mobility levels, rising income levels, increased social and leisure time, and the breaking down of national barriers within Europe. There seems to be agreement that European transport is in a state of crisis, and that this crisis is likely to get worse in the near future. There is increasing reference in the literature to the German term *Verkehrsinfarct* (traffic blockage), but as Ross (1998) comments, the awkward English equivalent (infarction) has anatomical rather than economic connotations. The much more appropriate French term *bouchon* (cork) gives a perfect image of the problem.

As we shall see in this Chapter, there seems to be uncertainty over the direction of policy. On the one hand, there is a lack of capacity, and many of the systems are incompatible, both in the technical sense and in an organizational sense. On the other hand, there is a realization that unlimited mobility is not desirable environmentally or socially. The EU (like many national governments) has not found the *Third Way*.

Transport policy at the European level has developed slowly since the Treaty of Rome (1957), but it is only in the most recent past (since 1992) that the Common Transport Policy (CTP) has been promoted by the European Union (EU). The three main components of that policy are:

1   competitiveness;
2   cohesion;
3   environment.

These clear underlying principles, which cut across many other sectors of EU policy, have recently been modified (CEC, 1998a) in a further communication from the Commission. The main purpose of this chapter is to provide the background context to the development of the EU CTP.

The main focus is at the strategic level and in the development of the Trans-European Networks for transport. This is where the EU has had most influence in determining future policy on transport in Europe, at least until recently when other policy imperatives, relating to sustainability, pricing, quality and safety have become more important (Banister, 1994; Banister and Berechman, 1993). For a more comprehensive survey of the broader policy and political background to the evolution of EU transport policy, the book by Ross (1998) provides a review of policy overall, and of each of the main modes of transport, together with a perspective of the system as a whole, concentrating on the major projects (constructed or under consideration), and the requirements for the new organizational framework.

4.2   European transport policy – phase 1 from 1957 to 1992

Transport was identified in the Treaty of Rome (1957) as one of the areas for development of a common policy. Since then, progress has been slow, with the Single European Act (1986) requiring the removal of physical barriers (at frontiers), reductions in technical barriers, and harmonization of fiscal barriers. In 1985, the European Parliament asked the European Court of Justice to recognize officially the lack of a European Transport Policy and that this failure was due to the inefficiency of the European Council of Ministers (CEC, 1985). In 1986, the Commission put forward proposals for a medium term plan on transport infrastructure (European Parliament, 1991). It described the principal deficiencies of the European transport network; the ways in which the Community could take action to resolve them; the ways in which the Community could declare an interest so that Community action would be possible; and it identified the needs for overall financial investments in infrastructures. The Council of Ministers was reluctant to accept that proposal, and in 1988 the Commission submitted a four-year plan extending to 1992 which coincided with the introduction of the Single Market. Again, there was resistance from the Council, and the Commission presented more modest proposals which concentrated available resources on a limited number of projects regarded as the most important. This proposal was accepted in November 1990.

Many international initiatives concerning transport came not from the EU but from the transport industry itself. For example, the proposal for an international network of high-speed trains came from the Community of European Railways. The role of the EU has been of secondary importance and restricted to issuing directives such as those on the environment, standards for road freight, cabotage, and reductions in custom's formalities. The Maastricht Agreement (1991) expanded transport's role to include common rules on international transport and improvements in transport safety.

The EU budget for transport infrastructure investment has always been limited and any increase in that budget has been resisted by Ministers due to a conflict with national interests and the notions of subsidiarity. Contributions have been made to specific projects, often under the European Regional

Development Fund (ERDF) and European cohesion programmes. The ERDF allocated 43 per cent of its expenditure (1983-1987) to infrastructure projects of Community interest (Vickerman, 1991). However, only 40 per cent of EU territory is eligible for ERDF financing. In Greece, 24 per cent of ERDF funding investment is for transport infrastructure, and the corresponding figures for Portugal, Spain, Italy and Ireland are 18, 47, 10, and 39 per cent, respectively (European Parliament, 1991). It is only in the air and telecommunications markets that the private sector has been fully involved, and it is here that most of the new investment took place (Table 4.1). The possibilities for an enhanced role for the private sector, either on its own or through joint ventures with the public sector, have not yet been fully explored for a wider range of infrastructure projects including road and rail (Gérardin, 1989).

Table 4.1 EIB financing for transport and telecommunications, 1986-1990 (million ECU)

Country	Overland transport	Air transport	Shipping	Telecomms[1]	Total
Belgium	–	6.0	–	–	6.0
Denmark	476.1	241.2	5.6	188.5	911.4
Germany	252.3	30.1	1.2	–	283.6
Greece	208.0	7.4	0.9	–	216.3
Spain	594.7	652.1	40.3	1203.8	2490.9
France	2448.5	45.1	15.8	85.3	2594.7
Ireland	150.7	144.9	–	135.3	430.9
Italy	1294.1	414.4	302.0	2311.5	4322.0
Luxembourg	–	–	1.6	–	1.6
Netherlands	–	367.3	–	–	367.3
Portugal	639.0	53.6	57.7	176.7	927.0
United Kingdom	640.3	731.0	77.4	44.4	1493.1
Article 18	–	–	–	660.8	660.8
Total	6703.7	2693.1	502.5	4806.3	14705.6

Note:
1 Telecomms includes telecommunications and telecommunications satellites; Article 18 projects are located outside the EU (such as submarine cables and satellites).
  Austria, Finland and Sweden were not members of the EU. This is the EU12 rather than the EU15 (Figure 4.1).
Source: European Investment Bank (1991).

The other main agency has been the European Investment Bank (EIB), which co-finances projects (up to a maximum 50 per cent contribution) designed to modernize Europe's economy. Between the date of its establishment (December 31, 1982) and 1985, the EIB allocated just over 20 per cent of all its financing operations within the Community to transport. More recently (1986-1990), the EIB further increased its support to over 15 billion ECUs (37 per cent of its total budget) for transport and telecommunications infrastructure and equipment (see Table 4.1). Assessment

Figure 4.1 Map of the EU15 and the accession countries

of projects is based on financial criteria related to their potential profitability. The total allocation to transport and telecommunications increased as follows:

1986	1945 million ECU
1987	1661 million ECU
1988	2980 million ECU
1989	4001 million ECU
1990	4518 million ECU

To enhance European integration, the EIB has given priority to projects which:

* help to develop regions in difficulties;
* achieve energy savings or other energy-related investment so as to reduce the EC's dependence on oil;
* assist in European economic integration or towards the achievement of Community objectives such as protection of the environment;
* modernize and promote sectors with high innovation potential including advanced technology (Abbati, 1986).

EIB loans are generally repayable over 8 to 20 years, and loans can be backed by financial guarantees or by the assets represented in the project itself.

The Edinburgh Council (December 1992) recognized the problem by setting up a new European Investment Fund to help fill the *missing links* in European infrastructure and also extended the lending facility of the European Investment Bank. It has made it easier for financial markets to back large infrastructure projects for Trans-European networks, including transport, telecommunications and energy. The EIB will contribute 40 per cent of the fund's capital of 2 billion ECU's with the remainder coming from the Community (30 per cent) and the private and public sectors (30 per cent). It is estimated that the Fund could support investment projects worth up to 20 billion ECU. The crucial assumption here is the expectation that the limited capital in the new Fund will generate this level of borrowing – a gearing ratio of 10 to 1 is very high. Nevertheless, this was an important step forward in EU thinking as it was the first time that a new financial instrument had been set up in this area. Previously, the Council had confined itself to laying down the objectives of an infrastructure policy and identifying the principal criteria for establishing whether a project is of Community interest. The EU has approved fourteen priority infrastructure projects. The new European Investment Fund has been approved and this means that action can now take place on the major new infrastructure projects.

However, across the EU there is still no infrastructure policy. The long-term loans provided by the EIB support individual projects submitted separately by public and private promoters in each EU country. Although it is recognized that international travel is only a small part of overall travel, some corridors are already at capacity, there are many missing links in the European network, and demand will increase dramatically as a result of the Single Market. Some strategy seems to be essential, particularly when transport policy is set against competition policy, regional development policy, and environmental policy within the EC. Congestion in the core area of the EU has resulted from:

- a high-density population and a high concentration of economic activities in those regions;
- north-south traffic crossing through this area concentrated in a limited number of congested corridors; and
- rapid and recent development of east-west flows related to the political and economic changes in central and eastern Europe.

4.3 European transport policy – phase 2 from 1992 to 1995

The Maastricht Treaty of the EU (Art. 2) states that the Union aims to 'promote a stable and non-inflationary growth which respects the environment' and it stresses the importance of an integrated approach to economic growth, quality of life, jobs, local development and the environment (CEC, 1993). The European Commission's interpretation of sustainable development is contained in the Fifth Action Plan for the Environment. As part of the required action, it calls for the integration of the principles of sustainable development into all of the EC's policies (CEC, 1992a). This includes the regulations governing the Structural Funds programme, which supports a large number of transport projects (approximately one-fifth of Structural Funds are used to support transport projects). As a consequence of this new imperative, the EU changed its approach to transport so that a Common Transport Policy would be based on *sustainable mobility* (CEC, 1992a). The new framework sets out strict environmental standards for all modes of transport, for quality standards on pollution, for encouraging environment-friendly modes, and for the promotion of guidelines for infrastructure and the development of urban transport. These guidelines for the development and assessment of Community infrastructure projects would:

> discourage unnecessary transport demand and encourage where appropriate the development of alternatives to road transport, such as railway, inland waterways and combined transport. Guidelines for the conversion and upgrading of relinquished infrastructure, particularly for the purpose of 'soft' transport, would be implemented.
>
> (para. 127)

The common strategy of sustainable mobility should:

> contain the impact of transport on the environment, while allowing transport to continue to fulfil its economic and social functions, particularly in the context of the Single Market, and thus ensure the long term development of transport in the Community. It should also contribute to social and economic cohesion in the Community and to the creation of new opportunities for the peripheral regions.
>
> (para. 128)

In the EU White Paper on a Common Transport Policy (CEC, 1992b), one of the main themes has been Trans-European Networks. Incompatibilities between national transport systems have been highlighted, including inadequate interconnections, missing links and bottlenecks, and obstacles to inter-operations. All of these lead to inefficiencies. The EU has had only a limited policy role mainly through the Committee on Transport Infrastructure (set up in 1978), but with the principal financial contributions coming from the structural funds and instruments that have been mentioned previously:

- ERDF credits (1975-1991) for transport infrastructure of 16 billion ECU;
- EIB loans (1982-1991) for transport infrastructure of 14 billion ECU;
- European Coal and Steel Community loans (1987-1991) to TGV track in France and Spain and to canals 1.2 billion ECU.

The EU proposes to establish and develop a:

Trans-European transport network, within a framework of a system of open and competitive markets, through the promotion of interconnections and inter-operability of national networks and access thereto. It must take particular account of the need to link island, landlocked and peripheral regions with the central regions of the Community. (CEC, 1992b, para. 140)

The goal has been to improve the integration of the Community transport system and not the improvement of the transport infrastructure in general. Much of the funding has continued to be allocated to the geographically isolated regions. On the crucial question of financing, the White Paper (CEC, 1992b) is pessimistic. The general level of investment in transport infrastructure has been stagnant at about 1 per cent of GDP. The volume of investment required for the period 1990-2010 is nearly 1500 billion ECU, or 1.5 per cent of GDP (CEC, 1992b, para. 143). This level is far in excess of the resources available to the EU even if its mandate would permit such intervention. Its role is limited to financing feasibility studies, loan guarantees, and interest rate subsidies. In addition, the EU may have a major dilemma. On the one hand, it sees under-investment in transport infrastructure, but on the other hand it is arguing for sustainable mobility and protection of the environment (Table 4.2). It could be argued that these two objectives are incompatible.

Table 4.2 Objectives of the Common Transport Policy

- the continued reinforcement and proper functioning of the internal market facilitating the free movement of goods and persons throughout the Community;
- the transition from the elimination of the artificial regulatory obstacles towards the adoption of the right balance of policies favouring the development of coherent, integrated transport systems for the Community as a whole using the best available technology;
- the strengthening of economic and social cohesion by the contribution which the development of transport infrastructure can make to reducing disparities between the regions and linking island, land-locked and peripheral regions with the central regions of the Community;
- measures to ensure that the development of transport systems contributes to a sustainable pattern of development by respecting the environment and, in particular, by contributing to the solution of major environmental problems such as the limitation of CO_2;
- actions to promote safety;
- measures in the social field;
- the development of appropriate relations with third countries, where necessary giving priority to those for which the transport of goods or persons is important for the Community as a whole.

The EU policies on infrastructure now extend beyond the Community members, and there is a specific provision for co-operation with third countries. The Prague Declaration adopted by the Pan European Transport Conference in 1991 emphasized the necessity of developing transport networks on a truly European scale and of integrating the greater European transport market. Measures were also taken with the European Economic Area agreement and transit agreements with Switzerland and Austria. Trade between East and West Europe has increased movements in both directions by more than 50 per cent (1990-2000), which in turn has placed considerable pressure on the links where little investment has taken place for the past forty years.

It should be acknowledged, however, that the function of EU policy is more one of stimulating and initiating, while the final responsibility for implementation and enforcement still largely rests with the individual Member States of the EU. At the same time, the CTP has become increasingly important, due to several 'package deals' (Hey, 1996). First, as a result of the internal market objective, transport markets were liberalized and the Trans-European Networks became a pre-requisite for the functioning of the internal market. Second, from 1987 onwards more financial support (for example, for the financing of transport infrastructure) was granted in order to compensate peripheral regions for the negative impacts of the internal market. Third, these funds were increased in 1992 in order to compensate those regions for economic disadvantages of the monetary EMS and EMU criteria.

In order to focus the policy assessment aspects of CTP, the above mentioned objectives can be summarized as follows:

1   *Efficiency*: subsidies should be reduced and market principles should be applied in the operation of the transport system and in assessing new investments; in this way the transport system should contribute to the economic efficiency of society and to an improvement in the competitive position of the economy.

2   *Regional Development*: the transport system is a means to stimulate economic development in more peripheral regions (especially CEC-countries and Southern Europe) and is used to stimulate the social cohesion within Europe.

3   *Environment*: the transport system must reduce its external (environmental) impacts, and the system should favour sustainable (environmental) development.

Although most of the EU CTP has been focused on infrastructure, this transition phase (1992-1995) also brought about other important changes in regulations, particularly on safety and the environment (CEC, 1995a). European regulation aims at reducing air pollution by road vehicles by setting emission reduction targets per vehicle, by reducing traffic congestion, and by reducing mobility growth. The first has been applied relatively successfully during the recent past in Europe, emissions of several gases being reduced by up to 50 per cent (OECD, 1993). However, the simultaneous rise in mobility has meant that the net energy consumption and emissions of CO_2 by transport have increased. The reduction of CO_2 emissions is seen as a major environmental challenge, and the stabilization target was agreed at Rio (1992) (reducing CO_2 emissions to 1990 levels by 2000). More recently the EU took the lead from Kyoto (1997) to set a target level of reducing CO_2 emissions by 8 per cent between 1990 and 2010 (Chapter 1).

The existence of and the quality of infrastructure are both prerequisites for using any mode. In the past, a large road infrastructure network has been constructed in Europe, which has induced a steep growth in the number of vehicle-kilometres and thereby in personal mobility. At present the road network is relatively dense in comparison to rail or air networks, which partly explains why the car has become the dominant mode of transport. The EU CTP is now aiming to close the gaps in the European (trans-national) network ('missing links', 'missing networks' and 'Trans-European Networks' – see Nijkamp *et al.*, 1994) for both road and rail infrastructure. The main justification for this is economic reasons, as building new infrastructure is promoted as a generator of economic growth and regional economic development. But this is only one element of the CTP.

4.4   European transport policy – phase 3 from 1995 to 2000

In 1995, the Commission launched its action plan for 1995-2000 (CEC, 1995a). As part of this new initiative, there has been a series of important debates opened up in the transport sector. Although the main aims of the CTP of 1992 have not changed fundamentally, there is a significant change in the focus of transport policy in the EU. The efficiency of the transport system still underlies much of the policy thinking, as this is seen as being essential to the competitiveness of Europe and to growth and employment. But a greater emphasis is being given to the social cohesion objectives, to safety (again), the environment, subsidiarity, and the accession countries.

Improving efficiency and competitiveness of the transport system is not only concerned with new infrastructure and the completion of the TENs, but with four other main policy initiatives:

1   liberalizing market access (particularly as it relates to railways, air and ports);
2   ensuring integrated transport systems across Europe (continuation of the TEN-Transport priority projects, but with public-private partnerships financing and operating these systems);
3   ensuring fair and efficient pricing within and between transport modes, in particular applying the principles of marginal social cost pricing;

4   enhancing the social dimension so that more balanced and sustainable development can be implemented across all the EU.

Improving quality in response to the needs of EU citizens means that priority is given to the following three areas of policy:

1   safety is a permanent concern of the EU in all forms of transport, particularly in the air, maritime, and roads sectors;
2   the development of sustainable forms of transport to limit the impact of transport activity on climate change. This work includes the development of accurate indicators of transport and the environment, and the strengthening of the environmental impact assessments of policy initiatives. Links are being made here with air transport noise and emissions, with waste reception in maritime transport, with the problem of heavy lorries in the roads sector, and with the emissions work of the Auto/Oil I and II programmes (CEC, 1998*b*);
3   protecting consumers and improving the quality of transport services through participation and representation of organizations in the development of the CTP. The two main sectors concerned here are aviation and local public transport. In the latter, a Citizens Network has been set up to establish best practice, including the integration and benchmarking of services.

Improving external effectiveness covers the links with the accession countries and the globalization of the world economy. Agreements have been negotiated with some of the accession countries so that markets can become more open during the transition period to membership of the EU. The enlargement of the EU must be achieved with minimum disruption. The globalization issues concern the effects on trading and market conditions as they relate to countries outside the EU.

As can be seen from the discussion above, the CTP has evolved substantially from 1992 to a much broader-based and more coherent approach (CEC, 1998*a*). The primary concerns of policy within the EU along the three original dimensions of competitiveness, cohesion, and the environment are still present. They form the first two of the new priorities (efficiency and competitiveness, and improving quality), but the two new dimensions relating to the accession countries and the role of the EU in global markets have substantially enhanced the scope of the CTP.

Further, the original concerns were primarily with the network and the means to provide a European infrastructure to link all the EU countries together, and to link with the countries of Eastern Europe (CEEC) and the

Soviet Union (CIS). This has also changed with a new emphasis on bringing down the barriers to free trade (and using pricing tools more effectively), making the systems compatible (interoperability), getting the best out of the different modes of transport (intermodality), making good use of the network (interconnectivity), promoting best practice in organizational structures (including logistics and technology), and in ensuring the responsible use of resources in transport. Strong links are now being drawn between the transport policy perspective and the new European Spatial Development Perspective (ESDP), as the combination of these two policy areas is necessary to achieve sustainable mobility and a balanced territorial development.

Recent priority areas for EU transport policy are also reflected in the content of a succession of European policy papers. The 1995 Green Paper on fulfilling the potential of passenger transport in Europe, 'The Citizens' Network', identifies how public transport may be made more attractive and usable, and looks at all levels of policy-making (local, national and European) that might achieve this goal (CEC, 1995a). The 1995 Green Paper on policy options for internalizing the external costs of transport, 'Towards Fair and Efficient Pricing', explores economic policy options for internalizing some of the external costs of transport such as air pollution, congestion, accidents and noise (CEC, 1995b). Promoting rail modernization, integration and use is addressed in the 1996 White Paper on a strategy for revitalizing the Community's railways (CEC, 1995c). It recommends Community action in five main areas: finance; market forces; public services; integration of national systems; and social aspects. The 1997 Communication on intermodal transport (Intermodality and Intermodal Freight Transport in the European Union), sets out a framework for the integration of transport modes to provide seamless and efficient door-to-door services (CEC, 1997).

The action plan sets out the initiatives it intends to take to ensure 'sustainable mobility' within the European Union, which it interprets as encouraging 'efficient and environmentally friendly transport systems that are safe and socially acceptable'. The document states that the efficiency of transport systems remains a fundamental objective for the competitiveness of Europe and for growth and employment, whilst at the same time promoting 'sustainable mobility'. The major priorities and initiatives of the action programme up to 2004 include the following:

- improving market access and functioning of railways and ports;
- strengthening environmental assessments of policy initiatives with important environmental effects, especially in the light of CO_2 emissions and climatic change, and actively supporting the Council of Ministers in setting up a strategy to reinforce further the integration of environmental issues into transport systems;

- ◆ encouraging Member States to speed up the implementation of the Trans-European Transport Networks priority projects defined at the Essen Summit, and encouraging public-private partnerships (PPPs) in the priority projects;
- ◆ taking steps to launch the first phase of a programme progressively to apply the principle of charging for marginal social costs in the light of the White Paper on Fair Payment for Infrastructure Use (CEC, 1995b);
- ◆ presenting new proposals on working time in the inland waterways and aviation sectors and synergy between transport and cohesion policies;
- ◆ ensuring transposition and implementation of the various legislative measures adopted by the Council;
- ◆ promoting safety in all areas of transport, particularly in relation to air, maritime and road transport;
- ◆ examining how to ensure adequate consumer participation in the development of the Common Transport Policy to protect consumers and improve the quality of transport services, giving special priority to civil aviation and the improvement of passenger information in terms of new commercial developments;
- ◆ examining how to update the regulatory framework for domestic public transport (for example by including quality targets in contract conditions) in order to improve the quality of local public transport;
- ◆ setting out a specific key action programme to carry out a number of targeted research projects aimed at improving the efficiency and sustainability of transport systems in the context of the fifth framework programme (FP5) for research and development (CEC, 1999); and
- ◆ negotiating agreements in the areas of civil aviation, heavy goods vehicles, coach services and inland waterways with Central and Eastern European countries.

However, there may still be inconsistencies in EU transport policy, particularly as it relates to the environment and the achievement of the challenging Kyoto targets for CO_2 reduction. As stated in the recent Communication on EU CTP (CEC, 1998b):

> it will be necessary to assess more globally to what extent existing policy measures will bring the transport sector in line with environmental objectives and what further well-focussed and complementary measures may be needed. Particular attention will need to be given to measures designed to reduce the dependence of economic growth on increases in transport activity and any such increases on energy consumption, as well as the development of less environmentally damaging energy alternatives for transport. (para 46)

These are the new challenges of the Common Transport Policy for the next five to ten years. It is a dynamic instrument for delivering an integrated transport system that both accommodates the needs of the planet and those of all its inhabitants. The policy discussion paper (CEC, 1998*a*) concludes that much progress has been achieved, but to sustain economic progress, social structures and a clean environment, significant further agreement at EU level is required.

4.5 Trans-European Networks

The concept of the Trans-European Networks was developed during the formulation of the Maastricht Treaty of the European Union, which specified a network of transport corridors forming the backbones of the European transport system. At the Council in Essen in December 1994, fourteen TEN priority projects were accepted (Figure 4.2 and Table 4.3), with special emphasis being placed on the improvement of those European axes.

1.	High-Speed Train/combined transport North–South	8.	Multimodal link Portugal–Spain–central Europe
2.	High-speed train PBKAL	9.	Conventional rail Cork–Dublin–Belfast–Larne–Stranraer
3.	High-speed train South	10.	Malpensa airport, Milan
4.	High-speed train East	11.	Oresund fixed railroad link Denmark–Sweden
5.	Betuwe-line: conventional rail/combined transport	12.	Nordic triangle multimodal corridor
6.	High-speed train/combined transport France–Italy	13.	Eire/United/Kingdom/Benelux road link
7.	Greek motorways pathe und via Egnatia	14.	West Coast main line

Figure 4.2 Location of the Trans-European Network priority projects

The timetables submitted by the Member States suggest that there will be a very substantial increase in expenditure on the fourteen priority projects during the period 2000-2006, with many of the larger projects moving into the full construction phase (Table 4.3). At present, three of the fourteen

Table 4.3 Investment in the Trans-European Network priority projects

Trans-European Network project	Investment pre-1998 (MECU)	Investment 1998-1999 (MECU)	Investment 2000+ (MECU)	Total investment (MECU)
1 High-speed train/combined transport north-south (Berlin to Nürnberg and from München to Verona – the Brenner Axis)	2505	1325	11245	15075
2 High-speed train (Paris-Brussels-Köln - Amsterdam-London: PBKAL)	3728	4118	9386	17232
3 High-speed train south (Madrid to Perpignan-Montpellier – Mediterranean Branch – and Madrid to Dax – Atlantic Branch)	240	1375	11757	13372
4 High-speed train Paris-Eastern France-Southern Germany (including Metz-Luxembourg branch)	59	170	3086	3315
5 Conventional rail/combined transport Betuwe line (Rotterdam to German Border)	360	870	2864	4094
6 High-speed train/combined transport France-Italy (Lyon-Turin. Turin-Milan-Venice-Trieste)	368	943	16949	18260
7 Greek motorways PATHE (Patras to Bulgarian Border)and Via Egnatia (East-West Axis)	2175	2351	4716	9242
8 Multimodal link Portugal-Spain-Central Europe	not available	not available	not available	6212
9 Conventional rail link in Ireland (Cork-Dublin-Belfast-Larne-Stranraer)	328	29	0	357
10 Malpensa Airport, Northern Italy	473	406	168	1047
11 Fixed rail/road link between Denmark and Sweden – Øresund fixed link	2505	1377	276	4158
12 Nordic Triangle	0	1260	3320	4580
13 Ireland-United Kingdom-Benelux road link	1670	247	1710	3627
14 West Coast main line (UK) high-speed train/combined transport north-south	287	532	2180	2999
Total for all fourteen projects	14698	15003	67657	103570

projects are close to completion (Malpensa airport – opened in 1998, the Øresund fixed link opened in 2000 and the Greek Motorways). All the others are under construction or at an advanced state of preparation and most are likely to be completed by around 2005.

The priority projects have benefited from substantial amounts of EU financial support, particularly those located in areas eligible for Structural and Cohesion Fund financing. The TEN Transport Budget, (around 1800 MECU1 1995-1999) has had a considerable impact in helping to launch major projects. The European Investment Bank (EIB) is the major source of loan funding for TENs projects, advancing 1400 MECU to the fourteen priority projects in 1997 alone.

The Community budget will continue to play a crucial role in getting projects off the ground and maintaining momentum. In a number of cases the Community contribution will be a determining factor in the financial viability of the project. The estimates of financial requirements (5000 MECU for the period 2000-2006) which the Commission put forward with the proposal to revise the TEN Financial Regulation reflect the forecast increase in activity, and the need to continue to recognize the strong Trans-European element in the projects concerned.

The contribution that these Trans-European Networks make to the cohesion objectives of the EU is important as they are designed to raise the quality of the infrastructure in each of the Member States. They are not necessarily the fourteen most critical projects, but they are symbolic of the wider European ideal. Most of the projects outlined above improve the infrastructure between two or more EU countries, all countries are represented, and most funding is for rail schemes (usually high-speed rail). In terms of sustainable mobility, it is necessary to make use of the most efficient forms of transport. High-speed rail seems to be in an anomalous position, as it uses more energy than conventional rail, but less than air and road, but its overall efficiency is dependent upon high occupancy factors. In energy terms, high-speed rail can be extremely efficient, provided that passengers have switched from road or air and provided that the trains are full (Banister and Banister, 1995). However, if new long distance travel is encouraged and spare capacity is realized for more air travel (as more slots become available as a result of new high-speed rail investment), then the energy arguments in favour of high-speed rail are far less clear (see Chapter 12).

4.6 Conclusions

Substantial progress has been made on the EU Common Transport Policy since the Treaty of Rome, particularly in the last decade of the twentieth century. It is clear that the EU sees itself as a major player in the integration of Europe and in promoting sustainable mobility, but there are still conflicts and dilemmas to be resolved. There is a continuing and growing conflict between the Directorate Generals (DGs) in Brussels and the elected Members of the European Parliament (MEPs). This conflict came to a head in 1999 with the mass resignation of all EU Commissioners and the appointment of a new set of Commissioners in the summer. However, it seems that there will be a probationary period and the MEPs are seeking to have a much greater control over the Commission. This conflict is apparent across all of the EU policy-making spheres, and transport policy action is a key part of that process. The input of the MEPs will become more regular and consistent, and it may take much longer for action to be taken as the decision-making processes become extended. Ironically, this new situation may be preferable to the Commission as its propensity to make major policy changes may be slower and more deliberate than the desires of the MEPs.

The second dilemma is within the Commission, where transport functions cut across several of the Directorates. Apart from the interests of the Transport Directorate, transport is a concern of Science and Research, Telematics, Environment, Competition and Regional Development. These other Directorates have considerably more power than the Transport Directorate and their budgets are also very substantial.[2] These conflicts are now being addressed by the new Commissioners as their portfolios have been rationalized to accommodate some of these differences, but transport will continue to be a policy area that is within the sphere of several Directorates, each seeking to achieve slightly different objectives and each seeking to claim responsibility for popular actions, but also seeking to avoid the blame for controversial actions. In addition to these difficulties within the EU, transport has also to be seen as an important area for national policy, which again may conflict with the wider European agenda. Nevertheless, the EU has moved very much from a reactive following role to a proactive leading role on transport policy, particularly on issues such as environmental quality, the Trans-European Networks, and the opening up of European markets to competition.

Note

1 At current exchange rates 1 ECU = 1 Euro = US1.00 = GBP0.60.
2 The transport portfolio has been combined with energy to form DG-TREN. The Commissioner (loyola de Palacio) is also responsible for European Parliamentary relations. This means that transport has been effectively downgraded as an area of activity for the EU.

Chapter 5

Impacts of transport on sustainable development

5.1   Introduction

Transport is one of the largest sources of environmental pollution in Europe. The large number of significant environmental impacts associated with transport range from local through to global and cut across a large range of issues. The extent of these impacts is illustrated in Table 5.1 (using the example of the United Kingdom). Many of these impacts are increasing. Others are beginning to decrease but these impacts may start to increase again in the longer term unless action is taken to reduce transport growth. Transport is also associated with a number of adverse social and economic impacts although these impacts are not the main focus of this Chapter. The environmental impacts associated with transport include energy and mineral resources, land resources, water resources, air quality, solid waste, biodiversity, noise and vibration, built environment impacts and health effects. Impacts across these nine categories are outlined below. Having outlined the environmental impacts of transport, the importance of establishing policy targets is discussed. Targets can help focus effective action to reduce the environmental impact of transport. These targets should be challenging, but not unrealistic, and they should be amenable to measurement, monitoring, and adjustment over time. They are central to the scenario building process described in Chapters 7 to 9. The relationships between transport policies, the organization and structure of the transport sector, economic conditions, and environmental impacts are illustrated in Figure 5.1. It shows that reducing the environmental impacts of transport requires action not just in terms of transport policy, but also in terms of the organization and structure of the transport sector as well as general economic policies.

Table 5.1 The environmental impacts of transport in the United Kingdom

Environmental categories	Environmental impacts	Transport's contribution (1995 unless otherwise stated)
1. Energy and mineral resources	• Energy resources used for transport (mainly oil-based) • Extraction of infrastructure construction materials	• 44.8 million tonnes of petroleum consumed by transport • transport accounts for approximately one-third of the UK's total energy consumption • approximately 120,000 tonnes of aggregates per kilometre of 3-lane motorway • 78 million tonnes of roadstone extracted
2. Land resources	• Land used for infrastructure	• approximately 4.2 hectares of land per kilometre of 3-lane motorway • 1725 hectares of rural land developed for transport and utilities per annum (1992)
3. Water resources	• Surface and groundwater pollution by surface run-off • Changes to water systems by infrastructure construction • Pollution from oil spillage	• 25 per cent of water pollution incidents in England and Wales caused by oil • 585 oil spills reported in the UK • 142 oil spills requiring clean-up in the UK
4. Air quality	• Global pollutants (such as carbon dioxide) • Local pollutants (such as carbon monoxide, nitrogen oxides, particulate matter, volatile organic compounds)	• 25 per cent of the UK's carbon dioxide emissions (CO_2) • 76 per cent of the UK's emissions of carbon monoxide (CO) • 56 per cent of the UK's emissions of nitrogen oxides (NO_x) • 51 per cent of the UK's emissions of black smoke (particulates) • 40 per cent of UK emissions of volatile organic compounds (VOCs)
5. Solid waste	• Scrapped vehicles • Waste oil and tyres	• approximately 1.5 million vehicles scrapped • more than 40 million scrap tyres
6. Biodiversity	• Partition or destruction of wildlife habitats from infrastructure construction	
7. Noise and vibration	• Noise and vibration near main roads, railway lines and airports	• approximately 3500 complaints about noise from road traffic • approximately 6500 complaints about noise from air traffic
8. Built environment	• Structural damage to infrastructure (such as road surfaces, bridges) • Property damage from accidents • Building corrosion from local pollutants	• more than £1.5 million annual road damage costs
9. Health	• Deaths and injuries from accidents • Noise disturbance • Illness and premature death from local pollutants	• 3500 deaths • 44,000 serious injuries • 49 per cent of people who can hear noise from aircraft or trains consider it a nuisance (1991) • 63 per cent of people who can hear noise from road traffic consider it a nuisance (1991) • between 12,000 and 24,000 premature deaths due to air pollution • between 14,000 and 24,000 hospital admissions and re-admissions may be associated with air pollution

Sources: Banister (1998); Central Statistical Office (1997); Committee on the Medical Effects of Air Pollutants (1998); Department of the Environment, Transport and the Regions (1997a, b and c); Department of Trade and Industry (1997); Maddison et al. (1995); OECD (1988) and Royal Commission on Environmental Pollution (1994).

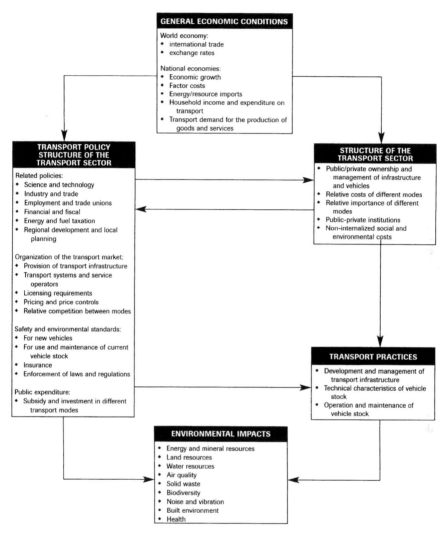

GENERAL ECONOMIC CONDITIONS

World economy:
* international trade
* exchange rates

National economies:
* Economic growth
* Factor costs
* Energy/resource imports
* Household income and expenditure on transport
* Transport demand for the production of goods and services

TRANSPORT POLICY STRUCTURE OF THE TRANSPORT SECTOR

Related policies:
* Science and technology
* Industry and trade
* Employment and trade unions
* Financial and fiscal
* Energy and fuel taxation
* Regional development and local planning

Organization of the transport market:
* Provision of transport infrastructure
* Transport systems and service operators
* Licensing requirements
* Pricing and price controls
* Relative competition between modes

Safety and environmental standards:
* For new vehicles
* For use and maintenance of current vehicle stock
* Insurance
* Enforcement of laws and regulations

Public expenditure:
* Subsidy and investment in different transport modes

STRUCTURE OF THE TRANSPORT SECTOR
* Public/private ownership and management of infrastructure and vehicles
* Relative costs of different modes
* Relative importance of different modes
* Public-private institutions
* Non-internalized social and environmental costs

TRANSPORT PRACTICES
* Development and management of transport infrastructure
* Technical characteristics of vehicle stock
* Operation and maintenance of vehicle stock

ENVIRONMENTAL IMPACTS
* Energy and mineral resources
* Land resources
* Water resources
* Air quality
* Solid waste
* Biodiversity
* Noise and vibration
* Built environment
* Health

Figure 5.1 Transport policies, structure, practices and environmental impacts (Based on: OECD, 1988)

5.2 Impacts of transport on sustainable development

5.2.1 Energy and mineral resources

In 1970, the transport sector accounted for 14 per cent of Europe's energy consumption. By 1995, it was responsible for more than 21 per cent. Energy equivalent to 285 million tonnes of oil was consumed by the transport sector in 1995 (OECD, 1997). The transport sector is now the largest and fastest increasing consumer of energy due mainly to the growth in road and air transport. The last decade saw large increases in the use of energy intensive modes such as cars and aircraft for the movement of passengers and freight. Over the same period there was a decrease in the use of energy efficient modes such as walking and cycling. Passenger vehicles became more fuel efficient but factors such as catalytic converters, higher safety standards, air conditioning and higher vehicle performance tended to counter the fuel efficiency gains from improved engine design.

In 1995, 78 million tonnes of road stone were quarried in the United Kingdom, almost one-third more than the tonnage quarried in 1985 (Central Statistical Office, 1997). According to the Royal Commission on Environmental Pollution (1994) the construction of one kilometre of a three-lane motorway requires around 120,000 tonnes of aggregates. The extraction of aggregates and road stone can damage natural habitats, scar the landscape and can also create noise and disturbance from quarrying and the transport of materials.

5.2.2 Land resources

Transport occupies substantial areas of land and the amount of land used for transport infrastructure currently probably amounts to over 20,000 hectares per year (approximately equivalent in area to a square whose sides measure 14 kilometres). Roads occupy approximately one-fifth of the urban surface area and railways take up around a further four per cent of the surface of large cities (Royal Commission on Environmental Pollution, 1994). Every kilometre of three-lane motorway requires 4.2 hectares of land (Banister, 1998). In addition to the land consumed for roads, significant amounts are also used for the storage of vehicles. The effects of this land loss include the loss of productive agricultural areas, the loss of biodiversity, and the fragmentation and severance of local communities (see below).

5.2.3 Water resources

Transport accounts for much of the consumption of petroleum products and must therefore bear a large part of the responsibility for oil spills in coastal and marine waters. The oil spill from the Sea Empress in February 1996 off the coast of Milford Haven is a recent example of a major water pollution incident with serious impacts on biodiversity, recreation and tourism. 72,000 tonnes of crude oil were released into the sea, of which between 3000 and 5000 tonnes reached the shore, affecting 200 kilometres of shoreline in the United Kingdom alone (Maritime and Coastguard Agency, 1997).

5.2.4 Air quality

Transport produces a number of emissions that are detrimental to air quality. These include global pollutants (such as carbon dioxide which contributes to global warming), national or regional pollutants (for example nitrogen oxides which produce acidification or 'acid rain') and local pollutants (such as particulates which contribute to respiratory problems including the increased susceptibility to asthma). Transport's contribution to environmental pollution in urban areas is particularly large, where transport is by far the most significant contributor of most emissions. The temporal trends in air pollutants from transport are mixed. Some emissions continue to increase, others are beginning to fall. However, some of the emissions that are decreasing may be a problem in the future if the growth in transport increases faster than improvements in technology (see, for example, Howard, 1990; Department of the Environment, Transport and the Regions, 1997d).

Carbon dioxide from the transport sector is produced by the combustion of fuels. CO_2 is the most important greenhouse gas and is responsible for global warming and climate change. Transport currently accounts for more than one-fifth of Europe's carbon dioxide emissions, most of which comes from road transport (European Environment Agency, 1999). In 1994, 1.79 tonnes of CO_2 were produced in the transport sector for every person in Europe. The transport sector is now the largest generator of CO_2 emissions in some European Member States (such as Austria and France). In 1994, transport-related CO_2 emissions were lowest in Greece, Portugal and Spain (1.28, 1.15 and 1.28 tonnes per capita respectively) and highest in Luxembourg (2.83 tonnes per capita). If the trends in CO_2 emissions from transport continue, a 40 per cent increase in carbon dioxide emissions from transport might be expected between 1995 and 2010 (CEC, 1998b). Although the total CO_2 emissions per capita in Europe have decreased over the last two decades due to reductions in energy consumption in other sectors (such as domestic and industrial energy consumption), the rapidly increasing emissions from the transport sector may soon lead to increases in total emissions.

Nitrogen oxides cause national and trans-national pollution, contributing to acid deposition and the formation of secondary pollutants, which give rise to photochemical smog and poor air quality. Almost half of all emissions of nitrogen oxides in Europe now originate from road transport (European Environment Agency, 1999). Emissions of nitrogen oxides in many European countries decreased between 1980 and 1995 as a consequence of the introduction of catalytic converters.

The transport sector is now the largest generator of NO_x emissions in almost all European Member States. In 1994, an average of 16.31 kilogrammes of NO_x per person was emitted from transport in Europe (European Environment Agency, 1999). Transport-related NO_x emissions were lowest in Austria (11.98 kg per capita) and highest in Finland and Luxembourg (26.53 and 24.6 kg per capita). Although the total NO_x emissions per capita have decreased in most European countries over the last two decades, there have been increases in total NO_x emissions in a few Member States (such as Ireland and Portugal). Emissions of nitrogen oxides are likely to continue decreasing in most countries for several years but could then begin increasing again if increasing levels of traffic outweigh the emission reductions achieved by catalytic converters.

Volatile organic compounds (VOCs) contribute to the formation of secondary pollutants, which give rise to photochemical smog and poor air quality. Almost one-third of all emissions of VOCs in Europe now originate from road transport (European Environment Agency, 1999). Emissions of VOCs in many European countries decreased between 1980 and 1995 as a consequence of the introduction of catalytic converters. Emissions are likely to continue decreasing for several years but could then begin increasing again if increasing levels of traffic outweigh the emission reductions achieved by catalytic converters.

The transport sector is also one of the largest generators of VOCs in many European Member States. In 1994, an average of 13.55 kg of VOCs was emitted from transport in Europe (European Environment Agency, 1999). Transport-related VOCs emissions were lowest in Austria, Germany and the Netherlands (8.91, 8.30 and 8.92 kg per capita, respectively) and highest in Greece and Luxembourg (21.09 and 22.44 kg per capita, respectively). Although the total VOCs emissions per capita have decreased in most European countries over the last two decades, there have been increases in total VOCs emissions in a few Member States (such as France and Portugal). Emissions of VOCs are likely to continue decreasing in most countries for several years but could then begin increasing again if increasing levels of traffic outweigh the emission reductions achieved by catalytic converters.

5.2.5 Solid waste

Transport accounts for a significant proportion of solid waste due to the high rate of vehicle scrappage. Millions of road vehicles are scrapped annually, resulting in millions of tonnes of waste material requiring recycling, reclamation and disposal. Vehicle residues for disposal are rapidly increasing as the proportion of steel used in vehicles declines. Plastics are increasingly being used in vehicle manufacture but few of these are recycled at present. Waste tyres present another major solid waste problem: millions of tyres are scrapped each year.

5.2.6 Biodiversity

Infrastructure construction and maintenance often leads to losses of vegetation-rich land including hedgerows and verges. Newly planted verges are generally not an adequate replacement. Where new infrastructure cuts across natural or semi-natural habitat, the effects on biodiversity will depend on factors such as the habitat's sensitivity, the siting of the infrastructure and the area of land used for construction. Transport infrastructure such as roads, airports or railways may act as a barrier to the movement of species which may result in the separation of populations and a decline in numbers. Rarer species may disappear if the population becomes too small.

5.2.7 Noise and vibration

Transport is the most pervasive source of noise for many people in Europe. It is estimated that around 80 million people (or 17 per cent of the population) in Europe are exposed to noise levels above 65 dB(A), which the OECD defines as an unacceptable noise level (CEC, 1992a). The exposure to noise varies by country: from around 4 per cent of the population in the Netherlands to 23 per cent of the population in Spain (*ibid.*). The most common sources of transport noise (in order of importance) are road traffic, aircraft and trains. Road traffic is generally considered to be more of a nuisance than most other sources of noise. Conclusive evidence of the health effects of noise is limited to cases of hearing loss and tinnitus caused by long periods of exposure to high noise levels – more than 75-80 dB(A) (Royal Commission on Environmental Pollution, 1994). It is unlikely that most people are exposed to traffic noise at these levels over a sufficiently long period to cause these health effects, although traffic noise may aggravate or contribute to stress-related health problems such as raised blood pressure and minor psychiatric illness (Taylor and Watkins, 1987; OECD, 1991). Sleep is also disturbed by transport noise for a number of people (Jones, 1990). In addition, transport movement causes vibration which may be another contributory factor to stress-related diseases (Royal Commission on Environmental Pollution, 1994). Excessive noise from traffic may also discourage social interaction in streets and reduce the attractiveness of walking or cycling. The costs of noise are thought to amount to between 0.1 and 0.5 per cent of Europe's GDP (CEC, 1992b; International Union of Railways, 2000 and Quinet, 1994).

5.2.8 Built environment

Transport's impact on the built environment includes the damage to property as a result of accidents, structural damage to transport infrastructure (such as road surfaces and bridges) and damage to property and monuments as a consequence of corrosive local pollutants. Road damage is dependent on factors such as climate, the road surface and the axle weight of vehicles using the road. Because road damage is related exponentially with axle weight, heavy vehicles with few axles cause most of the damage. Maddison *et al.* (1995) report that the annual road damage costs in the United Kingdom are in excess of £1.5 million.

5.2.9 Health

More than 44,000 people were killed and 1.6 million people were injured on Europe's roads in 1995. In other words, more than five people killed every hour and more than three people injured per minute on the roads. The costs of road casualties are thought to amount to between 2.0 and 2.5 per cent of Europe's GDP (CEC, 1995*b*; Quinet, 1994; International Union of Railways, 2000). The number of deaths and injuries on the road is decreasing in most European countries, although part of the reason is the decline in the number of pedestrians and cyclists using the road. There are significant differences in road safety statistics between European Member States. The proportion of people killed per capita on the roads in Portugal is more than double the proportion of people killed in the Netherlands, Sweden or the United Kingdom (Figure 5.2). The proportion of people injured per capita on the roads in Belgium is more than three times the proportion of people injured in the Netherlands or Denmark (Figure 5.3).

Research suggests that the deaths of thousands of vulnerable people may be brought forward each year and thousands of hospital admissions and re-admissions per annum may arise as a result of short-term air pollution containing ozone, sulphur dioxide or particulates (Committee on the Medical Effects of Air Pollutants, 1998). Transport is a major contributor to pollutants that form ozone as a secondary pollutant (such as nitric oxide) and one of the largest sources of particulate matter. The people most liable to be affected by air pollution are likely to belong to vulnerable groups such as pregnant women, the frail or the very ill. Air pollution levels normally experienced in Europe may not have any short-term effects on other groups but the long-term effects are still unknown.

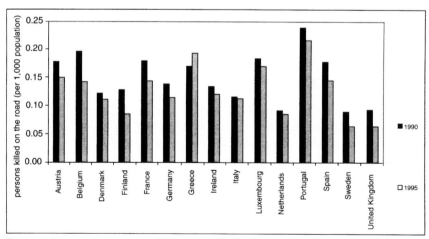

Figure 5.2 Persons killed on the road in the EU, 1990–1995 (Source: EUROSTAT, 1997)

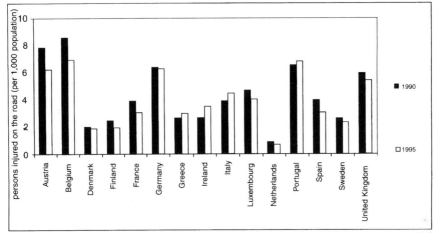

Figure 5.3 Persons injured on the road in the EU, 1990-1995 (Source: EUROSTAT, 1997)

5.2.10 Other

Heavy traffic disrupts home and community life. Research by Appleyard and Lintell (1969) showed that social contact on the street declines as traffic volumes increase. Behavioural differences such as use of front gardens and front rooms in homes were correlated with traffic volumes. Many families chose to move away from heavily trafficked areas if they could afford to do so. Transport corridors (a motorway or railway line for example) can cause the partition or destruction of neighbourhoods. Social contact and/or walk journeys may be inhibited where corridors are difficult or inconvenient to cross.

5.3　Environmental targets for transport

Targets can give policy a clearer sense of direction; they can add to the pace of policy implementation and development; and they can make explicit those aspects of policy that might otherwise remain opaque. (UK House of Lords, 1995, p.16)

Environmental targets are becoming increasingly important in the development and implementation of transport policy, particularly since the introduction of the concept of sustainable development into policy-making. Environmental targets are also being advocated as a way of promoting more sustainable transport policies. Environmental targets describe qualitative or quantitative environmental levels to be achieved in a particular area by a certain time. In the context of transport policy, environmental targets generally represent points of reference or 'staging points', as opposed to specific end-points. Environmental targets may relate to environmental levels established by scientific investigation (such as the dose-response characteristics of pollutants and health), attitudinal surveys (such as the quality of landscape), or a combination of the two (such as acceptable levels of noise). Thus, environmental targets represent a qualitative or quantitative statement of aspirations about the state of the environment and the quality of life.

The nature of existing targets varies considerably. Some are fixed, aimed at clearly specified objectives, whilst others are 'rolling'. The sanctions behind targets also vary; some have legal status and are backed by penalties; some form part of international obligations or agreements (such as national CO_2 targets), whilst others are more indicative.

The 1992 Rio Declaration commits all European countries to the concept of sustainable development in all areas of policy. The concept of sustainable development has led to a prominent role for environmental targets in several stages of the development and implementation of policy options, as well as assessment and review. The Royal Commission on Environmental Pollution (1994) recommends establishing environmental targets to provide a framework for the environmental appraisal of transport policies. The value of targets in policy implementation is discussed in the EU Expert Group on the Urban Environment's European Sustainable Cities Report (CEC, 1996). The report argues that two important functions of targets in the implementation of policy are securing commitment to a direction of change and helping to achieve policy goals. The report states that the effective implementation of policy depends on establishing the direction and rate of change, using indicators and targets. The EU Expert Group on the Urban Environment argues that targets are an integral part of policy assessment and review, providing 'staging points' against which policy performance can be measured (European Commission, 1996). Research into road safety targets suggests that more ambitious targets are associated with more successful achievement of objectives, by securing more commitment and/or resources for the achievement of the objectives (Box 5.1).

The process of developing and deriving environmental targets is at least as political as it is scientific. Jacobs (1993) observes that:

> limits are not always absolute or objectively 'discoverable'. The environment's capacities are not always fixed, and they cannot always be scientifically defined. Science can provide useful (if uncertain) information, particularly on factors such as 'sustainable' extraction rates for renewable resources or the 'critical loads' of pollutants at which serious damage to ecosystems is caused. But scientific evidence does not by itself make a judgement on society's goals. Ultimately environmental capacities depend on what society believes to be tolerable, for itself and future generations.

Box 5.1 Road safety targets and their effect on policy

National road safety targets have been adopted in various countries in recent years. These include Denmark, Finland, France, Great Britain, the Netherlands, Norway and Sweden. Targets have also been adopted at a local level in some of these countries. In Norway, road safety targets have been set by a number of county authorities. Elvik (1993) describes these in a study of the relationship between targets and accidents.

Targets were classified into three categories according to their type and ambitiousness: highly ambitious quantitative; less ambitious quantitative; and qualitative targets. Elvik presents the case that counties which set quantified targets were more successful in reducing the road accident rate than counties which set qualitative targets. Of the counties setting quantitative targets, the ones with highly ambitious targets achieved a larger reduction in road accidents. The study shows that road safety is associated with the type of target, the ambitiousness of the target, and the level of road safety spending in the county (a link between these three factors seems likely).

Elvik suggests that the chief policy implication is that the adoption of ambitious targets can assist the policy-implementation process by enabling priorities to be set more effectively, and enabling schemes to be implemented more successfully.

Thus, environmental targets should be developed in a systematic way, based on sound environmental data, and determined by participation and consultation on public aspirations about the state of the environment and quality of life.

In some cases (but not all) it may be possible to base local targets on existing national environmental targets or environmental standards (such as EU 'guide values' and 'limit values' of air pollutants). Setting targets requires striking the balance between unrealistically ambitious and undemandingly achievable levels. There is little point in setting targets that would be achieved in their absence, or in setting excessive, unrealistic targets that may discourage progress towards achieving them. Target setting requires reliable baseline data and a system for monitoring progress towards the target. At the local level, authorities may wish to adopt target levels set by national or international organizations (such as the European Union, World Health Organization or national government) or adapt them to reflect local conditions. A number of European environmental targets already exist. These include CO_2 emissions, NO_x emissions, dioxins, volatile organic compounds (VOCs), noise and biodiversity (Hey et al., 1999).

Environmental targets may not always be complementary, and the interrelation between targets should be carefully examined before they are adopted. Banister (1995) suggests a hierarchy or priority list of targets may be useful for assessing and comparing the contribution of different measures towards meeting a range of targets.

There is an increasing level of interest and activity in the use of indicators for policy analysis and decision-making. Many different types of indicators for a variety of sectors are being investigated and used. There is already a body of literature on indicators for the transport sector (for example OECD, 1993; USEPA, 1996; World Bank, 1995). These are illustrated in Table 5.2.

Table 5.2 Examples of environmental indicators from a selection of literature sources

Type of indicator:	Proposed by:
1. Resource Consumption:	
♦ proportion of energy consumed by transport	OECD (1993)
♦ energy consumption by mode	OECD (1993)
2. Pollution	
♦ proportion of global pollutants (CO_2, NO_x) from transport	OECD (1993); Pearce (1993); RCEP (1994)
♦ proportion of local pollutants (CO, VOCs, particulates) from transport	OECD (1993); Pearce (1993); RCEP (1994)
♦ proportion of waste from transport sector	OECD (1993)
♦ proportion of population affected by transport noise	OECD (1993); RCEP (1994)
3. Land:	
♦ land lost through infrastructure construction	OECD (1993); RCEP (1994)
4. Minerals:	
♦ aggregates production for transport infrastructure	RCEP (1994)
♦ oil production for transport	OECD (1993)
5. Air:	
♦ levels of local pollutants in air	OECD (1993)
6. Health:	
♦ transport injuries and deaths	Pearce (1993)
♦ ambient noise levels from transport	OECD (1993)

Note: The categories for Biodiversity and Built Environment (Table 5.1) are not included in this Table.

5.4 Conclusions

The range of transport's impacts on the environment has been deliberately drawn widely so that the full extent of the links is made clear. Within the broader context of sustainable development, the role of transport is evident and decisions taken in the transport sector (for example, about the location of new roads or airports) or in the development sector (for example, about the location of new housing) will be instrumental in determining future levels of demand. The basic argument here is that when addressing the problems of sustainable development and sustainable transport, it is not just a transport problem, but one that links in with decisions made in other sectors. Similarly, the impacts are not all related to transport alone, but they also have impacts on health, the vitality of urban areas, quality of life, biodiversity, and local ecology. The international nature of some of the environmental impacts of transport means that action at the international level to deal with these problems is necessary. This includes action at the European level.

Consequently, it is necessary to have targets, which are measurable and challenging, and which can act as clear indicators of whether change towards sustainable development and sustainable transport is taking place. Possible indicators have been described here for most of the environmental impacts linked to transport. What is lacking is the means by which the targets can be identified and aggregated to determine whether progress is being made. In many situations, progress on one target may result in a lowering of quality on another target. Judgement is still required to assess overall progress towards sustainable development and sustainable transport. The use of targets in scenario building is discussed in Chapter 8, together with the targets set for sustainable mobility at the EU level.

Chapter 6

The potential for achieving sustainable mobility

6.1 Introduction

Before describing in detail the scenario building process, it is important to describe the potential for achieving sustainable mobility. In this Chapter, we explore the contribution that the main sectors can make in this process – technology, passenger transport, freight transport, and organizational change. It also forms the foundation in terms of the comprehensive list of policy measures outlined later in (Chapter 9). For each of these sectors, we have categorized measures according to whether they are:

- *market-based instruments* – policies which rely on market incentives;
- *regulation-based instruments* – policies involving technical standards and regulations;
- *lifestyle-based instruments* – including policies which relate to quality of life, education and public information;
- *public infrastructure/services* – policies involving the provision of public infrastructure and/or public transport services.

In addition, we add comments on research and development, and the role that information technology will have in facilitating change. This same typology is taken up again in Chapter 9 as part of the classification of the policy orientation of the different measures (Table 9.1) that are used in the policy packages and paths (Chapter 10).

6.2 The role of technology in achieving sustainable mobility

6.2.1 Market-based instruments

Three categories of market-based instruments can be identified. The first category contains fiscally neutral instruments, such as 'feebates' (combinations of fees for fuel intensive cars and rebates for fuel-efficient cars). The second category contains instruments to reduce externalities in the short term (such as sulphur emissions). The third category contains instruments to reduce externalities that require a longer time horizon (CO_2 emissions for example).

These three categories have different impacts on technology and transport volumes. Feebates may improve technology but not necessarily transport volumes, particularly if used as a single measure. Without complementary instruments, feebates may increase transport volumes if fuel costs decrease. The second category of measures mainly affect technology but may limit transport volumes at least in the short term. The third category is likely to affect strongly both technology and transport volumes.

Under the assumption of a perfect market, a CO_2 tax is a very cost-effective instrument for reducing CO_2 emissions. However, considerable market imperfections mean that this instrument needs complementary measures, mainly directed at private vehicle use. A CO_2 tax is likely to affect the development of new vehicles, customer choice among available vehicle types, and transport volumes. Studies of customer behaviour, although not unanimous, indicate that customers do not take the whole lifecycle fuel costs into account when buying a new vehicle. Typically only the first three years are considered (Eriksson, 1992). To achieve the desired effect from a CO_2 tax would require costs to be two to three times as high as the shadow price. This would lead to unnecessary large adjustments of transport patterns with probably severe distributional effects. Because of this market imperfection it seems appropriate also to include a vehicle purchase tax differentiated according to fuel consumption (and possibly also vehicle weight). It would probably be easier to get support for such a measure if it were introduced in the form of a feebate. It is difficult to assess the precise levels of CO_2 taxation and feebates on new cars. The gradient of the feebate is dependent on the CO_2 tax.

A high CO_2 tax may result in a rather uneven distribution of mobility. This could be compensated to some extent (but probably not fully) if labour taxes were reduced so that there was no net increase in taxation overall. A general CO_2 tax probably would be included in any policy package, although the levels would differ depending on environmental values and degree of cooperation at the global level.

Vehicle weight reduction is one way of reducing emissions. It may be argued that the most general policy instruments (such as a CO_2 tax) should be used since it is difficult to forecast which technological solutions will be appropriate. The situation regarding vehicle weight is, however, somewhat special. To have great weight differences in the road fleet means, *ceteris paribus*, that more people are killed or injured in road accidents. To introduce a new generation of vehicles that are significantly lighter than the present stock of vehicles may therefore be less attractive. If, on the other hand, gradual development towards lighter vehicles is started now, the result may be both lower energy use and better safety as the weight span is simultaneously narrowed (which means that focus is on phasing out the heaviest vehicles). The car manufacturers are faced with a 'prisoner's dilemma' situation. Safety is apparently an important variable for potential customers. So for the car manufacturer it seems rational to produce cars that are heavier than the cars of their competitors. From a societal point of view this is however unwise since the total safety (and the environmental performance) is worsened by this. Policy instruments with a more direct effect on vehicle weight may therefore be needed. These may be economic incentives (a vehicle purchase tax or a yearly tax differentiated according to weight) and/or regulations (such as a maximum car weight).

To encourage the scrapping of old vehicles, economic incentives and regulations may be necessary. Bonuses for scrapping of polluting and heavy cars could be introduced, or a successively increased annual tax would encourage car owners to dispose of old vehicles. The former cannot be used continuously but would have to be used for a short period (maybe every fourth year or so).

6.2.2 Regulation-based instruments

CAFE (Corporate Average Fuel Economy) standards have been used in the USA since 1975. They require that the average fuel consumption of cars sold by a company in the USA should not exceed a certain limit. Compared to a carbon dioxide tax this instrument is less cost effective. The use of standards in the USA is the consequence of the political impossibility of high taxes on gasoline. Fuel consumption regulations may allow specific targets to be reached more easily than by the use of CO_2 taxes. A drawback with this type of regulation, however, is that traffic volumes may increase due to lower fuel costs. In addition, new cars may become more expensive while the cost of driving an old and polluting car is unaffected.

In Germany, a slightly different policy has been proposed in which there is a limit on vehicle emissions of CO_2 per vehicle-kilometre. This is differentiated according to vehicle weight. The constraints are then gradually lowered. If the limit is exceeded a relatively high penalty fee is incurred.

Emission standards have been the most common way of limiting emissions other than CO_2 (NO_x for example), although market-based instruments are also possible. Since the negative impact caused by emissions other than CO_2 depends on where they are emitted, road pricing is a more precise instrument than, for example, an additional fuel tax. In any case, since real world emissions are often much higher than test cycles would suggest, more realistic test cycles are needed. Because of the potential deterioration of exhaust cleaning devices, monitoring and regular control of emissions from old vehicles may be even more important.

6.2.3 Lifestyle-based instruments

Information about the environmental properties of products is important if people are to act more environmentally. Information about fuel consumption and emissions (ideally lifecycle emissions) for cars should be easily accessible. 'Eco-labelling' of public transport could also speed up technological development. Public support for car rental and car-pooling (possibly in the form of tax rebates) may also indirectly contribute to more fuel-efficient cars.

6.2.4 Effects on research and development

Most research and development regarding vehicle technology can be carried out by industry if given the proper incentives (such as a CO_2 tax or a system of taxes or rebates on new cars according to fuel consumption). In some cases, public funding may be needed. Public actors may be able to play an important role in creating initial markets for new kinds of vehicles. One such way is the purchase of innovative vehicles for their own fleets. They may act as a catalyst for the market. Environmental zones with access only for vehicles with zero or very low emissions may also be used. This could create market niches for battery and hybrid vehicles.

Since changes in fuel production patterns have long lead time, policy instruments need to be implemented promptly. Market-based instruments can be used but are not likely to be sufficient alone. The introduction of alternative fuel vehicles in public fleets may be used in order to create a basic niche for new fuels like methanol. Flexible fuel vehicles could be used during a transition period.

Examples of transport policy measures that are likely to affect technology are identified in Table 6.1, together with an indication of their likely timescale of effect impact on the policy targets.

6.3 The role of passenger transport policies in achieving sustainable mobility

6.3.1 Market-based instruments

Pricing gives clear messages to users of the transport system about priorities and there is a strong case for internalizing the external costs of transport. As a general principle, users should pay according to their use of the system, particularly when travel takes place under congested conditions. This means that fuel duty should be substantially increased so that petrol and diesel prices reflect the full environmental costs (including pollution). In the longer term, higher fuel prices would be reflected in purchase decisions on new vehicles and clear indications would be given to industry to provide more fuel efficient vehicles. By the year 2020, it might be possible to have an average car fleet efficiency of 10 kilometres per litre (current levels are 7 kilometres per litre), with some vehicles achieving 15 kilometres per litre. There would also be an indirect incentive to scrap older vehicles, or 'cash for clunkers'.

Vehicle tax and insurance charges could also be related to the fuel efficiency and the emissions of the vehicle. Some pricing could be linked to the emissions

Table 6.1 The potential effect of transport policy measures on technology and new fuels

Measure	Timescale
Market oriented:	
• Ecological tax reform charging resource use instead of labour	long-term
• Tax on CO_2	medium-term
• Feebates (or only fees) on new cars according to fuel consumption	medium-term
• Feebates (or only fees) on new cars according to weight	medium-term
• Incentives for scrapping of cars	medium-term
• Differentiated road pricing	medium-term
Regulation:	
• Standards for average fuel consumption	medium-term
• Emission standards	medium-term
• Better control of 'real world' emissions	medium-term
• Maximum weight for cars	medium-term
Lifestyle oriented:	
• Eco-labelling of cars	medium-term
• Eco-labelling of public transport	medium-term
• Support for car rental and car pooling	medium-term
Public services:	
• Research and development – vehicle technology	medium-term
• Research and development – renewable fuels	medium-term
• Creating environmental zones	medium-term
• Public procurement of environmentally friendly vehicles	medium-term

profile, so that gas and electric vehicles (including hydrogen cell vehicles) could have a much lower fixed charge (the annual tax charge) than a standard petrol or diesel vehicle. The advantageous position of the airlines should also be reviewed so that the appropriate environmental taxes are charged on kerosene and other aviation fuels.

Distortions within the system should be eliminated wherever possible. This means that all forms of subsidy to private and public transport should be phased out. In particular, the substantial tax benefits from owning (or leasing) a company car should be abolished as should access to free private parking at the workplace or shops.

Parking is the one policy option that is easy to influence in the short term. Pricing for parking, along with controls of spaces and type of parking, strongly affects modal choice. As a general rule, parking occupies valuable space and so should be charged for at the appropriate levels for equivalent commercial floor space within that particular area.

In the longer term, road pricing may provide the most appropriate single measure to internalize costs, but there are substantial political and operational problems with its implementation. Acutt and Dodgson (1996) review fifteen policy instruments aimed at reducing the environmental impacts of transport, eleven of which could affect CO_2 emissions (Table 6.2). They have combined pricing and other measures, but the table does give some indication of the options available in the passenger transport sector. Apart from reducing travel, these policy options have other impacts on air pollution, traffic congestion and on consumer expenditure, equity across groups, and public sector finance.

Many of the policies, such as congestion pricing and traffic restrictions could be used in larger cities where the provision of an efficient and effective public transport alternative is possible. But some measures might not be so appropriate in more remote areas of Europe where a sparse network with low levels of demand is more in evidence. Here, it may be more efficient to travel around in an 'environmentally clean' car, rather than in a public transport vehicle. This means the policies should be seen as forming parts of a package of measures that can then be applied in appropriate contexts.

6.3.2 Regulation-based instruments and public services

Physical restraint and demand management measures have been extensively used in cities and elsewhere to allocate space to priority users. Promotion of public transport and limitations on car use are common. Environmental objectives can be achieved through these measures, which would supplement pricing strategies. Included here are access control measures, parking restrictions, speed limits, bus lanes and routes, cycle and walking networks,

Table 6.2 Impacts of road vehicle policy measures

Policy	CO_2 emissions	Kilometres by car	Equity implications
1. Fuel taxes	Reduction	Reduce total	Problems in rural areas
2. Variable car excise taxes	Reduction	No direct impact	Improvements
3. Scrappage bounties	Reduction	Small reduction	Improvements
4. Road congestion pricing	Reduction	Reduction in priced area, but may increase elsewhere	Ambiguous
5. Vehicle use restrictions	Reduction	Reduction	Ambiguous
6. Parking charges	Reduction unless diversion a problem	Reduction in priced area, but ambiguous in total	Ambiguous
7. Parking controls	Reduction unless diversion a problem	Reduction in controlled area, but may increase elsewhere	Ambiguous
8. Land-use planning	Reduction if policy successful	Reduction if policy successful	Possible long-term improvement
9. Traffic calming	Possible increase in total	Reduction in residential areas	Improvements possible
10. Public transport subsidies	Small increase	Reduce total, especially urban	Improvements
11. Road construction	Increase	Increase	Could be negative

Source: Acutt and Dodgson (1996).

priority to some vehicles at road intersections, high-occupancy vehicle lanes, and many other proposals. Underlying these measures is the desire to reallocate road space to the most appropriate user, whether it is the pedestrian, the cyclist, the public transport user or the car driver. In the longer term, clear zones can be designated in cities where no cars would be allowed to enter. This would include city centres, local centres and residential areas. Pedestrianization and traffic calming are intermediate steps to the complete banning of all cars from environmentally sensitive locations. Only non-polluting vehicles would be admitted (such as electric vehicles and bicycles).

The second role that regulations have is ensuring that high standards are maintained through testing, monitoring, and benchmarking. Tough targets can be set on acceptable levels of pollution and energy use, with incentives (and penalties) being set for compliance. These measures would ensure the best available technology is being applied, with vehicles being maintained to a high standard.

Land-use planning and spatial development controls can be used to maintain city compactness so that trip lengths can be reduced. The key components of sustainable development concern the location of new development, which should be of a substantial size (over 25,000) or located near to an existing settlement, so that the existing set of local facilities, jobs etc can be used. Density and intensity of land use should be sufficiently high (over 30 to 40 persons per hectare) for car use to be reduced and for there to be more opportunities available for cycling and walking. Mixed-use developments can also help reduce trip lengths and car dependence, as can development which is located near to public transport interchanges, and corridors so that high levels of accessibility can be provided.

It has been demonstrated that about 20 to 30 per cent of the variation in travel patterns can be attributed to land use and physical characteristics, and much of the remaining 70 to 80 per cent is accounted for by socio-economic characteristics of people, including car ownership. But these two sets of factors are not independent of each other (Stead, 1999; Gordon, 1997). In summary, land-use factors most conducive to low travel distances include:

- high residential population densities;
- larger settlement sizes;
- development within short distances of local and regional employment, services and facilities.

If it is assumed that a new development is built according to more sustainable criteria, perhaps 25 per cent travel reduction can be achieved in these areas. Assuming that such savings only apply to new developments, the overall effect on travel demand may be of the order of a 5 to 6 per cent reduction (since around 75 per cent of the built environment will remain the same between now and 2020). A larger reduction in travel demand may be achieved if new development has synergistic effects on existing development, such as the provision of local facilities in the new development which might also be used by residents of neighbouring existing developments. Land-use planning and environment policies can also add to the attractiveness of local areas, which may encourage more locally-based activities (such as shopping and leisure), rather than at distant (often out-of-town) locations.

6.3.3 Information technology

Information technology may allow workers to spend more of the working week at home, thereby reducing commuting distances. Hall (1995) suggests that telecommuting might reduce total vehicle commuting distance by approximately 3-4 per cent. The impact of teleconferencing is much more difficult to assess. According to Himanen *et al.* (1996), substitution of 10 to 20 per cent of business trips by teleconferencing in Finland would result in a 1-3 per cent decrease in car kilometres and 7-15 per cent decrease in aviation passenger trips.

Various technologies may reduce business travel. These include video-conferencing, telephone conferencing, and e-mail. Better global communications might also promote additional travel by increasing the number of global business contacts. The evidence is ambivalent here.

Distance learning is of interest for schools, institutes, universities and enterprises. Virtual classes have been established in order to reduce school transport and also for security reasons. Interactive multimedia systems are widely used in education, in companies and also on factory floors for advisory purposes. They are used instead of specially arranged outside training. The future potential for reducing trips is very difficult to assess because Information Technology (IT) is constantly changing the means of learning and creating new opportunities for many to participate. Most school trips are made by walking, cycling or by public transport – they form typically less than 10 per cent of all trips (Salomon *et al.*, 1993). However up to 20 per cent of all car journeys during the morning peak are for education purposes.

Value added IT services like banking, consulting (for example in medicine, law, design, engineering, architecture and computing), marketing and providing product and sales information, interactive media, freelance editors and authors, and municipal services (public libraries, taxing, social services, registrars etc.) are all using the advantages of IT, with consequences for transport demand. The major influence on trips is among customers, who can get services at home or at their work place via IT networks, but the future potential for reducing trips is very difficult to assess.

IT also has potential in helping elderly and disabled people. In addition to the welfare benefits, IT may lessen the burden of the social sector by diminishing the need for home visits.

Shopping trips are typically 20 per cent of all trips, but are usually relatively short – around 10 per cent of daily distance (Salomon *et al.*, 1993). A reduction of 20 per cent in shopping trips would mean 2 per cent decrease in total distance. This might include catalogue, telephone, and internet shopping. There is the potential for technology to replace more shopping trips, but it is likely that many people will still prefer face-to-face shopping.

In terms of teleshopping, some key factors in influencing demand include:

- network marketing;
- access to technology;
- availability of the interactive multimedia systems;
- the interplay of local and global production;
- population distribution;
- land-use policy;
- trends in urban and rural living;
- goods delivery.

Home entertainment is possible with advances in home-based technology and may be more of a substitute for the cinema in the future, particularly with the introduction of more interactive technology. The speed of the progress of telematic multimedia with interactive digital television is a key factor. Entertainment has so far been the driving force of IT and it must be remembered that people are already spending more time watching television than shopping and many other activities. Leisure trips may be as much as half of daily travel (Salomon *et al.*, 1993), which means that even a modest change in travel distance and/or frequency might have a large impact on personal travel.

As technology increases the flexibility and range of choices offered to users, the impact may be to increase interaction and travel rather than reduce it. The behavioural response to all types of tele-activities is not well researched or understood. It is likely that the responses will be extremely variable with subtle adaptations in behaviour, rather than large changes. Access to technology is also very variable, but almost universal use of a wide range of new technologies can be assumed between the present and 2020. Possibilities include the networking of companies, the distribution of company activities to the periphery of Europe, the transformation of traditional high street activities, and a greater awareness of environmental issues in business. Companies may encourage employees to work at home by providing the necessary infrastructure and by restricting parking at the workplace.

6.3.4 Lifestyles and attitudes

Various aspects of lifestyle and attitude may have significant effects on passenger travel demand. Home location is dependent on lifestyles and attitudes, and influenced by land-use policies. Local transport supply, home location, and attitudes to various modes all influence mode choice. The availability of alternative modes to the car can be affected through infrastructure policies. The option for employees to compress their working week may also influence work travel demand. Hall (1995) suggests that this could result in a one per cent reduction in total distance travelled.

Kitamura *et al.* (1997) show that pro-environment or pro-public transport attitudes do not necessarily correspond to fewer trips per person – in fact, these attitudes often correspond with higher than average trip frequencies. These attitudes do correspond, however, with higher proportions of non-motorized modes. Kitamura *et al.* (1997) suggest that attitudes affect travel patterns more strongly and perhaps more directly than land-use factors. They suggest that a better understanding of attitudes to travel, the formation of these attitudes, and the effect of land use on these attitudes is necessary.

More fundamentally, attitudes need to change towards the car, in particular the right to own and use it, often at less than the full social cost. New forms of ownership are important including car pooling, shared ownership and rental cars. There should be no need to own a car in the city. Public support for restrictions on private ownership would allow communal ownership patterns to evolve. This means that the alternatives must be as good as the private car in providing high-quality door-to-door travel. Car free cities together with environmentally benign public transport, which is demand responsive and fully integrated with the passengers having 100 per cent accurate real-time information, is possible – smart cards and personal communicators are readily available.

In the passenger sector, examples of the potential policy measures that are available to decouple transport growth from economic growth, and to achieve the challenging environmental objectives are identified in Table 6.3, together with an indication of their likely timescale of effect on the policy targets.

6.4 The role of freight transport policies in achieving sustainable mobility

In recent decades a large number of (often expensive) services have been substituted by industrial products (such as washing machines, do-it-yourself tools and private cars) which have become affordable for an increasing number of people. More recently, leasing equipment of all kinds has become attractive and new kinds of full-service contracts in the fields of heating and cooling, transport and cleaning have emerged, speeded up with the boom of outsourcing. This in turn has led to efficient use of more durable goods and equipment by these outsourced companies.

In addition, the durability of goods is influenced by very contradictory trends. In terms of private consumption, more expensive high quality goods

Table 6.3 Possible passenger transport policy measures

Measure	Timescale
Market oriented:	
◆ Congestion pricing	medium-term
◆ Fuel tax	short-term
◆ Vehicle purchase tax	short-term
◆ Car ownership tax	short-term
◆ Parking tariffs	medium-term
◆ Excise for aircraft fuels	short-term
◆ Airport charges	short-term
◆ Tradeable mobility credits	medium-term
◆ CO_2 tax	medium-term
◆ Taxes and feebates based on fuel consumption and weight	medium-term
◆ Scrappage bonuses and tax increases	medium-term
Regulation:	
◆ Land-use planning	long-term
◆ Parking restrictions/control	medium-term
◆ Access control	medium-term
Lifestyle oriented:	
◆ Driver information systems	medium-term
◆ Commuter planning	medium-term
◆ Travel information	medium-term
◆ Traffic calming	medium-term
◆ Teleworking /telecommuting /teleconferencing	medium-term
◆ Teleshopping /telebanking /telecottages	medium-term
◆ Telematics /informatics available locally	medium-term
◆ Multipurpose personal communicators	long-term
◆ Transport chaining awareness	medium-term
Public services:	
◆ Advanced traffic management systems	medium-term
◆ Priorities for bus, tram and high occupancy vehicles (HOVs)	medium-term
◆ Segregated rights of way for transit	medium-term
◆ Cycle priority and roadspace	medium-term
◆ Pedestrian priority and roadspace	medium-term
◆ Lower speed limits and enforcement	medium-term
◆ Fare integration and schedule coordination	medium-term
◆ Increase rail capacity and speed	long-term

are gaining ground over cheaper, less durable goods in some fields. The outsourcing of services makes more durable goods economically attractive (several car producers are now planning more durable cars for the rental and leasing business). Miniaturization is a strong trend in many fields. Information technologies have favoured this tendency. Generally, our mobile society prefers more lightweight equipment.

The spatial structure of production and consumption is influenced by a large number of factors whose interrelationships are not well known. The transport impacts of business or political decisions are in most cases limited by the absence of information. A number of more sustainable freight strategies exist, which include:

- ◆ enhancement of regional consumer markets;
- ◆ strengthening of regional production networks;
- ◆ 'glocalization' of large companies;
- ◆ slowing down 'deterritorialization'.

The strengthening of regional consumer markets is mainly a lifestyle and marketing issue, but companies can also be encouraged to produce near to their markets. Food and building are the two fields in which such regional markets can most easily be enhanced, and they make up a considerable share of the total transport market. Information on the origin of products is an essential prerequisite for such a strategy. In subsidiarity terms, enhancing regional markets while maintaining European openness, can avoid a narrow regional clientele. However, such endeavours are often considered to be in contradiction to the internal market.

Regional production networks have been important motors of economic growth in recent decades. Industrial districts in which a large number of small and medium-sized enterprises (SMEs) co-operate, such as the textile and furniture industry in Emilia Romagna or the machine industry in Baden-Württemberg, have been described extensively as the most innovative production structures in recent years. Large companies have learned to make use of similar structures by regional sourcing. On the procurement side, such spatial production patterns produce less transport than global sourcing concepts.

There are no simple recipes for reducing transport distances in business decision-making since there is a large number of influencing factors and trade-offs, and each business is only one link in a longer chain. Large potentials for reducing transport remain undiscovered and/or unused. Despite the fact that the cost of transport is only a minor influence on business decisions, readily available information about possible, even minor, savings could have a considerable influence, as endeavours for systematically improving logistics within large companies have shown.

The 'glocalization' of large companies follows a similar logic. In the information society material flows lose their importance for holding together large companies: it is the management of information and knowledge that counts. Material flows can therefore be decentralized without jeopardizing the cohesion and the essential functions of a European or global company. Impressive examples can be found in the car industry (Polski Fiat, for example).

Recently, a series of big steps in the liberalization of trade as well as technological changes have strongly loosened the linkages between material production and a specific territory. The internal market, the GATT/WTO agreements, enormous improvements in telecommunication, strongly decreasing relative costs of transport (also largely due to liberalization), have all resulted in larger markets and a steep increase in freight transport. It might be asked whether these trends will continue at such a pace in the future. The euro may further push intra-European trade, and GATT/WTO regulations have not yet fully developed their impact on international markets. However, it seems that the major steps have been accomplished and that further liberalization might proceed at a more moderate pace and may more cautiously try not to push 'deterritorialization' much further.

6.4.1 Market-based instruments

Market-based policies can support all three sub-strategies (durability, miniaturization, lightweight) for dematerialization. For example, waste policies, which establish a responsibility of producers for the whole product lifecycle, lead to increased durability and replacement of material consumption by services (through re-use of packaging, modularization of products). Public procurement can utilize its considerable purchasing power for developing markets in this direction.

The impact of rising transport costs in spatial patterns of production and consumption would probably be rather limited unless more information is available. In the food sector, transport makes up approximately 8 per cent of the total cost, for other products it is much less. Specific incentives for the development of regional markets and typical regional products are conceivable. Policy levers to encourage the formation of regional production networks are also possible. Support by the structural funds is currently mainly founded on the 'export-base' theory and requires that companies sell beyond regional markets.

6.4.2 Regulation-based instruments

Regulation-based policies can contribute to dematerialization. For example, lighter cars could be introduced if new low-speed zones and higher safety standards were created. New standards in the construction industry could save material. Moreover, review of regulations is important in conjunction with lifestyle-oriented policies. However, durability or miniaturization cannot directly be imposed by regulations. A more regional orientation of the Common Agricultural Policy (CAP) would be very important. Transport impact assessments for all major business and policy decisions could contribute enormously.

6.4.3 Lifestyle-based instruments

Lifestyle changes can have a major impact on the substitution of goods by services. They comprise all kinds of awareness-raising and advertising strategies.

They can also encourage such lifestyles by systematically removing disadvantages that persist in tax systems, different kinds of regulations, accessibility of infrastructure, or availability of public services. Durability can also be influenced to some extent through such policies. For miniaturization it is more difficult.

Such policies may be of utmost importance for enhancing regional consumer markets. Providing information is essential for all strategies. To establish a system by which the 'transport content' of all kinds of products is made transparent through a kind of 'transport chain assessment' is essential for considering transport issues in business and policy decisions.

6.4.4 Public infrastructure and services

The provision of public infrastructure and services could provide an important contribution to all strategies. Considerable subsidies for road infrastructure in most countries in recent decades have contributed to increasing road transport speeds and reduced transport costs. Shifting these contributions would allow for investments in other kinds of infrastructure and services such as community development, regional development agencies aimed at building regional networks, and so on.

Proposals to reduce growth in freight transport often create fears that this would have negative effects on the economy and the labour market. Analysis shows that there are considerable countervailing trends and that policies aimed at decoupling freight transport from economic growth would largely result in accelerated structural change. Such changes create winners and losers – such acceleration may therefore increase conflicts. The losers represent the old, material-oriented industries, the protagonists of the era of mass production, but who still have considerable influence and power. The winners are linked to the rising service and information-based industries. The impact of decoupling, therefore, is chiefly limited by political and not by economic difficulties.

In principle the potential of decoupling is very large. However, estimates are very difficult, since knowledge and information is limited in these fields. On the basis of rough estimates for the different strategies, the overall potential for decoupling freight transport growth from economic growth could be somewhere between 35 and 50 per cent compared to present trends. That means, that instead of growing by 80 per cent between 1995 and 2020 freight transport might remain at levels similar to those in 1995 if appropriate measures are taken (Schleicher-Tappeser, *et al.*, 1998). Examples of freight transport policy measures are identified in Table 6.4, together with an indication of their likely timescale of effect on the policy targets.

Table 6.4 Possible freight transport policy measures

Measure	Timescale
Market-oriented:	
◆ Full lifecycle responsibility of producers for their products	medium-term
◆ Ecological tax reform charging resource use instead of labour	long-term
◆ Increase taxes and tolls for freight transport	short-term
◆ Use public procurement for regional networking and creation of regional markets	long-term
Regulation-oriented:	
◆ New category for light cars	short-term
◆ Concentrate transport-intensive industry along existing infrastructure	long-term
Lifestyle-oriented:	
◆ Information systems	medium-term
◆ Transport content declaration (TCD)	short-term
◆ Transport chain assessment (TCA)	medium-term
◆ Development of regional markets for agricultural products:	medium-term
◆ Regional origin declaration	medium-term
◆ Encourage and facilitate car-less lifestyles	medium-term
◆ Facilitate car rental and car sharing	medium-term
Public infrastructure/services:	
◆ Regional networking agencies	long-term
◆ Shifting structural fund priorities	long-term
◆ Reduced subsidies for road infrastructure	medium-term

6.5 The role of organizational change in achieving sustainable mobility

6.5.1 Infrastructure and transport markets

Infrastructure is the set of physical facilities that allow the movement of transport, especially immobile capital. The organization of the transport market has in the past been the privilege of the public sector, with some involvement of the private sector. Demand was uncritically accepted as given and transport planning was not strongly oriented towards changing an ever increasing rise in private car use. However, the transport scene has changed drastically. Changes in lifestyles and leisure, globalization, technology progress, development of telecommunications, and so on have led to an increasing dependency on transport and increasing mobility. At the same time, policy-makers are increasingly being confronted with the externalities and problems of mobility like environmental issues, congestion and social exclusion. Two major approaches in defence of a public policy interference with the transport sector may be distinguished: the public good argument (equity considerations and monopolization objectives are of paramount importance) and the externalities (both positive and negative) argument (OECD/ECMT, 1995).

In recent years we have witnessed a process of devolution reflected in privatization, deregulation and decentralization. We also see new forms of transport operation, such as outsourcing and franchising. Furthermore, we observe also that physical transport is only used to lay down the basis of added-value operation, where profits are generated in complementary facilities (shopping facilities, cultural amenities). For the future it seems likely that this process of devolution will continue for quite some time. Many countries are just at the beginning of this process. Thus the future organization of the transport market provokes the question of institutional regimes for different modalities, with the aim to generate added value from transport and related activities. In addition to an involvement of the private sector, we also observe a trend toward the supply of packages of transport related services (such as the logistic operator in freight transport, the tourist operator in tourism).

Negative externalities caused by transport arise from the organization of transport markets and infrastructure. In other words, the supply of transport can affect the demand for transport in general and the demand for certain modes. Policy measures, affecting the organization of transport markets and infrastructure, should aim at stimulating the use of alternative modes, reducing car and truck use and stimulating the use of capacity of both infrastructure and all forms of transport to a fuller extent.

In the freight transport sector, as in the passenger transport sector, the requirements are more and more in favour of motorized transport. As the average value/weight ratio of goods increases, it becomes economic to utilize faster modes (such as road and air). Complex systems of freight transport involving several vehicles and transfers of loads at regional and local distribution centres are becoming increasingly used across much of Europe. Future goods transport requires important quality factors. Punctuality and reliability are very important as storage is more or less eliminated in logistical systems. As average consignment sizes will be reduced, frequency plays a decisive role.

The changes in passenger and freight transport, as described above, demonstrate the growing importance of making interchange between one mode and another easier and of improving alternative modes (including new modes). In order to meet the requirements of both passenger and freight transport, transport has to be quick, reliable and door-to-door. Consequently, alternative modes have to be improved and transfer from one mode to another has to be possible, cheap and fast. Different strategies are possible:

* changing ownership structure;
* new and upgraded infrastructure;
* integration of different systems;
* land-use planning.

Possible policy strategies affecting the organization of transport markets and infrastructure will now be placed under the headings of the four different policy directions, market-based instruments, regulation, information technology and lifestyle/attitudes. Infrastructure and the organization of transport markets mainly concern the supply side, which means that most of the policy measures should be categorized as regulatory measures. Market-based instruments play a smaller role and a lifestyle orientation is less relevant here.

6.5.2 Market-based instruments

High levels of risk and uncertainty mean that the private sector has been reluctant to get involved in transport infrastructure investments. Arguments in favour of private sector involvement are that if the market forces firms to provide the best service at the lowest cost, they will perform better and enhance consumer welfare more than either regulated firms or state owned companies. However, the public sector still has a key role to play concerning accessibility issues, negative externalities, interaction with other sectors or national and international factors. All these roles are essentially passive and therefore, the more important position for the public sector must be to promote a partnership between the public and private sectors. It is in such partnerships that most potential lies. There are several different possible approaches and these are described in more detail by Banister *et al.* (1995).

Different systems of tendering or franchising can be classified. Total franchises include both the operation and provision of necessary infrastructure. This means that the franchisee is also responsible for capital costs. Operations franchises exist where the franchisee operates the system, but with rolling stock and infrastructure provided by the franchiser, normally a public authority responsible for the planning and financing of public transport. In franchising or tendering systems, companies compete for the market instead of in the market. Authorities can control fares and plan an integrated set of services with cross-subsidy, while competition for tenders or franchisees would provide the required pressure on costs. The use of various forms of franchising or tendering would be an effective means of solving the need for further efficiency measures in public transport operations without choosing the most radical alternative of full deregulation.

Changing the regulatory regime for public transport and rail, like different forms of franchising, can influence the performance of the service. In public transport, separation of controlling, maintenance and exploitation would achieve a more effective business operation. It would improve the quality, flexibility and market orientation of the internal business operation through competition and innovation. Competition would result in more efficiency and more demand orientated service. So, by changing ownership structure, a more demand-oriented service can be provided. This means that prices would reflect the costs of transport to a larger extent and the service would be demand orientated.

Road pricing, congestion pricing and parking pricing may be implemented in order to internalize the external costs of driving. This would increase the costs of driving, especially where congestion occurs. In order to reach the goal of reducing the use of the car these measures would have to be combined with a decrease in the costs of other modalities, especially public transport and the transport of rail freight. A more demand-oriented service in combination with pricing might reduce road transport.

Changes in the tax system can also be used to influence transport users. In this way, alternatives to traditional car use, such as car-pooling and car-rental, could be stimulated. Furthermore, in both freight and passenger transport the use of cleaner vehicles could be rewarded.

6.5.3 Regulation

Restraints and prohibitive measures are typical regulatory measures. Speed limits on roads, public transport priority in cities, access rules in cities, goods traffic constraints, parking restrictions, and increasing rights and space for bicycles and pedestrians are all examples of regulatory measures. Fare integration and schedule co-ordination in public transport, standards and procedures on inspection and maintenance, standards for emissions, noise and safety are included here. Important supplementary measures in the form of pricing and improving public transport would have to be implemented as well. Alternatives to environmentally polluting transport (such as cars and lorries in cities) should be available. This would also incorporate new distribution centres outside the cities and home delivery services within the city for the distribution of goods. Passenger transport could be improved by creating transition points outside of the city (park-and-ride) and high quality, fast public transport in the cities.

The availability of alternative modes to the car can be affected through infrastructure policies. Building new infrastructure for environmentally friendly modes (new vehicles, bicycles, public transport) would improve the performance of these modes. The high-speed train, underground transport and other innovations may be introduced if infrastructure is provided, and if introduction is supported by the creation of niche markets. Systems with a potential to improve performance and reduce its costs would then eventually expand outside the niche. If there are no natural niches, public authorities may help to create them, by for example defining environmental zones in urban areas. The expensive development of new products by industry has to be encouraged and supported by national (and international) policy. Large automobile companies will have difficulties supporting such development, except when opportunities in the market are clearly present. In addition, development of new vehicles and transport systems therefore offers new opportunities to companies outside the automobile industry, especially in smaller markets (niche markets). The development of new vehicles and systems can again be supported through national and international investment, subsidies and taxation policies.

When new vehicles and new infrastructure are introduced or when old systems are improved, the demand for transport will increase. In order to reduce mobility and decrease the external effects, other measures need to be implemented at the same time.

If we look at transport infrastructure a distinction has to be made between different modes. Building more roads has increased the ability for people to travel by car. It has not reduced congestion in peak hours as available road space is quickly filled. Even regions with the most extensive road networks have high congestion levels (OECD/ECMT, 1995). So building new infrastructure does not solve congestion problems and besides which an extensive network of roads would change cities beyond recognition. New and improved infrastructure for bicycles and pedestrians will, to a limited extent, reduce car use (on shorter distances) and will facilitate transfer to public transport.

Integration of transport networks starts with building appropriate infrastructure, upgrading existing infrastructure and ensuring appropriate use of this infrastructure. For road transport, the ability to use the entire road network requires little more than the absence of restrictive legislation. For rail, organizational issues are far more important. Road transport generally is too cheap, so measures are needed to increase its cost. For international rail transport, there is a need for an organizational form that offers the same degree of flexibility in marketing as for roads. In order to realize this degree of flexibility in marketing, co-ordination and co-operation between different European rail companies is needed. The resulting integration of the network and fast transhipment will increase the efficiency of rail. In terms of rail infrastructure, the major problems of the European network are the non-standard track, different power systems and different signalling and communications systems. Harmonization of the railways would increase the efficiency and the profitability. For planning new tracks land-use conflicts and noise have to be considered.

In order to improve the possibilities for door-to-door transport with means other than just motorized transport, it is important that the possibilities for intermodal transport are increased. Intermodalities between trucks and planes, or cars and planes, already exist. However, there is close competition between rail, car, bus and the lorry. Railways compete directly with air travel over medium distances (about 500 km) by offering high-speed services from city centre to city centre. Favouring intermodality means favouring the railways with both investment and regulation.

Improving intermodality and the creation of transition points play a key role in the regulation measures. For freight transport, it is important to realize the transition possibilities between ship, rail and truck. The integration and harmonization of railways in Europe, co-operation between different rail companies and the creation of terminals for transhipment are included here. It is also important to use the land-use system to encourage the location of new developments near existing activities to ensure compactness.

6.5.4 Information technology

New developments in communication and information technology can have enormous impacts on the organization of transport markets. These developments can affect traffic management and logistical processes in freight transport.

Information systems can have an enormous impact on the organization of transport markets. Driver information systems can ensure a more efficient use of existing infrastructure and an optimal use of transport means. Information systems can give information concerning parking space and congestion and on waiting times in public transport. Information can change choice behaviour of transport users and it can improve the quality of travelling and the reliability of public transport. The problem now is that every car can use the infrastructure at any chosen moment. Information systems can change this. Expectations are that future traffic information systems may lead to a 10 per cent reduction in congestion (Bovy, 1995). Another possible application of information technology is a system for automatic road pricing.

Information and communication technology play a major role in logistics. Production processes have changed and logistics are more and more important as a result of developments in technology. Developments in information and communication technologies can influence transport flows through shipments size, co-ordination, and consolidation. As the level of flexibility in production and the required techniques of logistical organization emerge, the need for vertical and horizontal co-ordination within the logistical chain will become greater and thus require the transport sector to cope with a higher standard of service, reliability, and performance. This can only be achieved through efficient and high-quality information regarding the logistical processes which will affect the choice of location of parts of the logistical chain, the organization of distribution networks, the frequency of shipments, and the utilization of transport equipment and infrastructure.

6.5.5 Lifestyles and attitudes

Policies based on information could alter attitudes towards environmentally friendly modes. As awareness is increased, changes in lifestyles and travel patterns would take place. However, these policies should be supplemented with other measures, which would support the messages given by the public information. For example, lifestyles and attitudes concerning home and business location could be influenced and reinforced by land-use planning. The quality of the public transport system and other providers of transport and infrastructure could also be used to change attitudes.

Changing the organization of the transport market influences lifestyles and attitudes concerning mode choice. The availability of alternative modes to car and truck can be affected through infrastructure policies. The creation of possibilities for transition and improving door-to-door transport could change the decision on the location of firms and housing. Technological standards, increases in fuel costs, and ownership taxes may change attitudes towards car ownership and the use of new environmentally friendly vehicles.

There are many policy measures relating to transport infrastructure and the organization of transport markets. There is often an overlap with the other aspects of transport policy. The organization of transport markets and infrastructure mainly concerns freight management, traffic management, and mode management measures. It is quite difficult to estimate the potential reduction in mobility due to these measures since they affect many actors, but it is clear that changing the organization of transport markets will definitely have long-term and far-reaching effects.

Part Two

The methodological framework for analysis

Chapter 7

Scenario building and methodological framework

7.1 Aim and main issues

Transport policy-making has begun to respond to the issues of sustainability but is increasingly being required to do more. Whilst the future policy-making environment is uncertain, it is necessary to identify the key issues of policy-making likely to be of importance over the medium and long term if effective strategic decisions are to be made.

The main task of this exercise is to construct scenarios for achieving the objectives of sustainable mobility and to assist in future decision-making about the Common Transport Policy and the development of the Trans-European Networks. The overriding aim of the exercise is to find ways *'to facilitate movements of persons and goods in agreement with a strategy of sustainable development. The concept includes mobility levels, but also the technical systems required to enable mobility'*.

The scenarios are meant to show what sustainable mobility may look like and how it might materialize. The idea is to add clarity and detail to the relatively vague concept of sustainability, and to provide a framework for analysing consequences for everyday life as well as conditions for the realization of sustainable mobility.

More specifically the study aims at identifying future key issues – in the context of sustainable mobility - for policy-makers at the European level, such as:

* *packaging* – how policies can be packaged to increase their effectiveness (by maximizing linkages and synergies);
* *timing* – the timescales required for the introduction of policies, and the time over which policies might have most effect;
* *implementation* – the public acceptability of different types of policies and the potential barriers to implementation; and
* *responsibilities* – the responsibilities of decision-makers and other stakeholders in policy development and implementation, the key organizations that need to act to achieve specific policy goals, the level of co-ordination between different levels of decision-making required.

For a sector (in this case transport) to be sustainable, the global concept of sustainable development has to be broken down on a per capita basis. The resources and risks have to be evenly distributed both within and between generations in order to comply with a sustainable development. It should be acknowledged in this respect, that there is yet no scientific agreement on a definition of sustainable development. However, it can be argued that sustainable development would achieve an equitable development that can continue in the long term. Four issues are usually stressed in this respect: ecological scale limits, inter-generational equity, intra-generational equity and increased or maintained quality of life (Hunhammar, 1997).

The end result of the exercise is a set of policy scenarios aimed at achieving regional development, economic efficiency and environmental protection objectives (which correspond to the policy targets presented in Chapter 8). In this way, European transport policies will be assessed for their consistency and feasibility by means of a qualitative scenario approach based on backcasting (this concept is discussed below). The scenarios are explicitly policy oriented and expert based, and aim to help European and other decision-makers by presenting policy choices clearly, while the additional impacts of several external factors are controlled. In this way, they may contribute to future decision-making processes at both European and national levels.

7.2 Why scenarios?

The European Commission defines a scenario as 'a tool that describes pictures of the future world within a specific framework and under specified assumptions' and a scenario approach as 'the description of at least two or more scenarios designed to compare and examine alternative futures' (CEC, 1993). More generally, scenarios are descriptions of possible future developments that seem plausible under different sets of assumptions and provide a background against which policy assessments can be made.

There is a growing awareness that in the long term, the development of society is characterized by substantial uncertainties. This often makes a prognosis-based approach inadequate. Scenario analysis is increasingly being used in long-range policy research, since it provides a way of identifying future issues and problems for policy-making in an environment of qualitative uncertainty.

Scenarios are distinct from traditional forecasts, which are normally based on trend extrapolation.[1] The scenarios develop alternative futures in a structured way, and help to identify policies that are robust across a wide range of possible futures. Scenario planning, therefore, is not concerned with one particular future. The choice between an approach of trend extrapolation and scenario development is affected by one's view of the uncertainties involved. Under a trend extrapolation perspective, uncertainty is a problem to be minimized, and what cannot be removed by research and expert opinion should be quantified so that it is tractable in rational decision models. If, on the other hand, future trend-breaks are perceived as plausible, uncertainty is primarily qualitative in nature. In this case it is important to explore futures that develop according to a different logic (scenarios).

The purpose and advantage of scenarios is that they are a kind of structured brainstorming technique, which may widen the perceptions of researchers as well as policy-makers regarding possible future opportunities, policy options and other related developments – they may also give more insight into their impacts. In addition, they may increase the mental willingness at least to consider a broad spectrum of developments. Scenarios are important tools for strategic policy analysis, especially in situations where policy-makers have too much biased and unstructured information. In the present study we have chosen to combine two partly different scenario traditions, namely explorative external scenarios and backcasting. These traditions are described below.

7.2.1 Explorative external scenarios

The contextual framework for this kind of analytical task is the need to develop a strategy or package of policies for a policy area and focal issue, based on long-term considerations. The focal issue here is how to design transport policy that reconciles economic efficiency, regional development and sustainability.

The development of explorative external scenarios is a common approach to structuring the long-term policy options. The scenarios are external in that they describe factors beyond the control of the transport sector, although they have a direct effect on the sector (see Figure 5.1). An example would be dominant societal values in the future that may affect travel demand and mode choice preferences. The scenarios are explorative in that they elaborate on possible developments and trend breaks rather than business as usual paths.

There are three important requirements that the scenarios should meet in order to be of help in policy analysis. First, they must be relevant to the area of study. It is possible to conceive of an unlimited number of different developments, but those that do not make any great difference to the policy issues of interest could be omitted. It is essential that each scenario chosen has a different (and considerable) impact on the key issues at stake. Second, the scenarios should be plausible. They must be acceptable as possible developments. Otherwise they will be of no use. The third requirement is that the scenarios are challenging. If they are too much like a 'business-as-usual' future they will not trigger unconventional thinking and, hence, be of little use.[2] The idea is that the scenarios should be trend breaking in some respect and thereby illustrate developments following different logic.

This scenario tradition was developed mainly by Shell International in the late 1960s and in the 1970s. It has since then been widely used in corporate strategic planning, for example, by the consulting network Global Business

Network (GBN). It has also been used in public sector policy analysis and planning. One recent example is the STEEDS project that used external scenarios in combination with a modelling framework as a decision support tool targeted for the European Commission, national Governments and private enterprises (Dreborg *et al.*, 1997).

In the explorative scenario tradition an expert panel is usually used either to generate the basis of the scenarios that are then developed further by the project team (bottom-up), or to validate or corroborate outline scenarios generated by the project team (top-down). In STEEDS the bottom-up approach was used. An example of the top-down approach is the NECTAR study about the geography of Europe's future (Masser *et al.*, 1992).[3]

The use of explorative external scenarios is particularly beneficial when the task is to find robust policy options in the face of qualitative uncertainty as regards important external factors. Hence, this approach is strongly linked to policy forming and decision-making. Usually the emphasis is more on adaptability than on finding a way to fulfil a vision, such as sustainability. Although the method in itself does not preclude this, the backcasting methodology is the usual way of analysing how to reach a radical societal goal.

7.2.2 Backcasting

The term 'backcasting' was introduced by Robinson (1982) and denotes a particular kind of scenario approach, where the scenarios are chosen to reflect desirable developments. According to Robinson:

> The major distinguishing characteristic of backcasting analysis is a concern, not with what futures are likely to happen, but with how desirable futures can be attained. It is thus explicitly normative, involving working backwards from a particular desirable future end-point to the present in order to determine the physical feasibility of that future and what policy measures would be required to reach that point. (Robinson, 1990)

Instead of starting with the present situation and prevailing trends, the backcasting approach implies starting by designing Images of the Future that show desirable solutions to a major societal problem. The date for these images is sufficiently distant to admit major changes to take place before that point of time. Then one tries to find a possible path between today and the Images. Defining the Images is the key innovative step. The term 'scenario' is used to cover both the Image of the Future and the trajectory leading from the present state up to that image. Backcasting has been used since the mid 1970s. An early example is a series of Swedish energy futures studies (Lönnroth *et al.*, 1980; Johansson *et al.*, 1983). Another more recent example is the OECD project EST (Environmentally Sustainable Transport), where several member states have performed parallel backcasting studies (OECD, 1998). Other transport related backcasting studies have been carried out in the UK (Peake and Hope, 1994; Banister, 2000*a,b*) and in Sweden (Steen *et al.*, 1998).

The backcasting approach is of special interest when the task is to find long-term solutions to a major societal problem and/or when policy-making involves substantial change. Sometimes backcasting studies are aimed at a broad audience, where the objective is not just to support decision-making but to stimulate a debate in society and to widen the perception of what is possible to attain in the long run. In this case, it is difficult to draw the line between internal and external factors, which is so essential in the approach of explorative external scenarios. Somehow, influences beyond the control of the body of relevant actors must be taken into account. Otherwise the study may degenerate into wishful thinking.

The main audience of this exercise comprises EU and national transport policy-makers. The main aim is the visualization of sustainable mobility – a far-reaching goal – but not just for the sake of stimulating a debate about the future, but as a basis for actual policy forming. Therefore, the decision was made to combine these traditions into a *modified backcasting methodology*, which is described in the next Section. This means, in short, that external factors are explicitly taken into account when the visions of sustainable mobility are outlined.

7.3   The applied scenario methodology

In a kind of pilot study two reference scenarios were constructed in order to highlight key policy issues and possible goal conflicts. The method involved a bottom-up approach, the use of questionnaires, and expert groups in order to provide a well-founded view of key policy issues and important external factors. The main lessons from this exercise were twofold. First, the exercise indicated that it is necessary to find ways to reconcile the three goals of the CTP – economic efficiency, environmental protection, and regional development. Decoupling transport growth from economic growth may help to reconcile these goals. Second, the work showed that the extent to which decision-making is co-ordinated has an important influence on the success or failure of policies.

The main task of developing Policy Scenarios of Sustainable Mobility involved the development of a modified backcasting methodology comprising of three main stages: the identification of *policy targets*, the definition of *Images of the Future*, and the development of *policy packages and paths*. The backcasting technique and three main stages are discussed in turn below. The pure backcasting model has, however, been modified in order to highlight the impact of certain external factors. The more general reasoning of the previous Sections is adapted to the present application.

It is obvious that transport policies may have a great impact on the development of transport in the long run. It is, however, also true that driving forces and conditions beyond the control of transport policy-makers will have an impact as well, and also influence the conditions for policy-making. This is the question of external versus internal factors, which is highly relevant in the context of transport policy analysis. In this context, external variables are factors that are outside the transport system of Europe. Examples of such factors are changes in values and lifestyles. A distinction can also be made between transport policy (internal) and other policy areas (external), but it is important to note that these are often interdependent. For example, land-use planning has a considerable impact on transport demand in the long run, while, conversely, large infrastructure programmes (which is part of transport policy) have an impact on residential patterns.

The essence of the combined backcasting-explorative approach is that different external developments (in relation to the transport sector) are chosen (the explorative element), and for each of these a 'solution' to the problems of the transport sector has been sought (the backcasting element). The solutions all meet a set of targets regarding environmental protection, efficiency and regional development (see Chapter 8). The result is, hence, Policy Scenarios that combine strategic policy elements and contextual elements[4] in a systematic way. The policies considered are both transport policies and other policies with an impact on the transport sector. The contextual elements are transport-external factors that have a large impact on transport in the long run.

The main components of the policy scenarios are:

1   the definition of goals or targets to be met by the end of the studied period of time;
2   a set of important external factors;
3   the main strategic elements associated with each scenario.

These three components are used to construct different Images of the Future that focus on the situation at the end of the period (Chapter 9). To build complete policy scenarios that include the trajectory from today up to an Image of the Future, a fourth building block is needed:

4   policy measures, paths and policy packages that would promote a development towards goal fulfilment (Chapters 10 and 11).

Policy targets were developed to provide directions for policy measures, paths and packages and to help construct the Images of the Future. The method involved a review of policy targets from literature, questionnaires and internal consortium workshops. The objectives of the Common Transport Policy (CTP) may be summarized by three terms: regional development, economic efficiency, and environmental protection. Therefore, the scenarios are focused on achieving targets for these three issues (Chapters 3 and 4).

In choosing external factors, we have tried to select those qualities of society that we believe have a profound and widespread influence in the long run on patterns of consumption, production and settlement and thus on transport. Hence, we have tried to identify factors affecting long-term structural features of society, rather than accidental or catastrophic events that could also have an impact on transport. The climate for co-operation at different levels of society, attitudes to the environment, and the balance between local and international lifestyles are fundamental and salient external factors. The external factors also include assumptions about the dominant level of policy-making (local, national or international) and the degree of cooperation between these different levels of policy-making. These external factors will not only influence transport directly but will also affect the conditions for policy-making (Chapter 2). More accidental external occurrences, such as a new oil crisis, may appear in almost any scenario and are not therefore included in any specific Image. However, a sensitivity test could be worthwhile. By subjecting all Images of the Future or policy scenarios to the same occurrence and assessing the likely impact on goal attainment.

The strategic elements include assumptions about changes in technology and decoupling between the present and 2020. By decoupling we mean a decrease in transport intensity of GDP that will allow the volume of transport to increase at a lower rate than the economy at large. Technological change pertains to reductions of energy use and emissions per person-kilometre and tonne-kilometre.

The Images of the Future are the key innovative step of the methodology because they show how the targets can be achieved. The Images of the Future describe the characteristics of society and transport at the target year (2020). They form the framework for identifying suitable policy packages and paths to reach the policy targets. Three Images of the Future were selected in this study, reflecting different assumptions about external factors and strategic elements. The Images were developed using mainly a top-down approach and external workshops were used to validate them.

The actual mix of strategies (technology and decoupling) in each Image of the Future was designed by first assessing the potential of new technologies for each Image, taking into account the key character of the Image and the associated external factors. Next, decoupling was calculated as a residual, in the sense that changes of transport intensity (which is closely related to decoupling) are assumed to fill the gap between the sustainability goals and what is achieved by the technological improvements. The resulting levels of decoupling are, of course, uncertain. However, assessments of the decoupling effect of various changes such as dematerialization, decentralized concentration and so on indicate that the decoupling levels of the Images are reasonable.

As part of the identification of Images of the Future, key issues and key states were also identified. The key issues specify important policy areas between the present and the target date (2020) for each of the three Images of the Future selected for examination in this study. The key issues include potential problems for policy-making, sectors where policy must be focused and important changes in transport demand. The key states specify the strategic policy steps between the present and 2020 for each of the three Images of the Future. The key issues and key states act as an intermediate step between the Images of the Future and the identification of policy packages and paths.

The process of backcasting provides the basis for identifying policy measures that are compatible with both the scenarios and the policy targets. These measures are assembled into packages and paths in order to maximize synergies, minimize any anticipated problems of implementation, and improve the acceptability of the policy changes. This process included consideration of time-lines, policy priorities, intermediate goals and the potential of different policy measures for achieving the targets. For each Image of the Future, policy measures, paths and packages were developed to meet the targets using a combination of a deductive approach starting from the Images of the Future and an inductive approach starting from possible policy measures.

The scenarios in our study concern the transport system in Europe up to the year 2020. This reference year allows us to assume some quite radical changes. A shorter time period may reduce the possibilities of analysing large shifts in the technical and institutional environment, while a later time horizon may limit the policy relevancy of the scenarios. The scenarios include both goods and passenger transport. However, the description is at a rather strategic level – we do not explicitly discuss the impact of special features on transport systems in each country or city. The goals chosen for the year 2020 should be seen as tentative and intermediate. In the very long run, more far reaching goals will probably be set (such as CO_2 emissions – IPCC, 1996). An important question in this context is how to avoid a 'lock-in' to solutions that fulfil the targets for 2020 but are unlikely to fulfil more stringent targets in the longer term.

Notes

1   The term 'forecasting' is sometimes used in a broader sense that covers different scenario traditions.
2   This does not mean however that none of the scenarios can represent a 'business-as-usual' future.
3   NECTAR is the acronym for Network for European Communications and Transport Activities Research.
4   We prefer the term contextual elements or factors to external factors. We are talking about factors that are external to the transport sector, but which are not external in relation to the scenarios. Instead they form a very essential part of them.

Chapter 8

Targets for sustainable mobility

8.1 Introduction

The backcasting approach we have used in this book requires targets for sustainable mobility as inputs to the process. These targets are used for designing images of the future and for assessing the impact of policy measures, paths and packages. Targets for environmental protection, regional development targets, and economic efficiency are included. The environmental targets are most compelling since the sustainable use of the ecosystem is a necessary condition for social and economic development.

The time horizon considered here is 2020. Rather extensive changes are needed in order to achieve a sustainable transport system within this time-scale. These include changes in terms of infrastructure, land-use patterns, vehicle fleet composition, and lifestyles. In this context the time period up to 2020 is relatively short. Consequently the targets for 2020 are to be considered as intermediate steps towards truly sustainable conditions, especially as regards CO_2 emissions.

8.2 Environmental targets

The environmental targets have a more scientific origin, although the values are influenced by political considerations. In this book our interpretation of sustainability in principle is scientifically based but other considerations also affect the choice of targets. First, scientific evidence of the consequences of, for instance, global warming is not complete (and probably never will be). Thus, policy decisions and target setting will always be carried out in a context of uncertainty. What societal attitude should be taken to risks is not a scientific judgement. One standpoint is expressed by the precautionary principle (Rio Declaration, Principle 15):

> In order to protect the environment, the precautionary approach shall be widely applied by States according to their capabilities. Where there are threats of serious or irreversible damage, lack of full scientific certainty shall not be used as a reason for postponing cost-effective measures to prevent environmental degradation. (United Nations Conference on Environment and Development, 1992)

This principle is especially applicable when irreversible global changes are among possible outcomes. In the case of global warming this might well be the case. The time lags in the global climatic system are also considerable. Even if emissions could be reduced immediately, the level of CO_2 in the atmosphere would continue to rise for decades, enhancing global warming and corresponding effects on ecosystems.

Secondly, it is clear that a completely sustainable transport system is not possible by 2020 (and probably never possible). The rate of change used here is in part decided by physical necessities, such as the turnover rate of vehicles, but is also affected by political considerations, such as the feasibility of rapid changes in modal choice. The strategy chosen is to identify intermediate targets for 2020 that are demanding but still feasible. We thus start from scientifically derived targets and then slightly adjust these to what seems feasible until 2020.

Many of the environmental issues associated with transport have been catalogued (see CEC, 1992c; OECD, 1993), whilst other issues are perhaps less well documented, although several recent sources cover these issues (see OECD/ECMT, 1995; Maddison *et al.*, 1995; World Bank, 1996). An inventory of key issues associated with transport and sustainable development has been compiled by reviewing recent literature, and is presented in Table 8.1, along with potential indicators for the development of targets for each impact.

Table 8.1 Key domains, issues and potential indicators for sustainable mobility

Domain	Issues	Potential Indicators
Social	Accessibility	Walk distances to local services/facilities
	Health	Report incidences of transport-related illnesses
		Number of poor air quality days
	Safety	Road accident rates (casualties and deaths)
	Noise	Proportion of population affected by noise
	Visual Intrusion	Proportion of population affected by visual annoyance
Economic	Congestion	Road vehicle-kilometres/road length
	Building corrosion	NO_x emissions
	Road and bridge damage	HGV vehicle-kilometres
Environmental	Resource depletion	Energy consumption
	Climate change	CO_2 emissions
		Loss of agricultural land
	Acidification	NO_x emissions
	Air pollution	Emissions of NO_x, VOCs, CO, and other pollutants
	Waste generation	Vehicles scrapped related to vehicles recycled
	Water pollution	NO_x emissions
	Infrastructure intrusion	Length of transport infrastructure

Since social, economic and environmental impacts are often interrelated, many of the impacts in Table 8.1 could be included in more than one category. Accidents, for example, are listed as a social impact of transport, but they also have an impact on the economy in terms of health care, sickness benefits, and other factors.

Since issues of sustainability are emphasized in this book, we focus on emissions of CO_2 and NO_x and the intrusion of infrastructure. Emissions of CO_2 are a long-term global concern where all emissions count equally wherever they occur. Emissions of NO_x pose more of a local or regional problem.

8.2.1 Scientifically derived targets

Although there will always remain uncertainties, scientific evidence on environmental effects and sustainable levels is becoming consistently more solid. It is now apparent that sustainability will require rather extensive changes to our present society.

In translating the concept of sustainability to the transport sector of Europe, several assumptions have to be made. This especially holds for emissions of CO_2. One crucial issue is the distribution of emissions among nations. The difficulty in this task was exemplified by the Kyoto negotiations. In the long run, it seems hard to advocate that Europeans should emit considerably more CO_2 per capita than the global average.

Table 8.2 Examples of carbon dioxide targets for 2020 and beyond

Source	Method	Period	Reduction target
Lichtenthäler and Pastowski (1995)	Strong sustainability equity considerations	1992-2050	65-80%
IPPC (1996)	Stabilization of CO_2 concentrations at 450 ppm (accepts 1°C increase in temperature)	1990-2100	15-70 % of accumulated CO_2 emissions (depending on scenario assumptions)
Enquete-Kommission Klima (1994)	Stabilization of CO_2 concentration at 400 ppm	1987-2020	40 % for economically strong industrial countries
Steen et al. (1998)	Stabilization of CO_2 concentration at 450 ppm	1995-2040	80% for Sweden and countries with similar emission levels

Another assumption concerns transport's share of total European emissions. It is not necessarily cost-effective to use the same targets for all sectors of society. First, the potential to cut emissions per unit of travel (such as CO_2-emissions per passenger-kilometre) may differ. Second, the growth trends may not entail similar dynamics in different sectors. It is not easy to estimate the combined effect of these factors. The drive for increase in volume is clearly greater for transport than in most other sectors. On the other hand it seems that the potential for efficiency improvements is rather large. We have assumed that transport should be given slightly less demanding targets than average.

In Table 8.2 some long-term targets based on scientific analysis are shown. The different reduction targets are in part due to different time frames and in part due to uncertainties. However, they are all rather demanding and require that present trends are broken.

8.2.2 Politically set targets

Scientific evidence regarding global warming is successively influencing the public agenda. However, environmental objectives are still often subordinated to short-term economic interests. The political targets are thus often rather modest in their ambitions. The reasoning behind official policy targets is in general more accidental than the more scientific approaches starting from interpretations of sustainable development. In Tables 8.3 and 8.4 some policy targets are shown. The EU stabilization target from 1990 is based on the assumption that emission reductions in former Eastern Germany, due to the industrial decline, could outweigh an increase in some other parts of the EU. The 25 per cent reduction target of the German Environmental Protection Agency is rather ambitious, considering the 15-year perspective. It is based on scientific evidence and was announced before elections to attract conservative green voters (Hey *et al.*, 1999).

Table 8.3 Examples of short-term environmental targets

Targets	The Fifth Environmental Action Plan of the EU (CEC,1993)	German Environmental Protection Agency for the Transport Sector (Gorissen, 1995)
CO_2 emissions	Stabilization between 1990 and 2000	−25% between 1990 and 2005
NO_x emissions	−30 % between 1990 and 2000	−80% between 1990 and 2005
Noise	Acceptable threshold of 65dB, no additional noise beyond 55dB	Acceptable threshold of 50 dB by 2030
VOC	−30 % between 1990 and 2000	−80% between 1987 and 2005
Nature protection	'Natura 2000' network, Habitat and birds directives	No additional net surface to be covered by roads

Table 8.4 Political carbon dioxide targets

Source	Period	Reduction target
WBGU 1996	1992-2020	25-30%
EU-Commission, 1996	1992-2020	11.5 %
EU commitment in the Kyoto agreement	1990-2008/2012	8% (total greenhouse gases)

8.3 Regional development and economic efficiency targets

The role of transport in regional development is not clear-cut. First, transport is but one means of achieving accessibility. By means of existing and emerging information technology, access can to an increasing extent be accomplished in a very time- and resource-efficient way. Second, the role of intra-regional versus inter-regional accessibility is widely discussed. Specific conditions will probably often be decisive in this debate.

There are different perspectives on the economic role of transport (Hey *et al.*, 1999). The transport sector might be considered as a resource and a transport-efficient economy in this interpretation minimizes its transport needs to maintain a certain growth path. That is, a decoupling of economic growth from mobility growth is the aim. In another perspective, transport might be seen as a sector contributing to general economic growth in society.

8.4 Target selection

The target selection process requires a set of selection criteria against which potential targets can be evaluated. Reviewing a selection of literature on social, environmental, health and sustainability indicators, Maclaren (1996) identifies a list of criteria commonly used to evaluate indicators in the selection process. The criteria include:

- scientifically valid;
- representative of a broad range of conditions;
- responsive to change;
- relevant to the needs of potential users;
- based on accurate accessible data;
- based on data that are available over time;
- understandable by potential users;
- comparable with indicators developed in other jurisdictions;
- cost-effective to collect;
- attractive to the media;
- unambiguous.

In addition to satisfying these criteria, it should also be possible to devise threshold and target values, identifying acceptable and desirable conditions, for each indicator. If thresholds and targets cannot be determined, the desirable trend direction should be stated (Mitchell *et al.*, 1995). Policy targets have particular value in focusing attention on the link between the policy-implementation process and the outcome, and influencing the achievement of policy (Stead, 1997).

In this book we focus on the goals of environmental protection, regional development, and economic efficiency. The environmental protection goal is the most impelling, in the sense that it has to do with the long-term survival of society. It is a kind of goal that may require new solutions, including structural change. This is the primary goal on which the scenarios are based. Economic efficiency is an important goal for any sector of society. Of course, an efficient transport sector contributes to the general economic development of society. However, a goal of this kind was not defined. Instead, a goal for the efficiency of the transport sector itself was chosen. The reason is that transport is just one of many factors influencing the general economic development. The goal of regional development is very important to the EU, especially in the face of enlargement. However, much as in the case of the economic development at large, transport is but one of many activities influencing regional development and equity. A total of seven policy targets were chosen and are summarized in Table 8.5.

Table 8.5 Policy targets for sustainable mobility

Environmental Targets:
- 25% reduction of CO_2 emissions from 1995-2020;
- 80% reduction of NO_x emissions from 1995-2020;
- No degradation of specially protected areas;
- Marginal increase of net infrastructure surface in Europe.

Regional Development Targets:
- Improve relative accessibility of peripheral regions (both internal and external). This general target includes cost and time, and allows for substitution of physical accessibility by telecommunications.

Economic Efficiency Targets:
- Full cost coverage (including external costs) of transport under market or equivalent conditions by 2020;
- Reduce public subsidies to all forms of transport to zero by 2020, except where there are particular social equity objectives.

The target chosen for CO_2 in this study is a reduction of 25 per cent between 1995 and 2020. It was chosen on the basis of a review of different political and scientific reference points. The target is considerably more demanding than the commitment of the EU given at the Kyoto agreement, but is still not in line with what can be regarded as the needed long-term reduction to avoid major climate changes. There is a qualitative difference between the CO_2 and NO_x targets for 2020. To bring emissions of CO_2 in line with sustainable development appears to be a much more difficult task than is the case with the emissions of NO_x.

The regional development target comprises both intra-regional and inter-regional accessibility. The relative importance of these will depend on specific circumstances. The possibility to substitute physical accessibility with telecommunications will prove crucial in order to reconcile this target with the environmental targets.

There are both positive and negative feedbacks between emissions of CO_2 and NO_x respectively. Measures affecting transport demand, such as the promotion of telecommuting, will have positive effects in both these dimensions. In terms of technical options there is, however, sometimes a trade-off between these targets. A case in point is the choice between petrol and diesel engines. Increasing the share of diesel cars will lower CO_2 emissions while at the same time NO_x emissions will increase. Aircraft provide another example where engine design may be influenced by the choice of emission targets and their relative importance.

Chapter 9

Images of the Future

9.1 Introduction – the role of Images of the Future

The construction of Images of the Future is the first step in the backcasting approach, the second being the elaboration of paths from the present to the Images (Chapter 7). A basic presumption is that Images of the Future should be constructed to comply with the policy targets. The aim is not to try to discern what is likely to happen but to outline possible solutions to a perceived problem, in this case the unsustainable transport sector. Images of the Future widen the scope of possible futures beyond extrapolations of present trends. They should be seen as examples which might help trigger public discussion of which solutions are preferable. Three different external scenarios are used here, resulting in three distinct Images of the Future.

In this Chapter two strategic elements for accomplishing sustainable transport are presented. These elements are 'technology' and 'decoupling'. The term technology covers vehicle technology and fuel mix. Decoupling means the breaking of transport growth (as measured in passenger-km and tonne-km) from economic growth. Between 1970 and 1995 the volume of freight transport grew as fast as GDP, while the volume of passenger transport grew even faster (see Chapters 3 and 5).

It is also necessary to take into account an uncertain global context. This is included in the scenarios by using contextual elements reflecting important external factors, largely outside the influence of the policy-makers concerned. The principal contextual elements used concern the degree of co-operation permeating different levels of society. Other important elements are the spread of green values and lifestyles. The strategic elements are then combined with the contextual elements. By combining appropriate strategic elements with the different external scenarios, the core features of three Images of the Future are identified. These Images are then further outlined in terms of the use of technology, transport volumes for the different means of transport, use of IT-supported services and so on.

9.2   Building blocks of the Images of the Future

9.2.1 Strategic elements for sustainable transport – technology and decoupling

The strategic elements in the scenarios are things that can be influenced through transport policy. The two principal elements are examined here: technology and decoupling.

Technology

Within the transport sector, there is a substantial potential for reducing emissions and increasing energy efficiency by means of vehicle technology and alternative fuels. In order to estimate their role in achieving the policy targets, the transport volumes in the indicative Reference Case for 2020 (shown in Table 1.1) have been combined with different potential outcomes regarding technology level and fuel mix. The resulting emissions of CO_2 and NO_x are presented in Table 9.1.

Table 9.1 Emissions resulting from potential changes of technology and fuel mix combined with reference case transport volumes

Case	Change in CO_2 emissions 1995-2020	Resulting CO_2 emissions in 2020 compared to the CO_2 target	Change in NO_x emissions 1995-2020	Resulting NO_x emissions in 2020 compared to the NO_x target
1 Only fossil fuels with current efficiency	+67 %	+123 %	+69 %	+747 %
2 Only fossil fuels with high efficiency improvement	+13 %	+50 %	-62 %	+92 %
3 Only fossil fuels with very high efficiency improvement	+2 %	+36%	-66%	+69%
4 Methanol introduced with very high efficiency improvement	-17%	+11%	-71%	+46%
5 Electric cars introduced with high efficiency improvement	+5%	+40%	-64%	+81%
6 Electric cars and methanol introduced with very high efficiency improvement	-23%	+3%	-72%	+38%

Note
The EU-15, Norway, Turkey and Switzerland are included in these figures. It is based on the assumption that fuel cell cars have been introduced onto the market, but have not yet taken a significant market share in 2020. Transport volumes in 2020 for these cases are assumed to be in accordance with Table 1.1. This is called a Reference Case (RC). There were no 'official' forecasts for the EU available at the time, so the Reference Case is a rough estimate based on decreasing growth rates compared to the preceding period covering 1970-1995. It is probably on the lower side of what a business as usual scenario would entail.

Transport volumes in the CEEC/CIS countries are likely to increase more rapidly than in Western Europe in the next few decades. Because current proportions of diesel cars, catalytic petrol cars, and non-catalytic petrol cars are somewhat uncertain, it has been assumed here that the respective shares in the EU are 20 per cent, 40 per cent and 40 per cent. Since catalytic converters (or equivalent) only became compulsory across the EU in January 1993, the share of catalytic petrol cars was actually likely to be somewhat lower than this in 1995. Given the underlying assumptions, it can be seen that new technology and fuels are very important. However, the target levels (identified in Table 8.3) are not reached in any of the cases despite rather bold assumptions (case 6). The conclusion is that, even if improved vehicle technology and new fuels are promoted intensely, the growth of transport volumes also has to be curbed in order to reach the environmental targets.

For alternative (non-fossil) fuels, the major options include electricity, hydrogen, ethanol and methanol. Other fuels like biogas may be important for niche markets. Electricity has a potential niche in urban vehicles. Hydrogen could be the fuel of the future, but complexity in distribution and storage makes it less likely to be fully introduced by 2020. Ethanol and methanol derived from biomass both have similar properties, but with present processes methanol gives a higher yield in energy terms. Methanol is also suitable for fuel cells and may during a transitional period be produced from fossil fuel. Methanol and electricity have been used in the Images of the Future. It should however be emphasized that the actual choice of alternative fuel(s) is by no means easy to foresee. A decision on a new principal fuel for road transport could be taken at the EU level, but the prospect would be enhanced if there were agreement between the EU, the US and Japan.

It can be concluded from Table 9.1 that the CO_2 target (-25 per cent between 1995 and 2020) is easier to achieve than the NO_x target (-80 per cent between 1995 and 2020), particularly if fuel cells are not introduced quickly. On the other hand these targets are only intermediate, and it seems that the NO_x target is much closer to what could be called a sustainable emission level than the CO_2 target. We have to keep in mind what strategies are appropriate for the development after 2020. That is, to what extent are the different policy scenarios consistent with further cuts in emissions after 2020? For example the relationship between the CO_2 and the NO_x targets seems crucial to the choice of engines in road vehicles, especially lorries and buses. Abandoning the diesel engine in city traffic would have air quality benefits. Given the policy targets for 2020, an option might be to abandon diesel engines for long distance lorries. However, in the longer perspective this does not seem very attractive, at least not until fuel cells permeate the market, since emissions of CO_2 would then increase significantly. In the subsequent Images, however, it is assumed that diesel engines in passenger cars will be phased out since a large part of car travel takes place in densely populated areas and there is a need to reduce the health effects of pollutants (such as particulates and NO_x). Exhaust treatment of diesel cars is improving regarding some substances but increasing car travel could offset some or all of this effect (see Chapter 3). Furthermore, the amount of very small particulate matter (PM), which is considered most dangerous, might increase even if the total amount of PM decreases. If different cars could be used for different purposes, enabled by convenient car rental or car pooling, there might be a niche for diesel cars as long-distance cars. Electric vehicles could then be the main choice for city driving. A problem in the calculations above is that NO_x emissions are notoriously difficult to estimate due to large 'off-cycle emissions'. These are caused by cold starts, high speeds, hard accelerations and malfunctioning exhaust treatment devices, which are not accounted for in test cycles. As a consequence actual on-the-road emissions might exceed test cycle levels by 100 per cent or more.

Decoupling

One of the reasons why a technological solution is not sufficient for reaching the policy targets is the trend of increasing transport volumes. The rate of mobility is currently outstripping the environmental improvements offered by technology in many cases (such as CO_2 emissions and noise). Current travel trends indicate increasing journey distances to carry out activities that were previously carried out with less travel (see Chapter 3). Thus, the rate of growth in mobility has to be curbed if sustainability is to be achieved. As car ownership and use increases, transport capacity is likely to be exceeded more and more. Thus, time constraints may to some extent become a travel-limiting factor in the longer term. However, for long-distance travel, particularly by air, time constraints will hardly ever become a limiting factor for the major part of the population. With current attitudes, it is difficult to discern a limit to the number of people's materialistic desires. The demand for mobility increases when incomes increase. In principle, all measures to make travelling cheaper, more comfortable or faster generate a larger amount of transport. This can also be formulated in the following way: the possibility of reaching places with less effort leads to more travel because it creates more opportunities in terms of contacts and activities. From the point of view of the environment and the utilization of resources, it may be claimed that faster transport is doubly problematic. It makes it possible to travel longer distances within a certain time, and energy use per distance travelled increases.

If the costs of transport continue to be low it is also difficult to see any spontaneous limits to freight transport demand. Further, in a situation with continued growth and unchanged attitudes and values it is difficult to see any saturation levels for transport volumes in the near future. The conclusion is that, if sustainable development is accepted as a principal goal, transport volumes must be limited. On the other hand, it is not obvious that all types of transport can or should be limited to the same extent. One way of solving the conflict between the environmental, regional and efficiency objectives is decoupling transport growth (tonne-kilometres or passenger-kilometres) from economic growth. By decoupling we mean a decrease of transport intensity, measured as tonne-kilometres and person-kilometres per unit of GDP (see Chapter 3). This requires that the growth rate of transport volumes is less than that of GDP. When the growth rates are equal, no change in transport intensity or transport decoupling has occurred.

As we have seen earlier (Chapter 3), passenger transport grew faster than GDP in the fifteen EU countries overall between 1970 and 1995. The quotient between passenger transport and GDP growth was 1.4. For freight transport, the corresponding value was 1.0, which means that the growth in GDP was matched by the growth of freight transport.

Transport intensity is not the same in all sectors and will change differently. Furthermore, when the economy grows the relative shares of different sectors will change, affecting the average transport intensity and decoupling. Growth tends to be strong in some new branches, such as IT related activities. These activities are characterized by low materials content and high content of knowledge and services. The result is relatively low transport intensity. Although this trend towards high-value-per-weight products might slightly contribute to decoupling, the environmental benefit might be more than offset if freight is shifted from road to air, which is quite likely in a business-as-usual scenario. Air freight is about twenty times more energy intensive than road freight.

In addition, transport distances tend to increase for most traditional sectors – the reasons being more cost efficient transport technology, changes in transport infrastructure, and the removal of certain trade barriers. Given these trends, it is highly unlikely that the decoupling required to reach the policy targets will take place spontaneously. Determined policy action will be needed in this area. Three factors that are likely to have an impact on decoupling are consumption patterns, production processes, and location decisions. These are discussed in turn below.

The amount of transport needed is dependent on the structure of demand for goods and services. One element is the distribution between goods and services. Consumers can use increased wealth to buy more services rather than goods. Services are often less dependent on transport and are more locally produced than goods. However services are not always preferable to goods from an environmental point of view. The most obvious case is leisure travel by air or car. In many sectors products can be substituted by services. This applies to some products (leasing systems, joint use of durable consumer goods, repair systems) and mobility (such as car-sharing initiatives and public transport).

The type of goods consumed also affects the need for transport as an input. There is a clearly discernible tendency that bulk production with high materials content is decreasing in relative importance, while high-tech products, with little materials content but a high content of know-how are increasing in relative importance. However it is not clear that the absolute volume of the former products is decreasing. After all, we will still need food, housing, and fuels in an information society.

Increased demand for locally-produced goods is another option to reduce transport. This is especially important for low-value-per-weight products such as agricultural products, food, building materials, and fuels. These kinds of goods do not contribute much to a dynamic economic development, but account for about half of the road freight volume in the EU measured in terms of tonne-kilometres (Schleicher-Tappeser *et al.*, 1998).

Given the pattern of consumption, the need for transport is also a function of how the production is organized and of how products are designed. Traditionally, economic growth in the open world market economies is associated with the globalization process. Often this process is associated with a concentration and centralization of production, which itself creates additional transport demand due to longer distances between producer and consumer and between different stages in the production process. This is the typical case of mass production where economies of scale exist.

Since the economic crisis of the 1970s, a new production paradigm has emerged: flexible specialization, characterized by flexible technologies for specialized and segmented markets, small production series, and flexible adjustment to changing consumer tastes. The economic success is determined by economies of scope, not economies of scale. The success of this type of production strongly influenced the reshaping of the European economic space. It is characterized by strong intra-regional links and the 'networking' of enterprises. Co-operation and clustering within industrial districts may create external benefits. The transport needs of such regional production clusters are ambivalent, as short distances between interlinked business become a strategic success factor, but regional production clusters are the basis for world market oriented success stories and hence require long-distance transport. In general they are more transport efficient than global activities, since the linkages of the production processes are regionalized.

Alternatives to globalization and flexible specialization are local production for local markets or a combination of global and local production: so-called 'glocal' production. Glocal production is characterized by large network firms which combine economies of scale and scope and maintain a network of local and global organizational units with close communication links. Information technology has a key role to play. Transport needs can also be reduced by the design of products. Material flows can be reduced by dematerialization or miniaturization of products, increased durability and design to make service and recycling easier.

The 'informatization' of the economy largely influences the location of firms and individuals, but the impact is unclear. On the one hand opportunities for teleworking and teleconferencing might increase, which would imply a decrease in transport. On the other hand, another consequence would be that proximity to suppliers, buyers or public transport is of less importance to locational choices. This would mean that spatial concepts like 'compact city' and 'specialization and concentration' will decrease in importance and that the minimum volume of travel demand needed for public transport modes is not reached. The spatial policy of the government must influence these locational choices.

The structurally determined daily journeys for purposes such as work or shopping can probably be reduced without challenging today's values. Most people would probably regard a reduction in this type of journey as a positive development, for example through increased doorstep delivery service and teleworking. Other journeys, particularly leisure journeys, are highly valued. The places people often go to have a value of their own and sometimes the travelling itself can have a value (beautiful scenery or enjoyable driving for example).

In conclusion, there is some potential to decouple transport growth from economic growth. It is however difficult to make quantitative estimates. Decoupling is crucial to fulfil all policy targets simultaneously as transport volume growth has to be limited in order to meet environmental targets.

9.2.2 The world outside the realm of policy-makers – contextual elements

We have employed the degree of 'co-operation' or 'polarization' as a core feature of the Images of the Future. This is essentially an external factor relative to sustainable mobility, transport policy, and the transport sector. The extent of co-operation or polarization will of course greatly affect the achievements and relative merits of different transport policies.

The concepts of co-operation and polarization essentially pertain to the way society copes with market failure and public goods and bads. Here agreements and common policies beside the market are often needed. The climate for co-operation will then be of crucial importance. Is there a spirit of co-operation and social responsibility or is the dominant behaviour free-riding?

Even those who want to act according to the common interest, may fail to do so because of the logic (structure of incentives) inherent in the situation. Hence, the 'rules of the game' may have to be changed. There is a rich literature on this problem area in economics, political science, ecology, and mathematics (game theory), dealing with the closely related issues of Collective Actions (Olson, 1971; Hardin, 1982), Prisoners' Dilemma

(Axelrod, 1984), and Tragedy of the Commons (Hardin, 1968; Ostrom, 1990).

Many environmental problems are related to so-called social dilemmas. One example is a situation called The Tragedy of the Commons. Originally, this concept refers to situations where a group of people share a common, natural resource (such as a lake for fishing). Over-use will ruin the resource. Hence, it is in the common interest to restrict use to what is sustainable. However, individuals will be tempted to take a greater share than is reasonable, because if s/he does not, the others may do so and ruin the resource, making him/her a loser. This is largely a matter of trust (or lack of trust).

Social dilemmas similar to the Tragedy of the Commons occur at all levels of human interaction: within groups of individuals, within and between businesses, and at all levels of political decision-making. Examples include:

- national governments choosing a policy regarding CO_2 emissions (global level);
- urban commuters choosing between a convenient, more polluting trip by car or a less convenient, cleaner trip by public transport (local level).

The attitudes to co-operation in such situations will be crucial to solving the problem. Here, different assumptions are made in different Images of the Future.

One example is lifestyles. It could be that international lifestyles spread and travel distances increase. Or it could be that people exhibit a more local lifestyle with a preference for locally-produced goods and services as well as for exploring their native district. The relative strength of these two lifestyles in the future will have a strong impact on the demand for travel and freight transport. Therefore we distinguish between:

- the case of a widely spread 'local' lifestyle; and
- the case of a dominant international lifestyle.

Another example of a potentially important factor is the strength and spread of green values. Is the emerging green consciousness more or less a fad or a profound shift? The following alternatives are identified:

- the case of a strong concern for the environment and future generations among broad groups in society – the preservation of the environment is seen as a necessary condition for the long-term wealth of human-kind, or even for its survival (Images I and III);
- the case of a well informed but pragmatic and more short-term view on the environment – the relation to other societal goals is essentially perceived as a trade-off, where the environment does not take precedence over the others (Image II).

We have not studied the case of dominant materialistic values and withering green attitudes, because it is less likely that a successful policy for sustainability will be possible in such a case. Broader public devotion to the idea of a sustainable development would probably be required for the policy targets to be reachable by 2020. If this is so, an important question is how a shift in values and attitudes might come about.

Increasing environmental awareness is dependent on a mix of experience, education and media reporting. New scientific findings on the harmful effects of emissions of particulates in urban areas or strong evidence of a global warming effect may change attitudes in the future. A deliberate and persistent public policy of information and opinion forming as well as the incorporation of an environmental dimension at all levels of the educational system may play an important role in the long term. Such policies fall outside the transport sector, which shows the interdependence between different policy fields.

9.2.3 Additional factors in the design of the scenarios

In addition to these basic components of the Images of the Future, there is a series of other questions that have been addressed in the design process. It is only possible to list them here:

1 *Innovations and Niche Markets*. The market uptake of new technologies and systems is often problematic, because of high costs compared to established technologies. Uptake of new technologies may, however, be hastened by the creation of niche markets where novel concepts can be introduced, start to grow, and enter a learning curve where costs will gradually decrease, making it possible to compete in other markets as well.

2 *Regional Development and Innovation*. The production style of flexible specialization does not automatically lead to a convergence of economic development within Europe. The success conditions are regionally embedded and cannot easily be reproduced over the whole European territory. However, regional production offers new opportunities for less developed regions although regional convergence is not guaranteed.

3 *Economic Efficiency in the Transport Sector*. An economic efficiency target in this study is full cost coverage of transport under market or equivalent conditions. Subsidies should be minimized and market principles should prevail in the operation of the transport system and in assessing new investments. This has important implications for the financing and operation of transport, as well as its organization. The role of governments may be reduced but it will always be present.

4   *Key Issues in the Development of the European Transport System,* which include:

- The continuing concern over CO_2 emissions as a key environmental issue at the global scale;
- The future of the railways and the role that High Speed Trains (HST) have in centralizing accessibility and growth in Europe;
- The future of aviation, which is the fastest growing transport sector (currently around 5 per cent per annum);
- Urban overload, leading to unacceptable levels of pollution and congestion;
- Freight transit in areas where capacity is restricted, such as the Alpine region;
- Developments in the CEEC/CIS countries and their interaction with the EU.

9.3   Choice of Images of the Future

Different developments in society at large will demand different policy approaches to transport issues. Therefore, the scenarios are designed to show different combinations of policy alternatives, combining strategic and contextual elements.

9.3.1 Strategic elements

There are two main categories of change needed to achieve the policy targets by the year 2020:

1   a reduction of energy use and emissions per person-kilometre travelled and tonne-kilometre of freight by means of technological improvements, new fuels, improved load factors and modal shifts (Technology); and

2   a decrease in transport intensity of GDP, that will allow the volume of transport to increase at a rate which is less than the economy at large (Decoupling);

All Images of the Future rely on both strategies, but in different proportions. Three combinations are examined:

1   a moderate pace of technological improvements combined with a considerable degree of decoupling (Technology+ /Decoupling+++);

2   a fast dissemination of cleaner technologies and fuels combined with a moderate degree of decoupling (Technology+++ /Decoupling+);

3   both fast technological improvements and a considerable degree of decoupling.

The case of Technology+++ /Decoupling+++ case might be hard to realize. This may to some extent be due to financial costs, but political inertia is probably a more important factor given the limited time span considered. Therefore, we have chosen as a third case a Technology++ /Decoupling++ solution.

9.3.2 Contextual elements

Successful handling of many environmental problems requires agreements and co-operation outside the market, either by political intervention or by 'grassroots' initiatives by those affected, or some combination of both. Hence the attitudes towards co-operation in society will affect the possibilities of meeting the environmental targets. Three alternatives are distinguished:

1 Local, regional, and EU co-operation, where policies are mainly driven by local and regional initiatives (bottom-up politics). Local and regional aspects are high on the political agenda, while global environmental issues are a little lower down. Green values are pushed by 'grassroots' movements rather than by national or EU politicians, who lag behind but try to meet the demands of the people. There is polarization at the global level, where the EU, the US, and Japan take different stands on questions such as global warming, and tend to protect their own markets against competition from outside.

2 Global and EU co-operation, with free trade and a striving for consensus on environmental issues. At the local and regional levels the attitudes towards co-operation are more passive, as the political agenda is mainly driven by national and EU politicians. The focus is more on high level problems (top-down politics). Politicians take the lead and try to influence opinions.

3 Local-global co-operation promotes an accord between local, regional and supra-national initiatives and objectives – a kind of harmony between bottom-up and top-down politics. Green values are widespread, with both local and international lifestyles.

In all cases there is co-operation at the EU level.

9.3.3 Combining the strategic and contextual dimensions into the Images of the Future

The Images of the Future result from the combination of the three strategies based on co-operation at the local, national/global, and combined levels, together with differing levels of technological development and decoupling (Table 9.2). In total there are nine combinations, but not all seem equally plausible. In the first column of the table, the emphasis is on decoupling rather than technological improvement. Radical decoupling demands behavioural changes (mode choice, choice of residential area and so on) which in turn requires 'grassroots' involvement and commitment. This is prevalent in D1, but less so in D2. Where there is co-operation at all levels, a balanced strategy (TD3) would seem to be preferable to scenario D3. Hence, our choice from this column is D1: EU co-ordination of Active Citizens (Image I).

Table 9.2 Nine Images of the Future obtained by combining contextual and strategic elements

	Strategic Elements		
Contextual Elements	Technology+/ Decoupling+++	Technology+++/ Decoupling+	Technology++/ Decoupling++
Local, regional and EU co-operation	D1	T1	TD1
Global and EU co-operation	D2	T2	TD2
Local-global co-operation	D3	T3	TD3

In the second column (Table 9.2), the general strategy emphasizes fast technological evolution and dissemination, while the degree of decoupling is moderate. This strategy seems to require global co-operation on such issues as regulation of CO_2 emissions (T2). Option T1 lacks international agreements in this area and is, therefore, less likely. T3 would be possible, but here the conditions are favourable for both technological improvements and decoupling, making a more balanced strategy attractive, as in scenario TD3 in column 3. Consequently, we have chosen scenario T2 as the most interesting and internally coherent case in the second column: Global co-operation for Sustainable Transport (Image II).

Finally, the cases in column 3 (Table 9.3) all exhibit a balanced strategy of fast technological development and a considerable degree of decoupling. However, in TD1 the conditions for really fast technological improvements are not so favourable while in TD2 popular engagement, which seems to be necessary for a far reaching decoupling, is not present. Both conditions are fulfilled in the case TD3, and this is our choice from column 3: Accord on Sustainability (Image III). In summary, three Images of the Future are selected for investigation:

Image I   – EU co-ordination of Active Citizens (D1)
Image II   – Global co-operation for Sustainable Transport (T2)
Image III – Accord on Sustainability (TD3)

These three Images of the Future are discussed in turn below.

9.4   Image I: EU co-ordination of active citizens

9.4.1 Society at large

There is a trend towards more 'local lifestyles' and green values among the general public. People increasingly take responsibility for the common good and attitudes towards collective actions are positive, especially at the local and regional levels.

The public push politicians to adopt stricter environmental regulations and standards, especially at the local level (urban areas). At the global level no agreement on harmonizing standards is achieved. People are willing to pay for greener products as well as for locally-produced goods. Settlement patterns and location of workplace and service functions are also affected. Many urban sub-centres have a higher degree of self-sufficiency than at present, and city centres are re-urbanized. There is an increased acceptability for urban public transport, bicycles, and electric urban cars.

Production is more local and mainly serves local markets, but is based on licences and the know-how of large international firms and networks (glocal production). There is also an increasing share for the service sector, with traditional manufacturing industry showing a declining share of total production. GDP grows at a moderate pace, whilst green GDP develops faster. Freight transport volumes begin to level out.

A tax base reform (in line with a dematerialization strategy) takes place in EU countries, shifting taxation from labour to the use of natural resources and energy, with the aim to stimulate conservation of resources. This, together with greater demand for green products, results in reductions in the use of energy, materials and hazardous substances by businesses.

9.4.2 General approach to transport policy

The shift in values and lifestyles leads to a higher acceptability for changes in residential and travel patterns, providing an opportunity to bring the growth of transport volumes under control. Therefore the prime political strategy *vis à vis* the environmental goal, is to promote a decoupling of transport growth from GDP growth. The shift in demand has in itself led to a considerable degree of decoupling of freight transport and economic growth. This is complemented by policy measures intended to reduce structurally-enforced travel, such as commuting to work and service trips. Here, urban land-use planning and measures to facilitate telecommuting are important. A policy for cleaner transport (pertaining to both personal travels and freight) is also important. This consists of three parts:

1   measures to promote a shift in modal split towards a higher share for cleaner modes (more public transport or a higher share for freight by rail for example);
2   measures intended to make each mode cleaner, by spread of cleaner technologies;
3   measures to increase load factors.

Measures affecting modal choice form an important part of the general policy. Cleaner technologies are supported by research and development funding, and niche markets for introduction of new vehicles, and systems such as car pooling with specialized vehicles are all created. There is no great need for new inter-regional infrastructure, the exception being the improved quality of links to the former CEEC countries. Railways and other public transport are kept in public hands but they operate independently from governments. The EU has an important role in co-ordinating regional and national policies and in harmonizing targets and standards in Europe (Tables 9.3 and 9.4).

Table 9.3   Characteristics of the transport sector in Image I

General	Total mobility is the same as 1995 but lower than the Reference Case
	Commuting and shopping travel decreases
	Leisure travel increases
	Cars are used less except in CEEC/CIS countries
	Car accessibility without ownership increases in popularity
	Niche vehicles, car rental, smart cards are used
	Car use for commuting is lower, but higher for leisure purposes
Urban	Concentration of development in cities and transport corridors
	Telecottages and teleshopping
	Reduction in work and shopping travel
	Shift to public transport and bicycle and higher vehicle occupancies
	Less space for cars in cities: limited parking
	Lower speed limits and priority to public transport
Long distance	Telephone and videoconferencing are more widespread
	Long-distance leisure travel is important
	Public transport is competitive in price but not fast
	Air travel growth is slower than at present
	Rail in combination with rental car is a popular combination
	Limited investment in HST: greater use of existing track
Freight	Local and glocal production
	Dematerialization and decentralized production
	Distribution load factors increase
	Intermodality is promoted
Vehicle technology and fuels	Electric vehicles account for 20 per cent of car travel
	Cars are 15-20 per cent lighter than at present
	Diesel vehicles reduced due to emissions problems
	City buses and lorries have hybrid drives (gas turbine, petrol engine, or fuel cell)
Organization and financing	Market incentives such as road pricing are introduced
	Public transport is publicly owned, but independent from government
	There is little new road infrastructure
	There is some reorganization of railways to CEEC/CIS countries
Regional development	Regions are less economically specialized and more self-sufficient
	Glocal production increases

Table 9.4 Image I in figures for the EU 15+3 countries

Transport volume (billion person-km or billion tonne-km):

Mode:	1995 actual	2020 Reference Case	2020 Image I	2020 Image I as a proportion of 2020 Reference Case	2020 Image I as a proportion of 1995 actual volume
Car (fossil)	3590	5380	2260		
Car (methanol)	–	–	–	0.5	0.8
Car (electric)	–	–	560		
Aircraft	400	1200	720	0.6	1.8
Bus	370	480	700	1.5	1.9
Train	290	350	660	1.9	2.3
Total Passenger	4650	7410	4900	0.7	1.1
Lorry (diesel)	1130	2260	1130		
Lorry (methanol)	–	–	–	0.5	1.0
Train	240	240	300	1.3	1.3
Inland Water	120	130	150	1.1	1.3
Total Freight	1490	2630	1580	0.6	1.1

Note: For Reference Case refer to Table 1.1

9.5   Image II: global co-operation for sustainable transport

9.5.1 Society at large

There is a certain degree of green consciousness and an acceptance of policy measures intended to mitigate the environmental problems (i.e. those related to transport). However, these issues are not based on popular opinion: they stem from political priorities and agreements. Politicians are relatively successful in forming opinions and there is an understanding that transport must in principle pay its full costs. Most people are not inclined to accept major changes in travel behaviour. There is some green demand but this is relatively small.

The international lifestyle gains strength and there is a trend towards segmentation of society into different lifestyles. Many enterprises cater for a specific segment of customers across the world (an early sign of this trend was in the 1990s when Swatch and Mercedes exploited a certain market segment to launch the Smart Car). Production is increasingly characterized by 'flexible specialization', and economic development is generally dynamic with a relatively high average GDP growth. However, economic growth lags behind in some regions in Europe. Despite a trend towards dematerialization, transport volumes continue to grow due to increasing distances. A high degree of accord develops in the relations between EU, the US, and Japan as regards international regulations and standards in order to cope with global environmental problems.

Table 9.5 Characteristics of the transport sector in Image II

General	Total mobility is higher than 1995 but lower than the Reference Case People are not willing to change their travel behaviour Car travel increases moderately Working hours become more flexible
Urban	Telecommuting is widespread Urban decentralization continues Urban areas are still dominated by the car Public transport has little market share
Long distance	Air travel grows in line with the global economy Business travel by air and HST is high Leisure travel by air and car grows rapidly Prices on intercontinental flights are higher as a result of CO_2 taxes
Freight	High volumes of goods are transported over long distances (but lower than the Reference Case) Trade across EU borders increases Rail gains a substantial market share Freight centres for intermodal distribution at periphery of cities Rail standards are harmonized across Europe (including communications, signals and organization) There is extensive use of IT and new management strategies
Vehicle technology and fuel	R+D projects generously funded at EU level There is co-operative research between the EU, the US and Japan to establish common technical standards All purpose cars are dominant – mainly hybrid electric with gas turbine, direct injection petrol engine or fuel cell power Battery cars become niche market vehicles Cars are 25 per cent lighter in weight than at present Methanol accounts for 20 per cent of total transport fuel use and is used mainly in lorries Fuel cells with on-board methanol reformers are introduced for lorries, buses and cars
Organization and financing	Market incentives and private sector initiatives are introduced Road pricing is introduced and roads are privately managed Rail and other public transport is privately owned The private sector builds new infrastructure with government guarantees New railways are constructed in southern Europe and existing railways are upgraded and modernized in CEEC/CIS countries. New HST services are introduced, mainly in the core area due to high construction costs Public transport in peripheral areas is subsidised
Regional development	Flexible specialization is based on knowledge and local resources, but is export-oriented Goods flows increase Investment in telecommunications increases

9.5.2 General approach to transport policy

The widespread environmental consciousness among leading politicians on the world stage makes it possible to reach agreements on international standards and norms for cleaner vehicles, reductions of CO_2 emissions, and to achieve similar levels of taxation of externalities, at least in the OECD area. The accord among leading politicians has widespread public support, which makes implementation of these measures possible. However, people do not accept measures that interfere with current lifestyles, such as using private cars and living in low-density residential areas.

Consequently, the prime policy regarding the environmental goal in Europe is to make transport cleaner. Although some measures are directed towards raising the share of cleaner modes, the emphasis is on promoting the development and introduction of cleaner technologies and fuels. As there is no shift away from the use of the private car, much of research and development is directed towards improving the technology of the conventional all-purpose car. However, there are also more far-sighted policies that are promoted by the EU, such as creation of niche markets for fuel cell vehicles. This is achieved by experiments with environmental zones (Tables 9.5 and 9.6).

Table 9.6 Image II in figures for the EU 15+3 countries

Transport volume (billion person-km or billion tonne-km):

Mode:	1995 actual	2020 Reference Case	2020 Image II	2020 Image II as a proportion of 2020 Reference Case	2020 Image II as a proportion of 1995 actual volume
Car (fossil)	3590	5380	3550	0.7	1.1
Car (methanol)	–	–	300		
Car (electric)	–	–	0		
Aircraft	400	1200	960	0.8	2.4
Bus	370	480	550	1.1	1.5
Train	290	350	700	2.0	2.4
Total Passenger	4650	7410	6060	0.8	1.3
Lorry (diesel)	1130	2260	0	0.6	1.2
Lorry (methanol)	–	–	1400		
Train	240	240	400	1.7	1.7
Inland Water	120	130	160	1.3	1.2
Total Freight	1490	2630	1960	0.7	1.3

Note: For Reference Case refer to Table 1.1

9.6   Image III: accord on sustainability

9.6.1 Society at large

A spirit of co-operation permeates all levels of interaction among individuals, locally, regionally, at the national and EU levels, as well as globally. Of course, some problems are still difficult to handle, but there is a respect for other parties' interests and a willingness to find win-win solutions. The high level of interest and initiatives in societal matters by the general public results in strong support for the principle of subsidiarity. At the same time the overarching political structures of Europe are powerful because of the consensus among leading economic powers of the world regarding many global issues, such as the environment. A kind of balance of power exists, based on a strong popular involvement in local and regional affairs and a more passive support for EU co-ordination and politics in high level issues.

9.6.2 General approach to transport policy

The opinion among people and the political climate at higher levels is such that the solutions of Image I and Image II could be combined with even better

Table 9.7 Characterization of the transport sector in Image III

General	There is strong support for decoupling and good conditions for technological development
	Total mobility is higher than in 1995 but lower than the Reference Case
	Commuting and shopping travel decreases
	Leisure travel increases
	Cars have high capital costs (such as fuel cell cars)
	Only half as much methanol compared to Image II is used which means that less land is needed for growing biomass
Urban	Development is concentrated in cities and transport corridors
	Shifts to public transport and bicycle occur, and vehicle occupancies increase
	Telecottages and teleshopping are established in decentralized locations
	There is less road space for cars in cities and limited parking
Long distance	Long distance leisure travel is high
	Air travel grows, as does rail and rental car
	There is limited investment in HST and better use of existing track
Freight	Local and glocal production increases
	There is dematerialization and decentralized production
	Load factors are increased, particularly in distribution
	Intermodality is promoted
Vehicle technology and fuels	Technological development is fast, with focus on niche vehicles
	Methanol restricted to 10 per cent of all fuel – mainly for lorries
	Fuel cell cars account for 4 per cent of fleet
	There is a high proportion of high-mileage vehicles, such as taxis and rental cars
	Cars are 15-20 per cent lighter in weight: feebates are related to weight
Organization and Financing	Market incentives such as road pricing are introduced
	Public transport is publicly owned but independent from government
	There is little new investment in infrastructure
	Investment in IT infrastructure is high
	There is more investment in research and development to achieve very low emissions from new vehicles
Regional Development	Regions are less economically specialized and more self-sufficient
	Glocal production and the globalization of certain markets increases

goal attainment as a result of synergy effects. However, financial constraints will restrict what is attainable. The regions and municipalities of Europe largely choose their own ways of coping with local emissions and congestion, while the targets are agreed at higher levels (Tables 9.7 and 9.8).

Table 9.8 Image III in figures for the EU 15+3 countries

	1995 actual	2020 Reference Case	2020 Image III	2020 Image III as a proportion of 2020 Reference Case	2020 Image III as a proportion of 1995 actual volume
Transport volume (billion person-km or billion tonne-km):					
Mode:					
Car (fossil)	3590	5380	2470	0.6	0.9
Car (methanol)	–	–	–		
Car (electric)	–	–	620		
Aircraft	400	1200	800	0.7	2.0
Bus	370	480	700	1.5	1.9
Train	290	350	660	1.9	2.3
Total Passenger	4650	7410	5250	0.7	1.1
Lorry (diesel)	1130	2260	500	0.5	1.1
Lorry (methanol)	–	–	720		
Train	240	240	300	1.2	1.2
Inland Water	120	130	140	1.1	1.2
Total Freight	1490	2630	1660	0.6	1.1

Note: For Reference Case refer to Table 1.1

9.7   Comparison of Images of the Future

These three Images of the Future differ from each other as they mix different priorities according to levels of co-operation, the top-down or bottom-up approaches, the importance of technology in achieving the targets, and the nature and extent of decoupling (Table 9.9). These elements are presented in the upper part of the Table (points 1-5). The consequences of adopting the different Images of the Future are also elaborated through the illustrative figures given in Table 9.9 (points 6-18), which give a flavour of the expected changes in activities, travel, modal split, distance, and the relative importance of other policy factors. It is important to realize that there is a wide range of choices that can be made, all of which can contribute directly and indirectly to sustainable mobility.

9.8   Discussion of targets, consequences and presumptions of the Images

9.8.1 Target achievement

The Images of the Future have been designed to meet the policy targets and it is now necessary to examine whether the targets can be reached, and if so, the

Table 9.9   Comparison of the Images of the Future

	Image I	Image II	Image III
1 Levels of co-operation	Local, EU	EU, Global	Local, EU, Global
2 Valuation of environment in the population	High	Moderate (although higher than today)	High
3 Structure of production system	Much local and 'glocal' production Dematerialization	Relatively much international trade. Some dematerialization	Much local and 'glocal' production Dematerialization
4 Technological development of vehicles	Moderate pace	Fast	Fast
5 Attitude towards change travel behaviour	Positive (given there are environmental benefits)	Negative	Positive (given there are environmental benefits)
6 Reduction of enforced travel (such as work travel)	Large	Moderate	Large
7 Modal shift, personal travel	Considerable	Small	Considerable
8 Modal shift, freight transport	Small	Considerable	Small
9 Car travel compared to 1995 (EU)	-20%	+10%	About -10%
10 Car travel in CEEC/CIS compared to 1995	About +70%	About +100%	About +80%
11 Cars per 1000 inhabitants (EU)	350 (1995: 420)	500	400
12 Average car mileage per year (1000 km)	13 (1995: 13)	11	12
13 Urban land use	Decentralized concentrations Relatively high share of public transport and bike	Some urban sprawl	Decentralized concentrations. Relatively high share of public transport and bike
14 Role of railways	Alternative to car. Low cost prior to high speed	Railways are an alternative to air travel High speed prior to low cost. More freight by rail	Alternative to both car and air transport More freight by rail
15 Infrastructure investment	Little transport infrastructure Much IT	More rail infrastructure Some IT	Little transport infrastructure Much IT
16 Public spending on research and development	Moderate	Moderate	High
17 Environmental risks	Fewer environmental risks	Large use of biomass Large high altitude emissions	Fewer environmental risks
18 The long view (possibilities to further reduce emissions after 2020)	Quite good	Limited	Quite good (already lower than targets in 2020)

level of difficulty likely in achieving them. Even though there are considerable problems with data, particularly in the CEEC/CIS countries, it is possible to make comparisons between the three Images of the Future. The fulfilment of the environmental and other targets is to a large extent dependent on the degree of decoupling. The NO_x target is more demanding than the CO_2 target, but also closer to what could be called a sustainable level. It is achieved for EU15+3 in all the Images of the Future, but to achieve the policy targets overall further cuts may be necessary to allow for increasing transport volumes in CEEC/CIS countries. The target on special protected areas is fulfilled in all Images of the Future, and the limited increase in new infrastructure will be achieved, but in Image II it requires the removal of some old infrastructure. A normative summary of the extent to which targets may be achieved for each of the three Images of the Future is presented in Table 9.10.

Table 9.10 Summary of target achievement

Targets	Image I	Image II	Image III
CO_2 emissions −25% EU 15+3	−35%	−39%	−43%
CO_2 emissions −25% CEEC/CIS	+26%	+36%	+24%
CO_2 emissions −25% EU 15+3+CEEC/CIS	−27%	−30%	−35%
NO_x emissions −80% EU 15+3	−77%	−79%	−82%
No degradation of special protected areas	Target fulfilled; few infrastructure investments	Target probably fulfilled; moderate infrastructure investments.	Target fulfilled; few infrastructure investments
No or minor increase of net infrastructure surface in Europe	Target fulfilled	Target may be fulfilled if some outdated infrastructure is removed	Target fulfilled
Improve relative accessibility of peripheral regions (both internal and externally)	Target fulfilled: main means is improved telecommunications	In general the target is fulfilled, but the social distribution of accessibility is rather uneven	Target fulfilled: main means is improved telecommunications
Full cost coverage of transport under market or equivalent conditions	Yes but operated by public sector	Yes but subsidies to infrastructure investments in peripheral regions are required	Yes but subsidies to research and development on advanced vehicles are required

Accessibility targets will be hard to achieve and success is likely to depend on the level of telecommunications substitution for travel, as this will increase intra-regional accessibility. A potential source of tension in Image II is the uneven distribution of accessibility resulting from the introduction of road pricing and market principles to transport. The efficiency target will be met, although there may be some problems in Image I with subsidies to public transport and infrastructure for CEEC/CIS countries, and in Image II with financing research and development and infrastructure.

In Image II, individual mobility is highly valued, even though transport demand is reduced through taxation, road pricing, and other economic incentives. This implies that mobility will depend to a great extent on individual incomes and consequently there is a risk of strong opposition if there is an unequal income distribution in society. One measure to decouple is a tax-shift, from labour to resource consumption. This is a case where major impacts will take place outside the transport sector but will have far-reaching implications for the transport sector.

Road transport volumes in the CEEC/CIS countries are expected to increase. At present, they have lower traffic volumes than the EU countries. This is likely to lead to increased traffic emissions in these countries, which is in conflict with the aim of lowering emissions and reducing environmental impacts. However, it would be unreasonable to require implementation of vehicle emission standards in the whole area of the EU and the CEEC/CIS. A transitional period should be allowed for CEEC/CIS countries taking into account the much lower levels of emissions in these countries. One way to reach equity, would be to set an emission limit for each country, based on an average limit per capita for CO_2, NO_x and VOC emissions from road traffic in those countries. A limit based on the present EU countries per capita emissions from road traffic, therefore, would give space for some increases in traffic volumes in the CEEC/CIS countries. The per capita limit could be lowered over time as a means of reducing overall environmental pollution in line with the policy targets.

9.8.2 The potential role of technology and decoupling

The relative contributions to goal fulfilment provided by new technology and decoupling are illustrated in Figure 9.1 (Image I) and Figure 9.2 (Image II). The three curves on each graph show the development of GDP, transport volume and CO_2 emissions.

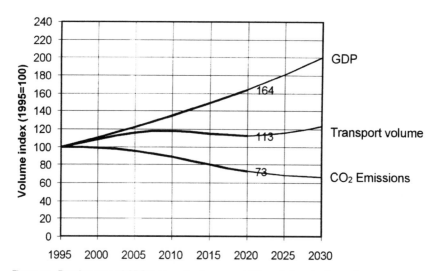

Figure 9.1 Development of GDP, transport volumes and CO_2 emissions for Image I

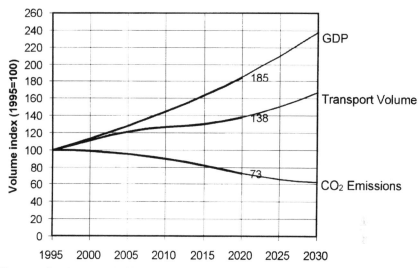

Figure 9.2 Development of GDP, transport volumes and CO_2 emissions for Image II

The vertical gap between the GDP curve and the transport volume curve represents the decoupling effect, whereas the gap between the transport volume curve and the emissions curve represents the effect of improved technology.

The development beyond 2020 is also indicated on the graphs. We can see how the transport volume curves begin to bend upwards again, as the decoupling potential of the structural and behavioural changes considered in the Images of the Future eventually is exhausted. It seems reasonable to assume that it will take some time for the typical contextual conditions (such as changes in lifestyles and values) of each Image to develop and have an impact on transport intensity. The same will probably hold for deliberate decoupling policies. Once the process is set in motion, however, the decoupling effect will accelerate for a period but gradually lose momentum and eventually come to a halt when the potential of the structural changes of society considered in the scenarios has been exhausted. Of course, a new wave of structural and behavioural change (policy induced or otherwise) may follow and possibly start before the waves have died away. This will probably also be necessary to reach the policy targets: technological improvements alone may not be enough to keep emissions at an acceptable level after 2020.

Figures 9.1 and 9.2 build on the assumption of an annual GDP growth rate of 2 per cent in Image I and 2.5 per cent in Image II . These are the standard values for the Images of the Future (Image III also has an assumed growth rate of 2.5 per cent). Of course, some deviations from these values are possible and compatible with the general features of the scenarios, but there should be a somewhat faster growth in Image II than in Image I. It should be noted, though, that a higher growth rate will require a higher degree of decoupling, provided that the goals are met and the technological improvements are given. This may be very difficult to achieve. Our estimate is that the required decoupling levels may be possible to reach at the standard growth rates (2 per cent and 2.5 per cent). However, at 3 per cent growth in Image I and 3.5 per cent in Image II, the need for decoupling would be so high that it does not seem to be realistic by 2020. Figure 9.3 illustrates this.

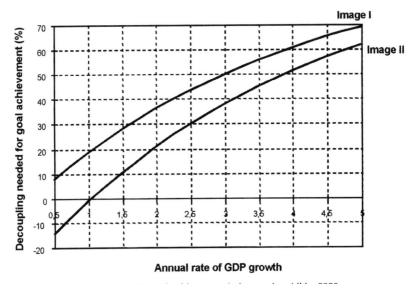

Figure 9.3 Decoupling required for goal achievement in Images I and II by 2020

9.8.3 Revisiting the construction of Images

Earlier in this Chapter (Table 9.2), nine alternative scenarios were identified according to the strategic and contextual elements. Three of them were chosen for elaboration. Image I had a focus on both decoupling and a bottom-up approach. Image II on technology and a top-down approach. Image III was a combination of both top-down/bottom-up and decoupling/technology. Here we will reconsider the basis for the choices of the Images of the Future.

The other six alternatives cannot be ruled out, even though the conditions for the policy measures are less favourable in these cases. In the case of strong decoupling, when the prevailing situation is in favour of top-down (D2) and not for bottom-up, the policy measures have to be oriented towards pushing citizens and other actors in a decoupling direction. This is a completely different situation compared to the bottom-up case (D1), where policy measures have the role of facilitating a desired development. In the D2 case, government action will be more oriented towards different general policy measures that will reduce transport volumes by regulation and/or pricing some transports out of the market.

A bottom-up situation that will push technology (T1) will be likely to be based on customer preferences expressed in the market. Customers will in this situation push development by demanding energy-efficient and environmentally-benign vehicles and transport services. Local policy measures, like environmental zones, can also be implemented. Co-ordination within customer groups can be achieved through NGOs. This process is likely to be much slower than the international harmonization of emission standards. It is therefore more unlikely that this alternative will reach the targets by 2020.

One major conclusion from this discussion is therefore that it is important for the success of a Common Transport Policy (CTP) that the prevailing situation regarding top-down or bottom-up is recognized and possibly also influenced over time. The Image III has been chosen as Technology++/ Decoupling++. In the following Section we will analyse under what circumstances both Technology and Decoupling can be strongly pushed (namely Technology +++/Decoupling +++).

9.8.4   Consequences for Image III – is strong decoupling and technology possible?

In Image III, there is political co-operation at the local, European, and global levels. This means that policy instruments in this Image could be a mixture of both bottom-up and top-down policies. There is strong support for environmental protection in this Image of the Future (Image I), which means that people take responsibility for the common good. Global agreement on targets concerning the environment receive at least passive public support.

It should be noted that the general prospect of achieving the targets in Image III is higher than in the other Images. The introduction of biofuels on a greater scale may be one of the more costly measures in Image III. Since targets in this Image appear to be achieved with some margin, an option might be to postpone this introduction and see if other technological improvements in combination with decoupling measures are sufficient to push down emissions until a time when a transport system based on hydrogen and fuel cells might be implemented.

The possibilities of simultaneously accomplishing relatively strong decoupling and much improved vehicle technology are at the centre of this Image. A specific issue is how new technology could be implemented rapidly before traffic volumes increase further. Policies intended to reduce transport intensity and volumes are employed mainly through the use of pricing and taxation (road pricing, ecological tax reform, feebates on new cars according to fuel consumption and weight, for example). Restrictions concerning parking, entry access, and goods traffic might also be applied. The production system needs to change towards more local and glocal production. Strong support exists for decoupling and there are good conditions for technological improvement. Emphasis on the concept of decentralized concentration induces the demand for telecottages and teleshopping facilities. Investments in information technology infrastructure are therefore quite high.

One potential synergy in Image III concerns the introduction of very fuel efficient, clean (but expensive) cars and the decrease of daily car travel in city areas. If more car use was by rented vehicle, pool car and taxi, this would increase the niche for expensive cars with low fuel consumption. A policy package could include tax incentives for rented vehicles and pool cars. Clean taxi fleets, which would increase in Image III, could have a substantial impact on emissions. If a strategy like this was applied, little public funding of research and development would be needed.

A shift towards fewer but more durable and lighter cars would also have some impact on dematerialization, which for instance could imply less transport in the production process, although increased export of cars outside the EU may counteract the benefits.

In terms of the renewal of vehicle fleets, there might be some difficulties in reaching desired fleet technology levels by 2020 due to the slow replacement of older vehicles. Longer vehicle life spans is positive from a resource and economic point of view but poses problems in environmental terms if today's cars are not as clean or fuel-efficient as in 10 or 15 years time. Furthermore, it seems that the heaviest and most powerful cars could remain in the vehicle stock longer than other types of car. This extension of a car's life span makes it the more urgent to change the incentives regarding fuel consumption of new cars.

In Image III it is assumed that cars will consume 40 per cent less fuel per kilometre than in 1995. This implies that by 2020 the fuel consumption of new cars should be roughly halved (taking into account the less efficient vehicles that will remain in the vehicle stock). If this is achieved without substantially increasing fuel price the consequence may be lower running costs and increased mileage. This may be consistent with Image II but not with Image I due to the strong decoupling emphasis. If fuel prices are increased substantially (more than doubled), old and less fuel-efficient cars will be very expensive to drive. Since these cars are often owned by the poorest section of society, the distribution of mobility will be even more uneven than at present. It is very doubtful whether this is politically acceptable. An alternative strategy would certainly include a higher fuel price but this would rely on other measures such as improved conditions for walking, cycling, and public transport, the replacement of trips by information technology and access to rented or shared cars. The distribution argument could also be used against road pricing in city areas. Besides improving the alternatives to car travel, simple regulation of the remaining car traffic could continue through congestion. A prerequisite would be very low emissions so that 'idling' vehicles standing in queues have much lower emissions. The apparent risk is that politicians would give way to claims for building new roads and increasing capacity.

In Image III, information technology is used heavily to replace travel and at the same time the travel generating effects of information technology are counteracted. The increased use of information technology to gain accessibility in combination with more flexible working hours implies more dispersed traffic patterns over time. This means that very little new road infrastructure would be needed and that (mainly) public resources could be saved. Because of the very fast expansion of the information technology sector, very little public funding would be needed. It is more a matter of creating a regulatory framework for the use of the technology. More local production of heavy (low value) goods, such as food, fuel, and construction materials, will decrease the need for long-distance road transport by lorry. An increase in teleshopping will increase the market for flexible and clean distribution vehicles. Through information technology, the co-ordination of goods flows could be achieved in order to minimize unnecessary travel. In general it seems that public funding does not have to increase if smart policies are introduced, possibly with the exception of biofuels.

Possibilities of both strong decoupling and technology

Image I is characterized by co-operation on local and regional levels (mainly bottom-up politics). Image II on the other hand is characterized by global co-operation (mainly top-down politics). If both these frame conditions materialize, then Image III is a feasible option. Originally it was argued that strong decoupling may not be possible to combine with strong technological development as the costs would be too high (Section 9.3.1). However, under certain conditions outlined below, a 'win-win' situation may be possible, involving both strong decoupling and technology. It was assumed in the study that the investments needed to pursue both strong decoupling and strong push of technology would be too high. Therefore Image III has a lower level of decoupling and technology than Images I and II respectively. Considering the proposed policy measures/packages earlier in this Chapter, it seems that in general they do not involve high investments. The proposed changes are very different from what can be regarded as business-as-usual. Therefore an Image with Decoupling+++/Technology+++ might be feasible.

Possible constraints

A tentative conclusion is that transport policy measures together with other actions in related sectors (such as land use and the development of industry) can achieve the targets set in the three Images. Options for a fourth Image of the Future (Image IV) with both strong technology and decoupling (Technology+++/Decoupling +++) may also be possible. In this case there is a good base for later achieving more far-reaching sustainability goals. To reach such an Image requires a high level of commitment and intervention of decision bodies across all sectors. The capacity for preparing decisions and implementing them is likely to be a bottleneck in realizing this Image. Transport policy at the EU level is only one of many competing areas of action.

If the conditions prevail for co-operation on all levels, this may be an attractive alternative. The issue addressed in the study is sustainable mobility, which is a subset of sustainable development. This deals with the question as to whether social and economic development is possible globally without destroying the ecological systems and depleting natural resources. It can be argued that heading for sustainability before it is too late is not a choice, but this is a question that should have high priority.

9.8.5 Important issues and conclusions

Vehicle technology

Images I and II have a different focus when it comes to priorities of research and development. The 'bottom-up' Image I favoured the development of niche vehicles such as electric city vehicles. Image II, which relies on international co-operation, results in the development and a widespread use of efficient multi-purpose cars. In the very near future a new generation of internal combustion engines will be phased into the car fleet (and are already marketed in Japan). These engines (such as lean burn engines) have about 15-20 per cent better fuel efficiency, although it is uncertain whether NO_x emissions will be reduced. Even so, this is not sufficient in the longer term. There are limits to engine efficiency in terms of fuel consumption, and the opportunities for weight reduction in vehicles is central to all Images of the Future. Environmental concerns have to be balanced against the safety implications. This process of technological development needs to be started immediately, with a phasing out of the least efficient heavy vehicles.

Vehicle fuels

In Images I and III, the decision on new fuels can be postponed because attitudes are in favour of modal shifts, and niche vehicles and lower transport volumes. In Image II, immediate action is required to provide an infrastructure for methanol to reach the environmental targets. However this implies higher fuel costs compared to Image I. Thus, a strategy stressing decoupling may give time enough to leap-frog directly to a transport system based on hydrogen produced by direct or indirect solar energy.

Transport infrastructure investment

There is a different profile in the investments in transport infrastructure between Images I and II. The emphasis on decoupling in Image I, means a higher share of public transport in urban areas and utilization of the existing rail network. In Image II car mobility is higher and the High Speed Train (HST) network in Europe is expanded.

Information technology

IT will fundamentally change everyday life in Europe. The crucial point is to ensure the full potential of IT in increasing accessibility and decreasing the need for physical movement, while at the same time avoiding any travel increasing mechanisms.

Land-use planning

The focus of land-use planning is to reduce the structurally-forced travel (such as work and shopping). If successful, such a policy will increase the scope for (more desired) leisure travel. Decentralized concentration (sub-centres with telecottages and local services connected by high quality public transport) is one interesting concept as it impacts on both transport volumes and emissions (encouraging a modal shift to environmentally benign modes). Measures to decrease travel can be achieved through demand management and planning interventions.

The longer term

The policy targets for environmental protection by 2020 are not final goals. As developing countries increase their standard of living, the environmental space and available resources for the developed countries (on a per capita basis) must be reduced. This means that long-term environmental targets are likely to be much tougher than the 2020 targets used in the scenarios. The need for further dematerialization will also increase if development is in line with sustainable development.

The rate of change differs according to different measures, and depends on the strength of political will. The turnover of cars is much faster than that for the built infrastructure. If changes are realized at the rate of replacement of worn out machinery, the costs can be low or zero. In each of the three Images of the Future we have assumed that most of the changes follow a 'natural' replacement rate although in some cases the environmental targets may result in earlier scrapping of vehicles.

The dynamics of change are also important. Will a continued development along lines before 2020 result in further improvements with respect to the objectives? One example is the introduction of fuel cell/hybrid cars. They are assumed to have quite a small share of the market in all Images of the Future by 2020. A further market penetration will improve the environmental situation even more.

In summary, the environmental targets should be viewed as intermediate targets, especially in terms of CO_2. In the long run more ambitious levels should apply. Therefore, when discussing and assessing the Images of the Future (and subsequently the scenarios) one should also consider the prospects of realizing very long-term goals (to 2050), as these may influence the choice of strategy even in the medium-term.

Chapter 10

Assembling Policy Packages and Paths

10.1 Introduction

In this Chapter the role of policy measures and the assembly of Policy Packages and Paths are discussed. Focus is on the thinking and the methodology used. The Packages and Paths themselves are presented in Chapter 11. We have not elaborated on policies for Image III in this Chapter or in Chapter 11. The reason is that they will primarily be a combination of policies for achieving Image I and II and the text may to a large extent be repeated from those Images.

First in this Chapter four different policy orientations are outlined which could be used by policy-makers with different outlooks. Then a review of different types of policy measures and their potential contribution to the achievement of the policy targets is presented. The timescale of their effects is also identified as well as their policy orientation. This is followed by a discussion about policy-making in an uncertain context. Although the delimitation of external factors is seldom clear cut, it is important to recognize their existence so that policy options being implemented are sufficiently flexible.

It is also realized that combining policy measures into Packages is crucial in order to find policies that could both reach the targets set and be politically accepted. The methodology developed for this process is also discussed. The policy scenarios, which consist of targets, Images and Policy Paths, are intended to guide policy-making, and relate to the longer-term goals of sustainability. Four principles for choosing initial measures are suggested. In the last Section the results from the validation process are presented.

10.2 The role of different policy measures

The role of policy instruments in achieving the policy targets is assessed in this Section. In order to show the enormous scope for action to achieve decoupling, a distinction is drawn between different basic policy orientations. By policy orientations, we understand the generic rationale which usually can be found behind different Policy Packages:

1   *Lifestyle-oriented policies.* Policy intervention is only a subsidiary help for the ongoing growth of 'post-material' lifestyles. A basic element of such lifestyles is a changed attitude towards mobility and material

consumption. Quality of life aspects play a central role. Part of this is an increasing acceptance of the claims that sustainable development has on lifestyles (which changes the balance between material consumption and resource use and environmental degradation). Public policy intervention is primarily an anti-discrimination policy in favour of such post-material lifestyles. The dynamics might be basically bottom-up. Information policies are an important element of this approach. Knowing the transport component of a product, or the transport consequences of a policy decision, may help to reorient behaviour.

2   *Market-oriented policies.* This approach assumes that people are willing to change their behaviour or lifestyles, if others do the same and if they have no material disadvantages. So a system of market incentives, such as fiscal reform or changed property rights will change the incentive structure. This approach will have some top-down elements, but it will also have to rely on the general acceptance of pricing as a fair mechanism to allocate goods and services.

3   *Regulation-oriented policies.* This approach relies upon technical standards and norms (for instance speed limits, maximum weight of vehicles), on innovative planning methodology (especially spatial planning and transport impact assessment), and government reform. The general approach is rationalistic, target and criteria led, and top-down.

4   *Public infrastructure/public transport.* The provision of infrastructure and public transport services is a policy approach that is strongly associated with regulation-oriented polices. The state provides infrastructure such as roads, rail, telecommunications, water supply, and services such as research, police and air traffic control. The performances offered are not directly linked to cost-covering payments. The actual delivery of infrastructure and public transport services may be contracted to private companies.

As a prerequisite to building Policy Packages and Paths, single policy measures are analysed along several dimensions. The result is shown in the comprehensive matrix in Table 10.1. The matrix is used to identify:

*   the extent to which each of the policy measures might contribute to the three broad types of policy targets (environmental protection, regional development, and economic efficiency);
*   the policy orientation of each measure; and
*   the timescale of effect of the policy measures – whether impacts are likely to be short, medium or long term.

In Table 10.1, we have identified 85 different policy measures under 9 headings, and they have been 'starred' according to the ten criteria. Most of the individual policy measures are well known, and those that are 'new' have

Table 10.1   **Potential policy measures for inclusion in Policy Packages and Paths**

Policy measures	Targets				Policy orientation			Timescale of effects		
	Economic efficiency	Environmental protection	Regional development	Lifestyle	Market-based	Regulation	Public service	Short-term	Medium-term	Long-term
1 Land-Use Planning										
Integrated planning	•	•	•	•		•				•
Regional development policies		•	•			•				•
Zoning regulations (single use, mixed use, densities, etc.)	•	•	•			•				•
Compact mixed land use	•	•			•	•				•
Development at public & intermodal nodes	•	•				•				•
Access to transport services	•	•	•			•	•			•
Pedestrian & cycle friendly developments	•	•		•		•				•
Designated areas for control over the pattern of development	•	•	•			•				•
Fiscal incentives for relocation in designated areas	•	•	•		•					•
Relocation of activities	•	•	•			•				•
Green belts		•				•				•
Regeneration of decaying areas (city centres, inner-city areas)	•	•	•	•	•	•				•
Improvements to housing and neighbourhood quality/facilities	•	•	•	•	•					•
Parking standards for new developments		•				•				•
2 Pricing/Taxation										
Road tolls for freight	•	•			•				•	
Congestion pricing	•	•			•				•	
Fuel tax	•	•			•				•	
Vehicle Purchase Tax	•	•			•			•		
Car ownership tax	•	•			•			•		
Parking tariffs	•	•			•			•		
Excise for aircraft fuels	•	•	-		•			•		
Airport charges	•	•	-		•			•		
Restrictions										
Parking restrictions/control	•	•				•			•	
Entry prohibitions/access control/environmental zones	•	•				•			•	
Goods traffic restraint	•	•				•			•	
Road capacity restraint/throttling	•	•				•			•	
Traffic management										
Advanced traffic management systems	•						•		•	
Driver information systems	•						•		•	
Bypassing sensitive areas		•	-			•		•		
Priorities for bus, tram & high occupancy vehicles (HOVs)	•	•				•				•
Segregated rights of way for transit	•	•				•				•
Commuter planning	•	•				•				•
Travel information	•	•					•			•
Traffic calming	•	•				•				•
Cycle priority & road space	•	•				•				•
Pedestrian priority & road space	•	•				•				•
Lower speed limits & enforcement	•	•				•			•	
Casualty reduction targets	•	•				•				•

Table 10.1   Potential policy measures for inclusion in Policy Packages and Paths (continued)

Policy measures	Targets			Policy orientation				Timescale of effects		
	Economic efficiency	Environmental protection	Regional development	Lifestyle	Market-based	Regulation	Public service	Short-term	Medium-term	Long-term
3 Infrastructure/Mode Management										
• Strategic environment assessment of plans and programmes		•				•			•	
• Fiscal & regulatory framework and investment for the promotion of environmentally friendly transport modes for passenger and freight transport	•	•			•	•				•
• Intermodality	•	•		•	•		•			•
• Park & ride	•	•		•		•	•			•
• Improvement of public transport	•	•			•	•	•			•
• Fare integration & schedule coordination	•	•				•	•			•
• Traveller information systems	•	•					•			•
• Deregulation	•				•	•				•
• Subsidies		•			•		•			•
• Concessions		•			•		•			•
• Investment in TENs		•	•		•					•
• Increase rail capacity and speed	•	•	•				•			•
• Harmonization of rail	•	•	•			•	•			•
• New rail freight tracks		•	•				•			•
4 Technical Improvements										
• Standards for emissions, noise and safety		•				•				•
• Fuel quality standards and alternative fuels		•				•				•
• Efficiency improvement of materials and energy (with a factor four)	•	•			•	•				•
• Dematerialization of products/miniaturization	•	•				•				•
• Standards and procedures on inspection and maintenance – test cycles	•	•				•				•
• Enforcement and monitoring	•	•				•		•		
• Research, dissemination and practical application	•	•				•				•
5 Telecommunications and Technology										
• Teleworking/telecommuting/teleconferencing	•	•	•	•						•
• Teleshopping/telebanking/telecottages	•	•	•	•						•
• Telematics/informatics available locally	•	•	•	•						•
• Infrastructure technology	•		•		•					•
• Vehicle technology – more efficient and/or smaller vehicles	•	•			•					•
• Multipurpose personal communicators	•	•	•	•						•
6 Behavioural Patterns										
• Activity patterns – leisure		•		•				•		
• Changing lifestyle (e.g. not travelling at weekends)		•		•				•		
• Home location		•		•	•			•		
• Job location		•		•	•			•		
• Promotion of local destinations		•		•				•		

Table 10.1   Potential policy measures for inclusion in Policy Packages and Paths (continued)

Policy measures	Targets				Policy orientation			Timescale of effects		
	Economic efficiency	Environmental protection	Regional development	Lifestyle	Market-based	Regulation	Public service	Short-term	Medium-term	Long-term
7 Freight Management										
• Logistic management of firms – increase load factors	•	•			•				•	
• Home delivery of goods/services	•	•			•				•	
• Freight distribution	•	•	•		•				•	
8 Information and Public Awareness										
• Campaigns for the promotion of environmentally friendly modes	•	•		•					•	
• Campaigns for reducing private transport externalities	•	•		•					•	
• Increase awareness of public transport services	•	•		•					•	
• Transport chaining awareness	•	•		•					•	
• Eco-labelling of vehicles	•	•		•					•	
9 General Economic Policies										
• Ecological tax reform	•	•	•	•	•				•	
• Tradable mobility credits	•	•		•	•				•	
• CO_2 tax	•	•			•				•	
• Taxes and feebates based on fuel consumption and weight	•	•			•				•	
• Scrappage bonuses and tax increases	•	•			•				•	

been introduced in Chapter 6 (e.g. on dematerialization). Most of the measures have an environmental impact, with the vast majority also helping to meet the economic targets. There seems to be far less scope with these measures for influencing regional development targets. About a quarter of the policy measures are lifestyle oriented, with about 35 per cent being market based. The majority of policy measures (about 50 per cent) require regulation, and a further 20 per cent come within the public service category. This suggests that to achieve each Image requires a mixture of policy measures, with a variety of policy orientations. It should also be realized that there is a clear difference in the timescales for the implementation of actions and the scale of the necessary changes. In all cases, action is required now, even though the effects of those actions may take many years to work their way through in terms of target achievement.

10.3   Policy Packages and Paths

Policy Packages are developed by combining sets of policy measures that are likely to work well together (i.e. which create synergies). Each of the Policy Packages is designed to relate to a specific Image of the Future. Policy Paths in this study are combinations of Policy Packages that lead from the present to one of the Images of the Future. In order to show the diversity of possible Paths it was decided to construct more than one path for Image I and for Image II respectively (see Chapter 11). However, before Paths can be constructed, Policy Packages are first identified.

10.3.1 Choice of policy in an uncertain future

The future is uncertain. In selecting appropriate policies for sustainable transport, this uncertainty has to be taken into consideration. Policy scenarios, or policy Paths, are based on a combination of elements where some can be chosen while others cannot and this process involves uncertainty.

The actual and future dominant policy level (local, national or international) and the degree of co-operation between these different levels of policy-making are contextual elements that cannot be chosen (Chapter 6). They reflect the way society copes with market failure, and with public 'goods' and 'bads'. The level of co-operation can of course be influenced and can change over time, but that will be outside the reach of a Common Transport Policy (CTP).

The relative priority between technology and decoupling can be chosen. However one of the major conclusions of this study up to this point is that both of these strategic elements have to be pursued if the set targets are to be reached by 2020. As most of the decoupling measures/packages should be designed so that adjustments can take place (such as land-use patterns), a relative long time perspective is needed. Implementation of these kinds of measures/packages cannot therefore be postponed. If sustainable mobility is the goal, decoupling activities have to start as early as possible. The choice is thus not between technology and decoupling, but between the relative priority and strength of policy measures.

A choice can also be made between different policy orientations. This study has divided the policy measures into:

- lifestyle-oriented policies;
- market-oriented policies;
- regulation-oriented policies; and
- public infrastructure/services.

Basic attitudes of the responsible policy-makers will always shape the course of developments. Therefore, it seems reasonable to take these policy orientations as construction principles for the different Paths. In practice these orientations always overlap. In conceiving first drafts of Paths it was found that there was a stronger affinity between market and lifestyle oriented policies on the one hand and between regulation and public service oriented policies on the other hand. It has therefore been decided to develop four Paths. Figure 10.1 shows the different combinations of choices associated with these Paths, together with the different futures which are themselves uncertain.

| | | UNCERTAINTY: Different futures | |
		Image I: focus on decoupling, bottom-up	Image II: focus on technology, top-down
CHOICE: →	market and lifestyle orientation	Path 1.1	Path 2.1
different → **strategies**	regulation and service orientation	Path 1.2	Path 2..2

Figure 10.1   Policy Paths – uncertainty and choice

10.3.2 The construction of Policy Packages

The construction of the Packages in this study has been achieved through the combination of two different approaches:

1   a deductive, systematic approach using the framework of the Images to define the outline of the Packages and Paths; and
2   an intuitive, inductive approach starting from the list of measures (developed in Section 10.2) following a creative process of inventing new combinations of policies.

Paths will contain a large number of policy measures that are needed to attain the targets. Since it is difficult to conceive and discuss all aspects at once, a two-step method has been adopted. First, several measures are combined into Policy Packages covering an issue or addressing a target group. Then, several Policy Packages are combined to form a Path. Figure 10.2 shows this process. Measures within a Package and Packages within a Path are meant to be interrelated.

Policy Packages can be imagined as a package of measures to be introduced and discussed in a parliament. They have to address a delimited issue, they must provide a convincing contribution to the solution of a perceived problem, they have to show a balanced impact on different groups of stakeholders in order to be acceptable, and they have to be understandable and convincing as a Package. Such a Package cannot be designed by a schematic application of rules – but it must be conceived as a creative and iterative process. As in practical politics, it is useful to start from a triggering issue and to begin with a central measure. Additional complementary measures can then be included so as to form a balanced Package, which is not too large and has an inner logic. New or modified kinds of measures are likely to be proposed in this process. The conceptual framework of this study can then be used for a more systematic appraisal of this Package which may again lead to adjustments.

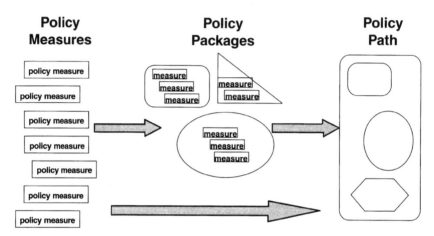

Figure 10.2 Methodology for the construction of Policy Paths

Several such Packages have then to be combined in a Path. A Policy Path is made up of both Policy Packages and single policy measures. The construction of Policy Packages and Policy Paths is an iterative process which could go on over many cycles. A further development of these Packages and Paths together with concerned stakeholders would be a challenging further step (Section 10.5). The discussions within the project team and with stakeholders in different countries have shown that the introduction of Policy Packages has been an important step in developing this methodology since:

♦   it allows discussions to be focused so as to achieve results within a limited amount of time;
♦   it allows for intuitive creativity in developing new approaches within a more systematic framework.

In Chapter 11, a number of Policy Packages are presented. This collection of Packages is illustrative rather than comprehensive and could be extended or modified. Some of the Packages appear in two different variants intended for different Policy Paths. The Packages are then combined with single measures to form the tentative Paths leading to the respective Images.

Clustering policy measures into Packages appears to be more relevant and entail more synergies regarding decoupling than technology. This is mainly because decoupling involves a deeper transformation of production and consumption patterns. These can only be reached by strategies which go well beyond traditional transport policies and require a cautious balancing of different interests.

10.4   Choosing initial measures – some principles

It is not reasonable to work out complete plans for a time-span of 20 years or more. Things will happen that are not possible to foresee, making plans obsolete. The scenarios, including Images, Packages and Paths, are intended to guide policy-making today, but with a view to long-term goals of sustainability. The scenarios also consider the developments of such contextual factors as values, lifestyles and climate for co-operation. The long view of this study could help to widen the scope of options considered, but the aim is to advise short-term policy-making.

In this Section we will discuss what measures could be implemented today as a first step that paves the way for later decisions and eventual goal attainment. We will not provide a detailed list of concrete measures, but rather discuss principles and give a few examples.

If governments and the EU commit themselves to the long-term goal of sustainable mobility in Europe, then a consistent policy should be developed aimed at this goal. This policy will have to evolve step by step and be adapted continuously to external factors that are more or less impossible to predict and control. It should be possible to take some measures now and to prepare for later steps. We suggest a few guiding principles for the choice of initial measures to be included in the starter Package:

1   the measure should not be too controversial today (principle of acceptability);
2   measures that are essential to goal fulfilment but will have a delayed effect should be implemented early (principle of inertia or long lead-times);
3   measures that will set dynamic processes in motion should be implemented early (principle of dynamic effects);
4   measures that tend to retain freedom of action in the future are often to be preferred to measures leading to lock-in solutions (principle of adaptability).

Only the first point is (close to) a necessary condition. The others are not really instrumental, but have different foci and are also important. Measures fulfilling the first principle may be qualified for inclusion in a starter Package by complying with either of the other principles. These will be discussed in the following Sections.

10.4.1 Acceptability

In this study we have assumed that measures intended to change people's travel behaviour will be accepted or at least tolerated by the majority. Now we want to elaborate on the subject of acceptability, by commenting on some key aspects:

1   In the long run, government policy generally requires the support of a majority of the general public. Admittedly, though, there are contrary examples. The Swedish restrictions on sales of alcohol are a case in point, and speed limits in some countries are another example. In such cases the actual question has generally not been a real issue in political election campaigns, either because it is a minor question or because the political establishment has a common view across party lines.

2   In many cases, such as the requirement to use seat belts in cars, political decisions have actually had an influence on attitudes. Politics is not just about reflecting prevailing preferences but also about forming opinions.

3   Judging from actual travel behaviour, one may be led to underestimate the support for change. Thus, some commentators have taken a rather pessimistic view on people's willingness to accept restrictions or higher costs on the use of private cars in urban areas. In cases of a conflict between the common good and the interests of the individual (in social dilemmas for example), the latter will win according to this view. The group of idealists will always be small, while the great majority is assumed to act with purely economic interests, always seeking to optimize their own benefits. These analysts tend to overlook the possible intermediate positions between that of the true idealist, always acting for the common good regardless of what other people do, and that of the selfish economic individual who does not care about the common good. People need to adopt the attitude that they want to act according to the common good provided that other people do the same. This is the key to a solution. If this group and the idealists together form a majority, then political initiatives promoting behaviour in accordance with the common good will be tolerated. There are studies indicating that a majority of commuters in some cities would welcome restrictions on private car use. This attitude is also increasingly prevalent among those who commute by car today. The discrepancy between attitudes and actual behaviour may be explained by the logic of social dilemmas.

4   The support or acceptance of a sufficient number of industrial and other interest groups and institutional actors is also required.

Linked with acceptability is the responsibility of all stakeholders to play a role in achieving the targets through implementing and supporting change.

This is particularly important in Image I, where it is assumed that individuals and firms are prepared to change the way in which they carry out their activities. Similarly, in Image II, strong leadership is assumed, with the EU and national governments demonstrating commitment to change through action.

10.4.2. Inertia and long lead-times

Inertia and long lead times is the main rationale behind taking the long view in planning and decision-making. When the greenhouse effect is being perceived as an emerging threat to society, one should start taking actions now, even if the consequences of those actions may take many years to have a positive outcome. We cannot wait until the problem is manifest. Because of the long time between decision and desired effect, the policy is also exposed to changing circumstances that are to some extent impossible to foresee. Some measures may also have unexpected effects. This calls for a strategy of flexibility and adaptability. Here we will focus on the long lead times and the need to take actions early. A major change of the built form (land use) has an enormous potential to influence travel patterns and mobility, but it will also take a long time to achieve. In 20 years time a considerable impact should be apparent, provided that policy measures are taken early. Several studies indicate that a spatial pattern of 'decentralized concentration' would minimize travel. This means a concentration of settlement, services and work places to centres that are nodes in a public transport system. Similarly, decisions taken now on the basis of the locations of new housing, services and facilities will substantially influence travel patterns in the future (Banister, 1997, Stead, 1999).

10.4.3 To catalyse positive dynamic processes

The most efficient way to achieve a change in, say, settlement patterns may be to trigger a new set of system dynamics. One example is the introduction of telecottages in urban sub-centres, thereby facilitating telecommuting. When more people stay in the suburb during daytime, the market for local services such as lunch restaurants and shops will grow. This in turn will attract more telecommuters and perhaps also new work places. The initial policy measure may be said to catalyse an accumulation process that may lead to more self contained sub-centres and less travel.

An important element of the dynamic process is the trigger mechanism, such as that proposed for a variety of teleservices. The same type of argument could be used with respect to road pricing where the final outcome is known (i.e. a full electronic road pricing scheme). The means to reach this objective requires creative thinking as to the process of implementation. Initially, road space could be reallocated to public transport services and parking charges in the city raised substantially, but new park-and-ride facilities would also be provided to give the motorist a choice. In stage two, cars would be allowed in the bus lanes if they pay and gradually more of the road space would be allocated to the paying motorist and public transport. As public transport is now more reliable, patronage would rise and further investments would be initiated to increase capacity. Eventually parking charges would be reduced and all the road space would be paid for by those motorists who continued to choose their cars. Such a dynamic facilitates implementation, gains public acceptability and gradually familiarizes users with road pricing, whilst at the same time providing choice through high quality public transport.

10.4.4 Adaptability to changing contextual circumstances

Decisions today should not unnecessarily restrict the scope for future decisions. When the impact of strong measures is hard to predict, a good strategy may be to make piece-meal changes and to test several solutions in small-scale experiments.

As with all of these conditions, there is no prescription or blueprint for the correct procedures to follow. Each situation requires separate analysis and implementation, including flexibility to change policy measures if intentions and outcomes do not match up. However, the goal of sustainable mobility must remain with support from all political, business, and public decision-makers. Adaptability is not an excuse for inaction or weak action – it is an argument for clear decision-making and leadership, supported by analysis and monitoring to check on the effectiveness of policy action.

10.5 The validation approach

10.5.1 Introduction

In the methodology for developing actor-oriented policy scenarios, validation plays an important role. As the policy scenarios deal with complex systems, and as qualitative estimates and statements play an important role, the involvement of a variety of actors is important for developing coherent scenarios and for identifying the key issues. At the same time the validation process is already part of the dissemination strategy of the project results. Three aspects of the study were validated:

1   the framework, including the overall methodology and the Images;
2   the Policy Paths including the technology and decoupling potentials; and
3   the overall conclusions and recommendations.

There were two main outcomes of the project, which were very much kept in mind during the validation:

1   a methodological framework for developing, discussing, and evaluating long-term transport policy strategies; and

2   concrete sustainability targets, Images, and Paths which help to identify key issues and to propose innovative approaches.

10.5.2 Validation of the framework

The framework has mainly been validated through a series of meetings with transport experts from the scientific community. Overall, the approach has been considered to be innovative, appropriate and useful. However, the complexity of the scenario construction repeatedly made it difficult to discuss the whole issue in a short time. The main points that emerged from these discussions are the following:

1   Decoupling is an important concept for future transport policy and considerable efforts in this direction are necessary in order to achieve the targets. However, there is considerable uncertainty about the true potential and the range of useful measures. Technology developments are difficult to forecast, as the use of technology depends on the general conditions and does not always correspond to the original intentions. The backcasting approach developed here is meant to complement the more conventional forecasts in other projects. It requires a way of thinking about future situations which is difficult and unfamiliar. It is considered to be particularly useful in transport policy where strategic thinking needs to be more aware of the complexity of choices and outcomes.

2   The policy scenarios and the targets should not give the impression of quantitative precision. They can only indicate orders of magnitude, key issues, key trends and key options. The Images of the Future are considered to be consistent and useful. It must be made clear that they are alternatives reflecting assumed frame conditions, and the choice of alternatives lies in the construction of the Paths.

A concise and condensed presentation of the framework has been presented and discussed. In terms of the research framework, the main results were:

1   The backcasting approach and thinking 20 years ahead are rather unfamiliar for most officers responsible for individual policies. However, many of them think that scenario approaches are increasingly necessary.

2   The framework could provide a useful support for meeting the growing need for a long-term policy strategy. The basic construction of the framework is consistent and useful. The concept of decoupling proposed by the study has now been introduced into official European policy.

3   The CO_2 target is more demanding than current official targets.

4   Decoupling strategies require the integration of transport policy with other policy fields. This seems to be increasingly an issue. When transport policy ceases to have only a supporting function and sets its own targets, it needs to have convincing arguments for requiring complementary measures in other fields. Backcasting scenarios can be useful in this respect.

5   As a management instrument that allows the development of policy strategies, the framework needs to be flexible in its use. A series of alternative Paths would be helpful. To fill the framework with a rich collection of measures, which can then be packaged to provide a kind of toolbox, could be a challenging and useful next step.

10.5.3 Validation of the Policy Paths

The purpose of the validation of Policy Paths has been to provide a mechanism for improving consistency, supplying expert information and helping to discover new approaches. The validation of the Policy Paths has also facilitated a more detailed exploration of the impact and the acceptability of proposed policies. Therefore at this stage, a wide range of stakeholders should be involved. The validation should help to balance Policy Packages, to minimize implementation difficulties, and to understand the differences between different countries and regions.

The number of Paths constructed in this study is somewhat limited and so is the extent of the validation. As a next step it would be challenging to go further into the iterative process and construct more Paths and validate them with a larger variety of stakeholders in different countries. Given these limitations, this study validated the Paths by holding:

♦   workshops with stakeholders;
♦   one-to-one discussions in Brussels with European transport policy officials.

The workshops gathered representatives from national government and NGOs. The discussions covered the following questions:

♦   are the Policy Paths consistent?
♦   are the proposed Policy Packages effective enough for meeting the targets?
♦   what are the consequences for different stakeholders, which conflicts will arise?
♦   are the policy measures adequately packaged and timed, and are additional/other policies needed?

The backcasting approach was considered to be very useful for discovering new political options and for elaborating strategies. The concept of decoupling was considered to be challenging and interesting. The following key issues emerged from validation discussions:

1   Stakeholders are not used to this type of thinking. Some discussion is needed before a useful assessment of complex Policy Packages in a longer time horizon becomes possible.

2   Discussion of the Paths produces interesting insights for both the researchers and the stakeholders involved.

3   It is difficult to assess the impact of longer lists of policy measures and it would be useful to break down the Paths into smaller Policy Packages.

4   More differentiated approaches in time and space (such as urban and rural) would considerably widen the scope of action.

5   Participants strongly shared the view that the increase of road transport has to be curbed. Policies acting on costs and on lifestyles were considered to be most promising.

6   Finding new ways of sharing responsibilities between different government tiers in the spirit of subsidiarity is considered essential for a more differentiated and adequate way of governing transport (in the field of taxes and tariffs for example). The approach of differentiated taxation as proposed in Path 1.1 was welcomed (see Figure 10.1 and Chapter 11).

7   Decoupling is a difficult task in highly interconnected industrial districts which are a characteristic of central Italy and other parts of the 'European core'. High-tech solutions for improved transport organization and for substitution of transport by IT are considered to be interesting approaches.

8   As a consequence of the whole post-war development in Europe, mobility is strongly perceived as an element of freedom and of the quality of life. Therefore decoupling should not be promoted as a limitation to the freedom of movement, but more as the discovery of new opportunities for improving the quality of life and the quality of transport. Confronted with a 'culture of mobility' a cultural shift has to be promoted cautiously. Lifestyle-oriented policies are therefore considered important.

9   Traditional theories concerning transport and economic development are still strongly rooted among the main actors. The emphasis in transport policy is therefore on the supply side. Demand-side policies (including tariffs and taxes) are mostly perceived as a support for supply strategies. The main actors therefore think that at least in the short term inducing a modal shift by improving public transport – which is considered to be of very low quality – is more important than decoupling.

10   The integration of transport issues into other policies is considered to be most important. Decoupling policies cannot be promoted by transport policy alone.

11   The internalization of external costs is considered to be a necessary but insufficient strategy. Given the present cost structures in transport, a simple internalization of environmental costs could lead to unwanted effects, such as penalizing rail travel. The considerable labour costs in public transport companies are not due mainly to operational necessities, but often to the important social function of public enterprises.

10.5.4 Conclusions from the validation exercise

The study has provided a useful framework for structured discussions of a wide variety of future transport issues. It seems to be a logical next step to use the results as a basis for discussion and validation with a much larger set of stakeholders in a series of different European Countries. The validation meetings that were carried out within the study have shown both the difficulties and the potential of opening the scenario building exercise to a much wider circle of participants. It takes considerable effort to convince stakeholders in responsible positions to spend time on discussing such long-term questions. Compared to the complexity of the issues, meetings have to be quite short, and the possible depth of discussion is limited. Decision-makers who do not perceive themselves as being strongly involved in transport issues are difficult to reach.

The backcasting approach and the concept of decoupling are not familiar to most stakeholders. On one hand, this has the disadvantage that it takes a long time to explain and discuss these concepts before being able to validate more concrete Policy Packages and Policy Paths. On the other hand, these concepts encounter much interest, as they challenge conventional views of the transport community and, as many participants have said, lead to new insights and innovative ideas that may influence their everyday decisions. Therefore, in each validation exercise, an appropriate balance has to be found between the discussion of the general framework, and the validation of specific issues to be looked at in more detail.

The reactions to the basic concepts and to the more specific propositions in the Policy Packages differ between European countries and regions. It is evident that a successful transport policy, especially when it is not limited to the transport sector but also relies on other policies, has to take into account national and even regional issues and differences. The Policy Packages and Paths have not yet been differentiated to respond to such detailed requirements.

Validation therefore cannot be conceived as a one-way exercise in which the project only gets input for improving the scenarios. It must also be considered as a means to disseminate results. Moreover, these discussions seem to be an interesting part of a transformation process in which views and perspectives concerning European transport issues are changing. However, the validation exercise has shown that the development of a common language for discussing endeavours for a sustainable mobility across different European regions, different policy fields, and different kinds of stakeholders is a challenging task which will take a longer time. A broad and systematic validation of the scenarios across different countries and different constituencies could be a viable and an important input to challenging conventional thinking, opening up new policy options (both in the transport sector and elsewhere), and in widening the perspectives of stakeholders.

Part Three

The policy implications

Chapter 11

Policy Packages and Paths

As explained in Chapter 10, the construction of Policy Packages and Paths is a creative and iterative process which includes both deductive and inductive elements. The construction of each package starts with a basic idea about policy orientation. Appropriate measures are then selected, or new ones are developed, through discussion. The overall impact of these measures is assessed through stakeholder analysis. Throughout this process measures are changed, added and subtracted until the Policy Package is sufficiently balanced to survive political discussions and lobby pressures. Every package originates from the study framework, which indicates the main targets, the predominant policy orientation, the transport sub-sector, the level at which action is required, and the time horizon for implementation. The construction of Paths is a more deductive process. Four Paths with different characteristics have been included in the study framework (Figure 10.1 and reproduced as Figure 11.1). Appropriate packages are selected and bundled and the study framework acts as a checklist for the development of Policy Packages.

11.1 Policy Packages

The policy packaging process is one of the most innovative and creative parts of this research. The basic argument is that achieving the challenging policy targets set for sustainable mobility, requires policies to be assembled as mutually supporting packages. Individually, policies may only have limited impact, and to introduce more fundamental changes in policy direction requires packaging of measures from a range of sources (Table 10.1). In this Section, we present ten different Policy Packages, ranging from actions that need to be taken at EU and national government levels, relating to macro-economic policy (such as Ecological Tax Reform), through to technology policy (such as low-emission city vehicles and door-to-door delivery services), to actions required at a more local scale (in the case of the 'Liveable Cities' Policy Package). Some Policy Packages have a strong element of pricing (in the case of long distance links), others relate to distributional issues (in the case of tradable mobility credits), and others relate to regulation (such as the Policy Package on minimizing specific emissions). The importance of the freight sector has been acknowledged through concepts of resource efficiency, subsidiarity, and dematerialization of the economy. These ten packages are intended to be illustrative of the potential for change in transport and the achievement of sustainable mobility at the European level. We now discuss each of these ten Policy Packages in more detail. The approach is challenging and synoptic, and the style of presentation is as 'punchy' vignettes, rather than detailed descriptions.

11.1.1 Policy Package: ecological tax reform

The transport market and the economy in general is distorted by externalities such as resource depletion and environmental damage that are not adequately reflected in overall costs, and taxation on labour has to compensate for a large share of externalities. An Ecological Tax Reform is a way of internalizing these external costs of transport.	
Designed for Image I: *Variant A* Image II: *Variant B* *Main policy orientation* Market-led	*Key strategy elements* Decoupling Passenger Transport Decoupling Freight Transport Technology

Internalizing externalities is a basic market-oriented policy strategy to reduce unwanted side-effects of economic activities. An application of this approach to the transport sector alone would help to improve the structure of the sector, changing the nature of transported goods by only slightly increasing transport costs. An Ecological Tax Reform applied to the whole of the economy would further lead to a general reduction of the material and energy intensity of our economies and reduce the need for transport. The Ecological Tax Reform proposed in this Package is a more general approach. The introduction of such a Package will not only be motivated by considerations concerning transport policy. Trends in Europe over recent years indicate that this direction is quite probable.

Two important considerations in the ecological tax debate are the utilization of the new tax revenues for alleviating fiscal pressure in other fields and the stability of tax revenues. Suitable bases for increased taxes on externalities are the consumption of energy and materials, CO_2 emissions, and the use of land. The Ecological Tax Reform proposed here is aimed at being fiscally neutral across society as a whole. That is, labour taxes should be reduced correspondingly. However, this interpretation does not imply that an Ecological Tax Reform should be fiscally neutral for every sector of society. On the contrary, the transport sector which is resource intensive would have to face substantially higher taxes, while labour intensive sectors would be taxed less.

Two variants of Ecological Tax Reform are presented here:

Variant A: In Image I, co-operation at the global level is not prevalent, and there is still some room for shifting taxes from labour to resources at EU and/or national level. In addition, the revenues from local road pricing could in some cases be used to lower local labour costs. Although some externalities such as emissions of NO_x could be cut substantially, it is congestion that is taxed (through road pricing). The main measures include:

- lower taxes on labour;
- increased taxes on energy, materials, and CO_2 emissions at national or EU level;
- local road pricing.

Variant B: This variant is aimed at Image II, in which comparatively high taxes could be levied on energy, materials and, not least, CO_2 since there is global co-operation on these issues. The global consensus (at least between the EU, the US and Japan) makes it possible to levy higher taxes on air transport than in *Variant A* and to introduce taxes on fuel for maritime and inland water transport. This considerably enhances the base for the CO_2 tax and increases economic efficiency, so that a reduction of CO_2 can be achieved at a lower cost. The main measures include:

- Lowered taxes on labour;
- Considerably increased taxes on energy, materials and CO_2 emissions at national, EU or global level.

Impacts on stakeholders

Differences in the application of Ecological Tax Reform between regions, countries or continents will cause differences in competitiveness between companies in the same sector in different regions. These differences will increase the pressure for the economies of the most advanced reformer regions to restructure in the intended direction. On the other hand, the resulting improvement of living conditions will raise the attractiveness of the reformer regions. A short look at other differences in competitiveness – such as the variation of exchange rates or the differences in labour cost – shows that the margin for tax shifts is considerable.

Considering the general economy, labour intensive and high-value-added sectors will increase in strength while resource-intensive sectors will face increased costs and may have to reconsider their strategy. Likewise, regions with a more service-based, transport-intensive or energy-intensive economy will be at an advantage. These effects are more pronounced in *Variant B* than in *Variant A*.

Frequent car users will generally pay more. A flat application of ecologically-based taxes would create distribution problems and might therefore raise considerable resistance. However, these difficulties can be overcome if labour taxes are reduced, particularly for low-income groups. This could lead to a more even distribution of mobility and income. People without a car, often the least affluent, would gain from such a strategy. Another problem is the strong dependence of rural areas on the car while urban residents have access to more alternatives. A geographically differentiated tax application through road pricing could address this problem to some extent. New information technologies offer new opportunities to deal with this potential problem.

The characteristics of this Policy Package are illustrated in Table 11.1. similarly, Tables 11.2 and 11.3 illustrate the characteristics of two other Policy packages (see below).

Table 11.1 Policy Package characteristics: ecological tax reform

Measures	Targets	Key elements	Transport type Passenger Urban	Inter-urban	Rural	Long-range	Freight Urban	Short-range	Long-range	Policy orienta-tion	Govern-ment level	Time horizon Start	Effect
Increased taxes on energy, materials and CO_2 emissions	ENV	DPA DFR	X	X	X	X	X	X	X	M	NAT EUR	2000 2010	2010 2020
Local road pricing	ENV EFF REG	ORG DPA DFR	X	X	X	X	X	X	X	M	LOC	2010	2020
Lowered taxes on labour	EFF									M	NAT	2000	2010
Ecological Tax Reform A	**ENV EFF REG**	**DPA DFR**	**X**	**X**	**X**	**X**	**X**	**X**	**X**	**M**	**EUR NAT LOC**	**2000 2010**	**2010 2020**
Much increased taxes on energy, materials and CO_2 emissions	ENV	DPA DFR	X	X	X	X	X	X	X	M	NAT EUR GLO	2000 2010	2010 2020
Lowered taxes on labour	EFF									M	NAT	2000	2010
Ecological Tax Reform B	**ENV EFF**	**DPA DFR**	**X**	**X**	**X**	**X**	**X**	**X**	**X**	**M**	**GLO EUR NAT LOC**	**2000 2010**	**2010 2020**

Targets	ENV	environment	Key strategy elements	TEC	technology
	EFF	efficiency		DPA	decoupling passengers
	REG	regional development		DFR	decoupling freight
Government level	LOC	local		ORG	organization
	REG	regional	Policy orientation	L	lifestyle
	NAT	national		M	market
	EUR	European		R	regulation
	GLO	global		S	service

11.1.2 Policy Package: liveable cities

This package aims at making cities more attractive by reducing the dependence on the car. Strategic measures include better conditions for walking, cycling and public transport, decreased space for cars and parking, land-use planning favouring mixed-use areas, local services and amenities, and decentralized concentration. Intensified Information Technology (IT) may play an important role.

Designed for	*Key strategy elements*
Image I	Decoupling Passenger Transport
Image II	Decoupling Freight Transport
Main policy orientations	Technology
Regulation	
Public Services	

The use of public space in cities is the main issue in this package. Reducing the volume and impact of car traffic has a high priority and may be achieved by simultaneously:

- improving alternatives to the car;
- limiting road and parking space for cars;
- limiting the environmental impact of motor vehicles (emissions, noise, accidents); and
- reducing the need for travel, particularly by the car.

The improvement of alternatives strongly depends on the space available. With regard to the process of implementation, the use of Information Technology (IT) to replace trips may play a crucial role. Reduced space for cars is difficult to achieve without alternative access to the activity required. If public transport is the alternative, it cannot be fast and reliable if car use is not restrained. Thus, a 'locked' position may occur. In this context, emerging IT presents a major opportunity to achieve an initial decrease of car travel (drawbacks like urban sprawl can be counteracted) which could make it possible to increase space for walking, cycling, and public transport. Some road space is replaced by dedicated lanes for public transport, cycling, and walking. The average speed of public transport is increased through these measures. The advantages are then reduced travel times, higher economic and environmental efficiency as well as increased capacity of the public transport system.

Environmental zones will be established which only allow clean slow-speed cars. The progressive extension of these areas will create growing markets for such vehicles and new technologies (such as electric, hybrid, and fuel cell vehicles). The Policy Package 'Low impact City Vehicles' explains this approach more in detail. Low-speed zones in residential areas make it more attractive and safer to cycle or walk. More generally it increases the quality of life in these areas, especially for children. Lower speeds and fewer conventional cars significantly reduce noise and injury.

Appropriate land-use planning such as decentralized concentration and high densities around public transport nodes enhances the efficiency of public transport. Teleoffices in local centres increase the possibilities for telecommuting. Less space for cars will also help to facilitate higher density development which in turn may help suppress car ownership. Mixing residential, working and shopping/service areas will reduce the need for commuting and shopping travel by bringing origins and destinations closer together.

Shopping by car can be reduced by the provision of neighbourhood shops and commercial delivery services. E-commerce could also play an important role. Planning regulations can provide improved infrastructure for delivery services. Reduced car traffic allows more recreation opportunities within cities or their immediate surroundings. The pressure for leaving the city for leisure purposes is then reduced.

The time horizon for the introduction of the measures proposed in this package will differ considerably. The effects of land-use regulations will take a long time compared to other measures (but may depend on land-use changes for most impact). The main policy measures include:

◆   improved conditions for walking, cycling, and public transport;
◆   progressive reduction of space available for cars;
◆   low-speed zones (30-40 km/h) in residential areas;
◆   environmental zones reserved for clean slow-speed vehicles;
◆   promotion of car-pooling, car sharing, and car rental;
◆   improved opportunities for telecommuting, teleservices, teleshopping, and doorstep delivery;
◆   promotion of home delivery services and co-ordinated distribution with very clean vehicles;
◆   land-use planning supporting decentralized concentration, mixed land uses, neighbourhood services and public transport; and
◆   upgrading of urban amenities and recreational facilities.

Impact on stakeholders

The urban environment will become safer, quieter and cleaner. This will be particularly attractive to families with children, and elderly people. Non-car drivers will benefit from improved IT-accessibility and improved physical accessibility.

The improved accessibility of everyday services through changes in planning and land-use regulations will reduce travel costs and time. Many people may save considerable amounts of time through telecommuting and home delivery services. Car drivers on urban-rural connections will be confronted with reduced direct accessibility. However, telecommuting and teleservices may substitute some of their travel. Changes in lifestyle will be necessary. Urban sprawl trends will be reduced. The characteristics of this Policy Package are illustrated in Table 11.2.

Table 11.2 Policy Package characteristics: liveable cities

Measures	Targets	Key elements	Passenger — Urban	Passenger — Inter-urban	Passenger — Rural	Passenger — Long-range	Freight — Urban	Freight — Short-range	Freight — Long-range	Policy orientation	Government level	Start	Effect
Improved conditions for walking, cycling, and public transport	ENV EFF	ORG DPA DFR	XX	X	X		X			R S L	LOC	2000	2010
Progressive reduction of space available for cars	ENV	ORG DPA DFR	XX	X	X		X			R	EUR NAT LOC	2000	2010
Low-speed zones (30-40 km/h) in residential areas	ENV	ORG	XX				X			R	NAT EUR	2000	2010
Environmental zones reserved for clean slow-speed vehicles	ENV	TEC ORG	XX				XX			R	LOC EUR	2010	2020
Promotion of car-pooling, car sharing, and car rental	EFF ENV	ORG	XX				X			R S	EUR NAT LOC	2000	2010
Improved opportunities for telecommuting, teleservices, teleshopping/doorstep delivery	ENV	TEC DPA DFR ORG	X	X	X	X	X	X	X	L R S	LOC NAT EUR	2000	2010
Promotion of home delivery services and co-ordinated distribution with very clean vehicles	ENV	ORG	X				XX			M L R	LOC REG NAT	2000	2010
Land-use planning supporting decentralized concentration, functional mix, neighbourhood services, and public transport	ENV EFF	DPA DFR ORG	X	X	X		X	X		R	LOC REG	2000	2010
Upgrading of urban amenities and recreational areas	ENV	DPA	X		XX	X				S	LOC	2000	2020
Liveable Cities	**ENV EFF**	**ORG DPA DFR**	**XX**	**X**	**X**		**XX**	**X**		**R S**	**LOC REG EUR**	**2000**	**2010**

Targets	ENV	environment	Key strategy elements	TEC	technology
	EFF	efficiency		DPA	decoupling passengers
	REG	regional development		DFR	decoupling freight
Government level	LOC	local		ORG	organization
	REG	regional	Policy orientation	L	lifestyle
	NAT	national		M	market
	EUR	European		R	regulation
	GLO	global		S	service

IT-related industries will flourish. Equipment for teleworking, tele-shopping, and teleservices will be in great demand since distribution to shops and home delivery services require extensive use of IT to optimize load factors and route selection. This could also increase economic efficiency quite significantly. Public transport companies will improve their economic position, because of increased demand and higher efficiency. The vehicle industry will sell fewer conventional cars. However new markets will develop for clean slow vehicles (passengers and freight), for integrated public transport systems, for semi-public transport systems (fleet management, reservation and rental systems, call systems), and for traffic management (access management, guidance systems). The oil industry may resist such changes. Densely populated and well-connected areas will flourish whereas less well-connected areas will face decline.

11.1.3 Policy Package: low impact city vehicles

This Policy Package aims at a better match between transport demand and the type of vehicle used. This could significantly increase resource efficiency.

Designed for	*Key strategy elements*
Image I	Technology
Image II	Organization
Main policy orientations	
Regulation	
Market	

The average all-purpose car is currently designed to transport five people with luggage at speeds above 100 kilometres per hour. The same car is used in city traffic for transporting one person at much lower speeds. High speed not only requires larger engines but also more complex, heavy construction. To better match performance with demand a new category of Low Impact Vehicles (LIV) is created. These vehicles would typically be small (2-seater) cars with a maximum speed of 50 km/h and low-emission motors – mainly electric. They would be cheap, easy to handle, clean, and require less parking space. Spaces perpendicular to the streets could be used. Lower safety requirements are acceptable when their use is restricted to areas where the maximum speed for all vehicles is 50 km/h. On the other hand their use could be allowed in environmental zones where only bikes and low impact freight vehicles have access. Lower driver requirements could widen their use to elderly and disabled people or children over fourteen, thereby considerably enhancing their mobility.

However, even these vehicles have an excessive capacity. For one person with little luggage, a bike may in most cases be sufficient. Therefore safety and convenience for cyclists is of prime importance in order better to adjust transport services to demand. Low-speed zones are one measure that improves cycling conditions. Wider use of electric cycles may also be possible. High costs for car use, restricted parking space, and different types of cars for different uses would raise the attractiveness of car rental and car sharing compared to traditional car ownership (additional incentives such as a lower sales tax or subsidized parking space for non-private cars could also be used). This in turn would lead to a more intensive use of equipment and to more efficient management of the car fleet. More durable vehicles (in terms of passenger-kilometres), quicker innovation due to shorter lifecycles, and lower material intensity would be additional positive effects.

Cheap rental of LIVs would be an ideal complement to fast public transport in less dense areas. With changing transport habits and growing markets, LIVs could even become a viable option for local transport in rural areas. The main measures in this package include:

- introduction of a new category of Low Impact Vehicles (LIV);
- support for car pooling, car sharing, and car rental;
- concerted action to promote very efficient and clean vehicles for taxi fleets, rental fleets, and public car fleets;
- dedicated parking space for LIVs and a stepwise reduction of parking space for conventional cars;
- low-speed zones in residential areas (30-40 km/h);
- environmental zones only for very clean vehicles in central areas; and
- improved conditions for walking, cycling and public transport.

Impacts on stakeholders

Accessibility for the elderly and people with disabilities would improve as a result of the introduction of easy-to-handle LIVs. The same may be possible for teenagers if they were permitted to use these vehicles. Most people in urban areas would have to adapt to not having a car of their own. They would, however, have relatively easy access to a wide range of vehicles for different purposes.

The impact on car companies is not clear – it will depend on their ability rapidly to adjust part of their production to a rather different kind of vehicle. New companies with a knowledge of innovative materials (such as plastic composites) and electric propulsion may emerge. Cycle manufacturers would gain from improved cycling conditions. There is substantial potential for the providers of IT-based information, as well as companies involved in rental, reservation, access management, speed control, and fleet management systems. Service providers in these fields will flourish.

The consequences for public transport companies are clearly positive: LIVs and public transport are likely to benefit from each other, although LIVs may have advantages over public transport in less densely populated areas. Restrictions on conventional cars in combination with changing habits will lead to an increase in the use of public transport, especially in inter-urban transport. Driving between urban and rural areas with conventional cars will be subject to increasing traffic restrictions in cities. This may lead to an increase in the use of park-and-ride schemes. The characteristics of this Policy Package are illustrated in Table 11.3.

Table 11.3 Policy Package characteristics: low impact city vehicles

Measures	Targets	Key elements	Passenger				Freight			Policy orientation	Government level	Start	Effect
			Urban	Inter-urban	Rural	Long-range	Urban	Short-range	Long-range				
Introduction of a new category of Low Impact Vehicles (LIV)	ENV	TEC ORG	XX	X						R	EUR LOC	2000	2010
Support for car pooling, car sharing, and car rental	ENV EFF	ORG	XX	X	X	X				R	EUR NAT LOC	2000	2010
Concerted action to promote very efficient and clean vehicles for taxi fleets, rental fleets, and public car fleets	ENV	ORG	X	X						S R M	NAT NAT LOC	2000	2010
Dedicated parking space for LIVs with shorter lots – stepwise reduction of parking space for conventional cars	EFF ENV	ORG	X	X	X					R	LOC	2000	2020
Low-speed zones in residential areas (30–40 km/h)	ENV	ORG	X				X			R	LOC NAT	2000	2010
Environmental zones only allowing very clean vehicles in central areas	ENV	ORG TEC	X				X			R	LOC NAT	2010	2020
Improved conditions for walking, cycling, and public transport	ENV EFF	ORG	X				X			R S	LOC	2000	2010
Low impact City Vehicles	**ENV EFF**	**TEC ORG**	**X**				**X**			**R S M**	**EUR NAT LOC**	**2000 2010**	**2010 2020**

Targets	ENV	environment	Key strategy elements	TEC	technology
	EFF	efficiency		DPA	decoupling passengers
	REG	regional development		DFR	decoupling freight
Government level	LOC	local		ORG	organization
	REG	regional	Policy orientation	L	lifestyle
	NAT	national		M	market
	EUR	European		R	regulation
	GLO	global		S	service

11.1.4 Policy Package: long-distance links – substituting for air travel

This package is directed at reducing long-distance passenger travel by substituting highly energy intensive modes with less energy intensive modes and other forms of communication. It also involves the reduction of travel distances.

Designed for	*Key strategy elements*
Image I: Variant A	Decoupling Passenger Transport
Image II: Variant B	Decoupling Freight Transport
Main policy orientation	Technology
Market	

The increase in air travel and air freight transport causes particular concern for sustainable development because:

♦ the environmental impacts of aircraft are considerable;
♦ the modal share of air transport is still very low but growth rates are much higher than all other modes; and
♦ air transport has an 'extraterritorial' status, being exempted from taxes that are charged to all other modes.

Long-range leisure travel and airborne freight transport is growing at a high speed, partly as a consequence of current charging mechanisms. As important economic structures rely on cheap air transport, attempts to internalize at least a part of the considerable externalities will become increasingly difficult in the future. Rapid action to correct market distortions and to provide alternatives is therefore necessary in all Images of the Future. In Image I, the possibilities to internalize externalities associated with international travel are more limited than in Image II because of the difficulties in obtaining international consensus and co-ordination. Nevertheless, even in Image I there are margins for the EU to levy significant taxes on air fuel. However, additional measures may also be needed to limit the growth of air travel.

Given existing capacity problems, restrictive policies on airports may offer another opportunity. Although environmental pressures near airports are high and expansion plans always cause strong local resistance, employment opportunities often lead to decisions in favour of further airport development. Restrictive policies at the local and regional level would require a high degree of co-ordination. Limitations within the European flight control system are more promising.

Among other transport modes, only rail has the potential to offer serious alternatives to air transport. European railways currently suffer from a lack of harmonization and co-ordination. The considerable improvements brought by high-speed trains on a very limited number of routes have not kept up with air travel growth. Faster rail services on existing infrastructure (with tilting technology for example), technical harmonization, organizational co-operation and improved conditions for competition, and Europe-wide operating carriers could all help make better use of unexploited potentials on long-distance routes. Considerable innovation for improving passenger comfort, flexibility, freight tracking and handling will be necessary. The present conservative 'rail culture' needs to change (perhaps quite radically) in order to be able to respond to these challenges. Long-range air transport of some goods may also be substituted by maritime transport.

However, the present growth rates in long-range air transport may not be be fully substitutable by other modes. Acceptable ways of avoiding high levels of air freight include:

+ strategies concerning freight flows such as those described in the 'Promoting Subsidiarity in Freight Flows' Policy Package (Policy Package 6 – Section 11.1.6);
+ strategies such as those described in the 'Liveable Cities' Policy Package may have some effect on long-range leisure travel, and lifestyle-oriented policies, raising costs, and limiting capacities may also have some impact (Policy Package 2 – Section 11.1.2);
+ increased use of telecommunications may reduce the growth of long range business travel.

Under present conditions, improved telecommunication opportunities seem to induce more travel than they save. As communication technologies are improving, their substitution potential could increase when air travel costs are increasing substantially. Training and demonstration may enhance developments in this sense. The main policy measures of this package include:

+ steadily increasing tax on air fuel (possibly implemented inside the EU);
+ restrictive policy on airport development;
+ organizational improvement of European railway links (including EU regulations enhancing co-operation between operators, providing a framework for competing and European-wide rail carriers);
+ technical harmonization of European railways;
+ better use of existing rail infrastructure (which can be achieved through innovative rolling stock, electronic controls, and organizational measures);
+ demonstration of teleconferencing facilities;
+ promotion of local leisure activities; and
+ making residential areas and their surroundings more attractive for leisure and recreation (see also the 'Liveable Cities' Policy Package 2 – Section 11.1.2).

Impact on stakeholders

Organizations involved in air transport will not support this Policy Package (although air transport will still grow quite rapidly). There will be strong pressure on railways to reform their structures and to offer faster and more customer friendly services and, if successful, they could gain a larger market share. Restrictions may motivate airlines to diversify in the transport market and/or invest in new technology engines to reduce noise and energy use.

11.1.5 Policy Package: fair and efficient distribution of mobility – tradable mobility credits

Increasing transport costs create social and geographical distribution problems. Differentiated approaches are required which avoid these problems. This Policy Package provides a flexible solution combining simple market mechanisms with new information technology.

Designed for	*Key strategy elements*
Image I	Decoupling Passenger Transport
Main policy orientation	Organization
Market	Technology

The kinds of taxes used today cannot easily be raised to sufficiently high levels that really would make a difference without certain groups being considerably disadvantaged (such as rural populations or low-income groups). As motorized transport is both a basic need and a luxury good, measures to contain it must take account of spatial and social equity considerations. Given widespread car ownership, the tax system should lower the fixed costs and raise the variable costs of car use in order to give incentives to use other modes of transport and to travel less by car.

Spatial equity problems can only be addressed by differentiating mileage-related taxes between different areas: urban areas will require higher rates than rural ones. Differentiated electronic road pricing is one potential solution to this problem. Where revenues from road pricing are hypothecated, local authorities would be free to fix road fees which would depend on variables such as the level of congestion, air quality, vehicle occupancy, and so on. A meter could show actual cost in each car, not least to act as a stimulus to find alternative cheaper ways of making the journey.

Given the present structure of mobility, a minimum car mobility should be ensured at prices not very much above the present ones for social equity reasons. Effective incentives for decreasing overall mileage cannot be directly coupled with monetary costs because this would create unacceptable social inequities. Introducing 'tradable mobility credits' (TMCs) might solve the social distribution problem: every person gets a limited number of credits for paying road fees and other mobility services at reasonable prices, corresponding to slightly less than present average mileage. Establishing a market for these credits will lead to higher costs for those who travel further and to extra incomes for those driving less. A similar system was intensively discussed in Switzerland in the 1980s. Numerous variations on such a system are conceivable.

Encouraging the use of public transport may be coupled with a similar system of TMCs as they could also be used for paying for public transport services. This would effectively decrease car mileage if public transport is attractive. Smart cards would present an excellent form for realizing a system of TMCs. The cards could easily be sold (or recharged) by public authorities according to allocated quotas. These could also be used for the payment of road pricing fees, public transport journeys, and traded between individuals. A strong differentiation in taxes (road pricing fees) for vehicles depending on geographical area and vehicle emissions becomes easier to implement with such a system. The introduction of TMCs could be a strong incentive for the use of clean vehicles such as proposed in the 'Low Impact City Vehicles' Policy Package.

High variable costs for car use, the widespread use of smart cards across different transport systems, and different kinds of cars for different uses would raise the attractiveness of car rental and car sharing compared to traditional ownership. This in turn would lead to a more intense use of equipment and to more efficient management of the car fleet. More durable vehicles (in terms of passenger-kilometres), quicker innovation due to shorter lifecycles (in terms of years), and less material intensity would be the consequence. The main policy measures of this package include:

- replacement of car taxes and basic insurance (except CO_2 tax on fuel) by differentiated road pricing;
- introduction of Tradable Mobility Credits (TMC) for the payment of road fees; and
- extension of the TMC system to public transport journeys.

Impact on stakeholders

People travelling less than average by car would benefit from such a system, particularly families with small children and elderly people, who often suffer most from the externalities of transport and whose personal mileage is often well below the average. If travel credits were unused, there would be the option of selling them – an incentive for travelling less. People travelling more than average would have to spend much more on travel (or change their travel habits). Urban and rural inhabitants could both take considerable advantage from such a system since differentiated solutions are possible.

Very important new markets would be developed in information technology and related equipment for establishing an efficient road pricing system and for managing the TMC system. Stepwise development of such systems will take at least ten years. Car producers would be confronted with decreasing car sales and considerably challenged to provide cleaner and more durable cars with sophisticated electronic equipment. New generations of navigation systems would probably be combined with the road fee payment systems. Strong incentives to substitute car ownership by car rental could affect the products and services offered by car manufacturers.

11.1.6 Policy Package: promoting subsidiarity in freight flows

Policies for decoupling freight transport from economic growth cannot limit themselves to traditional transport policy. Structural approaches are required to reduce the travel distance of goods.

Designed for	*Key strategy elements*
Image I	Decoupling Freight Transport
Main policy orientations	Organization
Market and Lifestyle: *Variant A*	
Regulation and Public Service:	
Variant B	

Reducing the travel distance of goods might be achieved through a strategy of 'regionalizing' material flows. As different approaches are needed at different scales for different products, subsidiarity may be a better term to use. The policies address the spatial patterns of production and consumption and the impacts are only likely in the medium and long term.

Consumers are targeted through awareness and information campaigns, promoting the use of local products. Information systems and declaration requirements have to be developed by public authorities in order to allow for responsible consumer choices. European agricultural policy needs to be reformed to promote opportunities for purchasing regional products. The concentration of retail companies which has taken place in Europe (particularly northern Europe) over the last 30 years, has strongly contributed to large-scale increases in material flows. This process has been aided by land-use planning and urban policies, technological developments, by changing lifestyles, a neglect of local cultures, and an ideology of homogenization. Changing the frame conditions in the above-mentioned policy fields may create advantages of more flexible small-scale structures of production and consumption.

In terms of the production, economic development policies at all levels could encourage regional networking and co-operation of companies.

Sourcing strategies strongly determine the transport input to manufactured goods. Information systems which trace the transport input of goods over the whole lifecycle could considerably help inform better choices. Likewise, a transport impact analysis of major political decisions could help inform and improve current understanding of the relationship between transport and development.

Transport will remain a neglected service function as long as it remains relatively cheap in comparison with manufactured goods. Continued subsidy of transport has led (and continues to lead) to inefficient structures of production and consumption. Differentiated pricing of transport according to regional contexts (by differentiated road pricing for example) may considerably widen the margins of action for attributing real costs.

Public spending plays a very important (mostly underestimated) role in many markets. Public procurement may be used very effectively for strengthening subsidiarity in the flow of goods. However this must not create anti-innovative local or regional protectionism. Differentiated approaches in the spirit of a balanced subsidiarity are conceivable. Two variants of this Policy Package are identified here:

Variant A: This variant is mainly lifestyle and market-oriented in which price mechanisms are widely used. In agricultural policy, regional marketing is encouraged by differentiated subsidies. Road pricing and an increase in transport costs also play a role. Structural development programmes favour companies that use local sourcing of products and services. There is a strong information campaign aimed at changing lifestyles and consumer preferences.

Variant B: This variant has a stronger emphasis on regulation and service-oriented policies. Here price mechanisms are less important. A strong emphasis is placed on the rapid introduction of product labelling, showing the origin of the product and its transport content. Standards for public procurement also play an important role.

The main measures in this package include:

• Promotion of 'regional' consumer markets – governments at all levels promote regional consumer markets by improving public awareness and information, by campaigning for reform of the Common Agricultural Policy, by introducing the notion of flexible subsidiarity in internal market regulations, and by promoting adequate distribution structures through land-use planning.

• Promotion of company networking and industrial districts – networking and local sourcing is encouraged by economic incentives, regulation, and the provision of specialized infrastructure (technology and training centres, for example).

- Information system on the transport content of all goods – parallel to the introduction of Environmental Management and Audit Scheme (EMAS), a European system for tracing and declaring the transport content of all goods could be established within ten years.
- Product labelling, including the origin of all components – this could be made compulsory within five years.
- Transport impact assessment for major political decisions – introduced at all political levels.
- Mainly *Variant A:* Differentiated road pricing and increases in road transport costs, which would allow the cost of road freight transport to be increased considerably, particularly in sensitive areas.
- *Variant B:* changes in public procurement could be revised in a way that allows European exchange of knowledge and information at the same time as limiting flows of goods in the spirit of local production and subsidiarity.

Impacts on Stakeholders

Freight traffic along long-range transport corridors would be reduced. Urban and rural populations would have better access to local products and services, and would be less reliant on the car. Certain social groups such as the elderly, the disabled, the young, and the less affluent would benefit. Large-scale distributors would lose opportunities and are likely to be some of the strongest opponents to such policies. Structural change will be accelerated so that traditional material-intensive and mass-production oriented industries will have difficulties in adapting to change (less so for flexible, high-tech oriented industry). The vehicle industry may oppose such a policy, while the IT industry may discover large new markets in information systems and road-pricing systems. New systems for more flexible local logistics may also create new opportunities. Small or medium-sized enterprises (SMEs) will probably be more advantaged from such policies than large companies.

Generally, entrepreneurship and local employment may be strengthened. The development of agriculture throughout Europe may become more even and less favoured regions may have increased opportunities. Consequently, areas with high intensity export-oriented agricultural production may oppose such policies. Railways will find it more difficult to compete since long-distance transport of mass-products form their traditional market. *Variant A*, which envisages an increase in transport costs, may encounter more general political opposition. In *Variant B*, the rapid introduction of labelling may encounter resistance in industry.

11.1.7 Policy Package: promoting dematerialization of the economy

A basic strategy for reducing the need for freight transport is to reduce the material throughput of the economy. This requires approaches which go far beyond traditional transport policy.

Designed for	*Key strategy elements*
Image I	Decoupling Freight Transport
Main policy orientations	Organization
Market and Lifestyle: *Variant A*	Technology
Regulation and Public Service:	
Variant B	

Dematerialization is a current trend which can be seen in many sectors. Three sub-strategies can be used to enhance it:

1   substitution of products by services;
2   increased durability of products; and
3   miniaturization.

Generally, dematerialization of the economy not only contributes to the solution of certain transport problems, but also reduces a wide range of environmental problems. Therefore, combined efforts between different policy fields are conceivable. This Policy Package addresses all three strategies. The general awareness and information concerning the problems caused by material consumption and the opportunities to reduce it can be overcome by labelling. Some kind of Transport Content Declaration (TCD) or Material Flow Accounting would be very helpful in this context.

The substitution of products by services can be encouraged by changes in the economy. Economic and fiscal policies are still strongly oriented towards a hardware-producing economy, rather than a service-oriented economy. Shifting the tax burden from labour to material consumption, shifting development policy priorities away from infrastructure and hardware investments to the improvement of the human and social capital could make a big difference here. A series of more specific changes (such as labour regulations, insurance for borrowed or rented equipment, and professional service standards for example) could support a general shift in the service dimension of consumption. The internalization of external environmental costs will help to curb the material intensity of the economy. Full lifecycle responsibility of manufacturers for their products will be helpful (these have been introduced into waste policies in some European countries). These policies will also tend to increase the durability of products and stimulate the more intensive use of them. Systems for sharing and rental of equipment will lead to more intense use, and this may in turn lead to technical development towards more durability.

Miniaturization can only be marginally influenced by public policies. However, many technical and safety standards prescribe an oversized use of materials which, on a closer investigation, may be reduced considerably with new technology, particularly in some sectors (such as construction). Changing the conditions of use for certain products could reduce material consumption (lower speed limits would allow the construction of lighter vehicles, for example).

Lifestyles may be influenced not only by awareness and information campaigns but also by providing opportunities for other *genres de vie*. The permanent availability of cars and frequent waste collection inevitably reduces the awareness of individual material consumption. Encouraging car-free lifestyles by improving public transport, facilitating car sharing and rental or providing home delivery services would not only reduce private car use and ownership but may also change the attitude towards the everyday consumption of materials.

Strengthening trends towards dematerialization would also change the structure of freight transport. Transported goods will diminish in size and increase in value. This will reinforce the trend towards more careful and flexible handling and shorter transport times. This in turn may create problems for the railways and intensify the trend towards air transport. Balancing policies for these two modes will therefore be important in order to avoid additional environmental problems.

Variant A: This variant is mainly market and lifestyle-oriented, in which economic policy plays a predominant role.

Variant B: This variant relies more on regulation and public services. It emphasizes manufacturer responsibility for recycling and disposal of goods after use, the introduction of increasingly stringent standards, and a shift in structural development policies towards investments into human and social capital.

The main measures in this Policy Package include:

- Incentives for the rental and sharing of goods and services – tax and other polices aimed at encouraging hardware investments are linked to incentives that allow intensive use of equipment. Legal frameworks for service contracting are improved.
- *Variant A* – the tax burden is shifted from labour to materials, energy, and emissions of CO_2. European co-ordination of taxes on energy and waste policies could be very helpful.
- *Variant B* – development policy (including structural funds) gives priorities to human resources. Improving learning and co-operation on optimal service delivery become the main focus of development policies at all levels.

♦ *Variant B* – product responsibility for manufacturers across the whole lifecycle is introduced. Manufacturers of all kinds of products are made responsible for all recycling, dismantling and/or disposal costs of their products after use, leading to the development of more responsible technology and more service-oriented marketing strategies.
♦ *Variant B* – standards which affect material consumption (such as cars and building) are revised.

Impacts on stakeholders

Dematerialization of the economy is an approach that allows for coalitions with a variety of actors in environmental policy. There are also strong political forces which call for effective policies for reducing unemployment and alliances seem possible to achieve changes in the tax system. The consequences of this Policy Package will be quite different for different sectors of industry. Traditional, hardware-oriented industries will be exposed to increased pressure to reorientate. IT and service-oriented industries will benefit from new opportunities. More service-oriented industries may oppose dematerialization policies. The pressure for developing new service-oriented and communication-oriented skills for large parts of the working population will increase. Economies which are already advanced in this direction will tend to be more competitive and stable. The changes may create political conflicts with those representing and depending on traditional industries. Small and large companies may be equally affected (both positively and negatively). A strong shift in tax policy as envisaged in Variant A may cause broader political opposition than the regulation-oriented approach (which affects more specific stakeholders).

11.1.8 Policy Package: minimizing specific emissions

This package aims at a significant reduction of specific emissions from road and air transport. It is particularly intended for Image II, where the all purpose car has a strong role.	

Designed for
  Image II
Main policy orientation
  Regulation
	Key strategy elements
	  Technology

Emission standards are related to specific test cycles but deviations from these occur in practice due to high speeds, accelerations, cold starts, and other causes. Actual emissions are in fact often much higher than those observed in test cycles, particularly for conventional cars. Stricter emission standards only affect a (decreasing) part of actual emissions and may not necessarily be the most cost-effective measure.

To ensure durability of exhaust treatment systems, manufacturers must have long-term responsibility for their proper functioning. Regular control of emission levels should be made compulsory. An option may be to use on-board engine diagnostics which are now common in new cars. Information about the benefits of a smooth driving style should be disseminated. Education of drivers combined with economic incentives for fuel efficient driving could have significant benefits both for CO_2 and other emissions.

If diesel engines do not comply with the strong measures needed to reach emission targets, they must be phased out from use in city traffic. This does not seem unlikely, although it is difficult to predict technology development in this area. They may still be used for inter-city freight but not in local distribution.

Hybrid vehicles, which are less sensitive to driving style, could be promoted by more flexible certification levels or by lower sales taxes for example. All measures leading to reduced vehicle weight will also have beneficial effects on emissions. However, more fuel-efficient engines do not necessarily imply lower emissions. Higher combustion temperatures may decrease fuel consumption but, *ceteris paribus*, tend to increase emissions of NO_x. This is especially problematic for aircraft because treatment of exhaust gases is not possible.

The main policy measures in this package include:

- long-term producer responsibility for emission levels;
- information regarding the effect of driving style on emissions and fuel consumption;
- introduction of more realistic test cycles;
- promotion of hybrid vehicles, which do not have the same problem with off-cycle emissions;
- drastic reduction of the sulphur content of diesel fuel; and
- feebates on new cars, dependant on emissions and fuel consumption.

Impacts on stakeholders

Car manufacturers might resist the more long-term responsibility for emission levels, although additional costs will probably be rather small. Car owners will be spared the risk of having to buy new exhaust systems, although the price of new cars may increase slightly. Airlines may face increased costs due to more complex engine designs.

11.1.9 Policy Package: resource efficient freight transport

This Policy Package aims to increase the resource efficiency of freight transport and reduce haul distance. This Package consists of two variants.

Designed for	*Key strategy elements*
Image II	Technology
Main policy orientations	
Market: *Variant A*	
Regulation and Public Service:	
Variant B	

This package is mainly intended for Image II. Although freight transport volumes are lower than in the reference case they are considerably higher than both in Image I and compared to 1995. This difference is mainly due to longer distances rather than increased goods volumes.

Longer distances improve the competitiveness of rail, but considerable efforts will be necessary in order to exploit this opportunity fully. Technical and organizational harmonization of railways over Europe is enhanced and supported by a number of other policies. In order to meet sustainability targets, the use of combined transport is increased considerably. Promoting European standards and technologies for automatic flexible freight handling and tracing will therefore have a high priority.

Substituting individual shopping travel by home delivery is another important strategy in this package (see also the 'Liveable Cities' Policy Package 2 – Section 11.1.2). Co-ordination of distribution including home delivery will be encouraged in order to increase load factors. Information technologies and e-commerce will contribute significantly to this. Integrated information systems may lead to shorter supply chains.

Integrated logistic services between the production and distribution stages of products will be based on information systems. An important political task will be to support the development of standardized interfaces that ensure inter-operability of different company systems in order to avoid new monopolies, to ensure the access of SMEs to such systems, and to improve the acceptance of these technologies.

Two variants of this package have been developed: *Variant A* is more market-oriented. An important component is increased costs for road transport. In *Variant B*, which is more regulation and public service oriented, direct support for railways is more important.

The main policy measures in *Variant A* of this Policy Package include:

♦ support for the development of technologies and standards for automatic flexible freight handling and tracing;

- promotion of integrated logistical systems;
- European rulings on common standards for railways, improved regulatory framework for Europe-wide operating carriers; and
- introduction of mileage-related taxes for road freight vehicles, tax levels that effectively raise transport costs (achieved with GPS-systems) – taxes may depend on time of the day or geographical area (see also the 'Fair and Efficient Distribution of Mobility' Policy Package 5 – Section 11.1.5).

The main policy measures in *Variant B* of this Policy Package include:

- active government involvement in defining standards for automatic flexible freight handling and tracing (hardware and software);
- establishment of a public IT infrastructure for integrated logistics;
- corresponding to public physical transport infrastructure (road and rail) an IT-system is established for facilitating the exchange of logistics related information. It should serve as an infrastructure for the operation of integrated logistics systems by companies or networks. This will be particularly important for the survival of small transport companies and logistic efficiency of small producing companies;
- European ruling on common standards for railways;
- public investment in additional infrastructure (tracks and intermodal nodes);
- improved regulatory framework for Europe-wide operating carriers (through a European regulation agency); and
- priority given to home delivery in local traffic management schemes and co-ordinated urban distribution with clean vehicles.

Impacts on stakeholders

Railway companies have historically been reluctant to forfeit their national monopolies. European rail policy has shown that considerable organizational obstacles have to be overcome in order to provide efficient trans-European rail services. However, a policy with clear priorities at the European level giving an important role to rail in freight transport may help to overcome such attitudes. Railway engineering industries will support harmonization.

With the market-oriented package (*Variant A*), small transport companies may have economic difficulties due to high logistics costs and/or greater dependence on large logistics companies. With *Variant B*, on the other hand, large logistics companies and large producing companies will probably oppose many of these policies. Efforts to promote co-operation in distribution will have limited success in Image II and will need strong incentives.

11.1.10 Policy Package: customer friendly transport services

This package aims at making public transport and intermodal travel more convenient. Intensive use of IT makes public transport more flexible and accessible.

Designed for	*Key strategy elements*
Image II	Organization
Main policy orientations	Technology
Regulation	
Public Service	

Technological innovation allows the development of personal communicators with smart card facilities. Each person will have a dedicated multipurpose personal communicator (MPC) that can be used for all forms of communication and information services. The MPC will have real-time information on travel services and facilities, including multimodal travel so that journeys can be planned in advance and modified as circumstances arise. This requires co-operation of all public transport providers so that door-to-door journeys can be booked with a single transaction. Car rental firms should also be integrated into the system. The intention is to encourage multimodal journeys which are flexible and convenient. Standardization and full compatibility between functions and locations should be completed by 2010. The MPC has an advisory function in that it can suggest alternatives, in terms of where to go, when to go, special deals, or even journey sharing possibilities. The MPC can also be used for individual banking facilities, shopping, booking leisure, and other activities. Support infrastructure will be required, and consideration needs to be given to the noise nuisance and potential health risks.

The main measures in this Policy Package include:

- European standards for mobility information between transport companies and personal communication devices;
- European public transport information system, combining local, regional, national, and European systems;
- increased flexibility of local public transport with the help of information systems;
- separated lanes and absolute priority for public transport through traffic regulation;
- improved opportunities for cycling;
- luggage deposit and other facilities at major public transport interchanges; and
- improved integration of public transport, semi-public transport (such as

taxis), car rental, car sharing, and car pooling with the help of integrated information, booking, and payment systems.

Impacts on stakeholders

IT industries will have a strong interest in establishing and marketing these information systems. Mobility information and booking systems could be a strong argument for selling personal communication devices (multipurpose mobile phones with internet features) to a wide market. The impact of these measures on the sale of cars may be limited. The vehicle industry may discover new opportunities in developing new forms of car use and in operating fleet management systems. However, if the systems are too technically complicated inexperienced people may have difficulties in using them.

11.2 Policy Paths

11.2.1 Overview

The analysis framework allows us to conceive of a large number of Policy Paths with different characteristics that could possibly be used for reaching the Images of the Future defined earlier. None of these Paths can be described in all its details here. Most measures allow for considerable flexibility in their application and continuous assessments would be necessary regularly to

Table 11.4 Combining the Policy Packages into Paths

		Path 1.1	Path 1.2	Path 2.1	Path 2.2
Image		I	I	II	II
	Lifestyle	X	X		
	Market	X		X	
	Regulation		X		X
	Services		X		X
1A	Ecological tax reform A	X			
1B	Ecological tax reform B			X	
2	Liveable cities		X		
3	Low impact city vehicles		X		
4	Long distance links – substituting for air travel	X	X		
5	Fair and efficient distribution of mobility – tradable mobility credits	X			
6A	Promoting subsidiarity in freight flows A	X			
6B	Promoting subsidiarity in freight flows B		X		
7A	Promoting dematerialization of the economy A	X			
7B	Promoting dematerialization of the economy B		X		
8	Minimizing specific emissions			X	X
9A	Resource efficient freight transport A			X	
9B	Resource efficient freight transport B				X
10	Customer friendly transport services			X	X

adjust the strategy and reach the policy targets. A further development of the approach described here is the development of a database management tool that allows new targets and policy options to be set, monitored, and evaluated. To give an impression of the possible variety of Paths and their respective difficulties, two different Paths have been constructed for each Image of the Future (see Figure 10.1). In the previous Section, we have outlined ten Policy Packages to give a feel for the range and depth of the alternatives available. From these packages, in combination with additional individual policy measures, it is possible to construct the Policy Paths to meet the targets set for sustainable mobility (Table 11.4).

11.2.2 Paths towards Image I – Path 1.1

This Policy Path includes five of the Policy Packages developed in the earlier part of this Chapter (Section 11.1):

- Ecological Tax Reform *Variant A* (Policy Package 1);
- Long Distance Links – Substituting Air Travel (Policy Package 4);
- Fair and Efficient Distribution of Mobility (Policy Package 5);
- Promoting Subsidiarity in Freight Flows *Variant A* (Policy Package 6);
- Promoting Dematerialization of the Economy *Variant A* (Policy Package 7).

In Image I, transport intensity is considerably lower than today. Decoupling strategies are therefore most important in the Policy Paths (Table 11.5). Both Paths 1.1 and 1.2 rely mainly on bottom-up initiatives. This is slightly more pronounced in Path 1.2 where local initiatives on local/city level are crucial, not least to achieve more 'liveable cities' with diminished reliance on car travel. In Path 1.1, there is greater emphasis on using market incentives, while the dominant policy orientations in Path 1.2 are regulation and public services. In both cases, policy is intended to facilitate environmentally benign lifestyles (common in Image I).

The widely used market incentives, such as local road pricing, could induce distributional conflicts, if complementary measures were not also introduced. If cars become cleaner and more fuel efficient, it is likely that the least affluent (those with the oldest vehicles) will have to pay the highest costs in any road pricing system. In the context of an Ecological Tax Reform, this can be compensated through labour tax reductions. Another solution which has been included is the introduction of Tradable Mobility Credits. However, the introduction of this would probably take some time, so that careful introduction of measures in the transition phase is very important. A wide range of policy measures and packages make it more probable that the targets can be reached. However, efforts to reduce freight transport intensity are essential and will not be an easy task. Some elements of the 'Liveable Cities'

Policy Package could be added to help through the transition phase before the more market-based measures have an impact (Table 11.5).

11.2.3 Paths towards Image I – Path 1.2

This Policy Path again includes five of the Policy Packages developed in the earlier part of this Chapter (Section 11.1):

+ Liveable Cities (Policy Package 2);
+ Low Impact City Vehicles (Policy Package 3);
+ Long Distance Links – Substituting Air Travel (Policy Package 4);

Table 11.5 Path 1.1: focus on decoupling and bottom up: market and lifestyle orientation

Policy Packages	Targets	Key elements	Passenger Urban	Inter-urban	Rural	Long-range	Freight Urban	Short-range	Long-range	Policy orientation	Government level	Start	Effect
1A Ecological tax reform A	ENV EFF REG	DPA DFR	X	X	X	X	X	X	X	M	EUR NAT LOC	2000 2010	2010 2020
4 Long distance links – substituting air travel	ENV EFF	DPA ORG				X			X	M R L	EUR NAT REG LOC	2000	2010
5 Fair and efficient distribution of mobility	EFF ENV	DPA ORG	X	X						M	EUR NAT REG LOC	2010	2020
6A Promoting subsidiarity in freight flows A	ENV EFF	DFR					X	X	X	M L	EUR NAT REG LOC	2000	2020
7A Promoting dematerialization of the economy A	EFF ENV	DFR					X	X	X	M L	EUR NAT REG LOC	2000	2020
Path 1.1	**ENV EFF REG**	**DPA DFR ORG**	**X**	**X**	**X**	**X**	**X**	**X**	**X**	**MM LL R**	**EUR NAT REG LOC**	**2000**	**2020**

Targets	ENV	environment	Key strategy elements	TEC	technology
	EFF	efficiency		DPA	decoupling passengers
	REG	regional development		DFR	decoupling freight
Government level	LOC	local		ORG	organization
	REG	regional	Policy orientation	L	lifestyle
	NAT	national		M	market
	EUR	European		R	regulation
	GLO	global		S	service

- Promoting Subsidiarity in Freight Flows *Variant B* (Policy Package 6);
- Promoting Dematerialization of the Economy *Variant B* (Policy Package 7).

Regulation allows for more differentiated interventions than market-oriented policy measures but careful evaluation of the results is necessary to avoid unwanted effects. Urban policies are very important in this path (Table 11.6).

Table 11.6 Path 1.2: Focus on decoupling and bottom up: regulation, public service and lifestyle orientation

Policy Packages	Targets	Key elements	Passenger Urban	Inter-urban	Rural	Long-range	Freight Urban	Short-range	Long-range	Policy orientation	Government level	Start	Effect
2 Liveable cities	ENV	ORG	X	X	X		X	X		R	LOC	2000	2010
	EFF	DPA	X				X			S	REG		
		DFR									EUR		
3 Low impact city vehicles	ENV	TEC	X				X			R	EUR	2000	2010
	EFF	ORG								S	NAT	2010	2020
										M	LOC		
4 Long distance links – substituting air travel	ENV	DPA				X			X	M	EUR	2000	2010
	EFF	ORG								R	NAT		
										L	REG		
											LOC		
6B Promoting subsidiarity in freight flows A	ENV	DFR					X	X	X	R	EUR	2000	2020
	EFF									L	NAT		
										M	REG		
											LOC		
7B Promoting dematerialization of the economy A	EFF	DFR					X	X	X	R	EUR	2000	2020
	ENV									L	NAT		
										M	REG		
											LOC		
Path 1.2	**ENV**	**DPA**	**X**	**X**	**X**	**X**	**X**	**X**	**X**	**R**	**EUR**	**2000**	**2020**
	EFF	**DFR**								**S**	**NAT**		
	REG	**ORG**								**LL**	**REG**		
										M	**LOC**		

Targets	ENV	environment	Key strategy elements	TEC	technology
	EFF	efficiency		DPA	decoupling passengers
	REG	regional development		DFR	decoupling freight
Government level	LOC	local		ORG	organization
	REG	regional	Policy orientation	L	lifestyle
	NAT	national		M	market
	EUR	European		R	regulation
	GLO	global		S	service

Comparison of Paths 1.1 and 1.2 (Image I)

The outcome of both Paths is not so different. The widespread use of market instruments in Path 1.1 may cause less resistance than the many regulations in Path 1.2, which would require extensive debate at the local level. As local regulation, especially in urban transport policy, plays a more important role in Path 1.2, it is a more bottom-up approach than Path 1.1, which requires a good framework for road pricing at the European level. In both Paths, old material-intensive industries will have to make considerable changes to be able to adapt and this will be a source of resistance. As these industries are often regionally concentrated, this may also cause political tensions between regions. On the other hand, knowledge-based and service-oriented industries will clearly benefit. Both strategies correspond to an acceleration of the structural changes that are already going on. With the growing strength of the service sector and IT industries, chances of political feasibility for these policies will increase. Employment arguments will play a major role in the

Table 11.7 Path 2.1: Focus on technology and top-down: market orientation

Policy Packages		Targets	Key elements	Transport type — Passenger: Urban	Inter-urban	Rural	Long-range	Transport type — Freight: Urban	Short-range	Long-range	Policy orientation	Government level	Time horizon — Start	Effect
1B	Ecological tax reform B	ENV EFF	DPA DFR	X	X	X	X	X	X	X	M	EUR NAT	2000 2010	2010 2020
8	Minimizing specific emissions	ENV EFF	TEC ORG	X	X	X	X	X	X	X	M R	EUR	2000	2010
9A	Resource efficient freight transport A	EFF ENV	ORG					X	X	X	M R	EUR NAT REG	2000	2020
10	Customer friendly transport services	EFF ENV	TEC ORG	X	X						R S M L	EUR NAT REG LOC	2000	2010
Path 2.1		**ENV EFF REG**	**DPA DFR ORG**	**X**	**X**	**X**	**X**	**X**	**X**	**X**	**M R S L**	**EUR NAT REG LOC**	**2000**	**2020**

Targets	ENV	environment		Key strategy elements	TEC	technology
	EFF	efficiency			DPA	decoupling passengers
	REG	regional development			DFR	decoupling freight
Government level	LOC	local			ORG	organization
	REG	regional		Policy orientation	L	lifestyle
	NAT	national			M	market
	EUR	European			R	regulation
	GLO	global			S	service

public debate on these policies. Therefore it will be very important to give evidence for new employment opportunities arising from these strategies in both Policy Paths.

11.2.4 Paths towards Image II – Policy Path 2.1

This Policy Path includes four of the Policy Packages developed in the earlier part of this chapter (Section 11.1):

- Ecological Tax Reform *Variant B* (Policy Package 1);
- Minimizing Specific Emissions (Policy Package 8);
- Resource Efficient Freight Transport *Variant A* (Policy Package 9);
- Customer Friendly Transport Services (Policy Package 10).

As this Path uses mainly market mechanisms, the 'Minimizing Specific Emissions' Policy Package may be enhanced by including the introduction of tradable permits or feebates for new cars and aircraft according to fuel consumption or weight. Decoupling strategies may be too weak for achieving the targets alone. Therefore some elements of other Policy Packages (such as 'Promoting Subsidiarity in Freight Flows A' and 'Promoting Dematerialization of the Economy A' developed for Image I) could be included, particularly if it is realized that the basic group of four Policy Packages is not sufficient to achieve the policy targets (Table 11.7).

11.2.5 Paths towards Image II – Policy Path 2.2

This Policy Path includes three of the Policy Packages developed in the earlier part of this Chapter (Section 11.1):

- Minimizing Specific Emissions (Policy Package 8);
- Resource Efficient Freight Transport *Variant B* (Policy Package 9);
- Customer Friendly Transport Services (Policy Package 10).

In order to strengthen the 'Minimizing Specific Emissions' Policy Package, a regulation-oriented approach might also be incorporated, including:

- CAFE[1] standards or uniform reductions of average specific fuel consumption for cars and aircraft;
- introduction of methanol by, for example, funding research and development and by public procurement of methanol vehicles.

As in Path 2.1, the decoupling strategies may be too weak for achieving the policy targets with just the Policy Packages included here. Therefore some elements of other Packages (such as 'Promoting Subsidiarity in Freight Flows B' and 'Promoting Dematerialization of the Economy B' Policy Packages developed for Image I) could also be included here (Table 11.8).

Table 11.8 Path 2.2: Focus on technology and top-down: regulation and public service orientation

Policy Packages	Targets	Key elements	Passenger — Urban	Inter-urban	Rural	Long-range	Freight — Urban	Short-range	Long-range	Policy orientation	Government level	Start	Effect
8 Minimizing specific emissions	ENV EFF	TEC ORG	X	X	X	X	X	X	X	R	EUR	2000	2010
9B Resource efficient freight transport B	EFF ENV	ORG					X	X	X	R S	EUR NAT REG	2000	2020
10 Customer friendly transport services	EFF ENV	TEC ORG	X	X						R S M L	EUR NAT REG LOC	2000	2010
Path 2.2	**ENV EFF REG**	**DPA DFR ORG**	**X**	**X**	**X**	**X**	**X**	**X**	**X**	**R S M L**	**EUR NAT REG LOC**	**2000**	**2020**

Targets			Key strategy elements		
	ENV	environment		TEC	technology
	EFF	efficiency		DPA	decoupling passengers
	REG	regional development		DFR	decoupling freight
Government level	LOC	local		ORG	organization
	REG	regional	Policy orientation	L	lifestyle
	NAT	national		M	market
	EUR	European		R	regulation
	GLO	global		S	service

Comparison of Paths 2.1 and 2.2 (Image II)

Paths 2.1 and 2.2 are both directed towards Image II. Although some policy elements are similar they have quite different policy orientations. The general potential for decoupling is better in Path 2.1, mainly due to Ecological Tax Reform which also affects transport volumes. It is uncertain whether the same technological progress can be achieved if market mechanisms are not widely used as in Path 2.1. The consequence is that it will be impossible to reach the targets by following Path 2.2 without introducing renewable fuel, such as methanol, on a wide scale. In Path 2.1, there is some chance that this step could be postponed. This, however, appears to be a rather costly strategy. As measures for decreased fuel consumption of new cars and aircraft, such as CAFE or uniform relative reductions, are relatively inefficient from an economic point of view, it may be concluded that it will be significantly more costly to follow Path 2.2 compared to Path 2.1.

In both cases, rather severe measures will be necessary in order to reach targets in time. In Path 2.1, which relies more on price mechanisms, this may also lead to distributional problems. However, measures such as the Tradable Mobility Credits in Path 2.1 do not seem to have much chance in the general political climate in Image II. Some elements of Ecological Tax Reform, as currently discussed in many European countries, will be necessary in both Policy Paths. Furthermore it is assumed that teleactivities will develop substantially in the years to come and provide some alternative to physical transport.

11.3 Conclusions

It has only been possible to sketch the character and briefly compare the different Policy Paths in this Chapter. However, it is clear that there are different ways to reach the policy targets for sustainable mobility. Different political constituencies with preferences for different policy orientations may all find their path to a sustainable mobility future. This opens opportunities for political agreement about targets without defining the specific strategies used to reach them. However, the Paths have also shown that the technically oriented top-down approaches in Image II open fewer options for a flexible policy than the more comprehensive approaches that are possible in Image I.

Important lessons must be learnt from this process of policy packaging and the development of Policy Paths. Some of the lessons relate back to the four principles of acceptability, inertia and lead times, dynamics, and adaptability, which were outlined in Section 10.4. It is noticeable that there are some common elements to several Paths. These common elements should perhaps be given special attention, as they are likely to be components in all futures that might help achieve more sustainable mobility. These common elements should be implemented early, as they will also have greatest impact and need to be carefully structured so that their expected impacts match their actual outcomes.

Note

1   CAFE = Corporate Average Fuel Economy – mandatory standards for fuel efficiency in the USA since 1976. Sales weighted average fuel consumption of all cars has to equal or better 8.55 litres/100 km (RCEP, 1994, para 8.50).

Chapter 12

Policy actions and conclusions

12.1 Transport in a changing world[1]

In his impressive work on 'The History of Knowledge', Charles van Doren (1991) argues that there is no reason to believe that the geographical action radius of modern man will come to a standstill. He foresees an accelerated mobility of people in the next century mainly induced by fast transport and communication technology, by more leisure time, and rising levels of welfare. Is the behaviour of *'homo mobilis'* compatible with constraints emerging from ecological, spatial or social considerations?

The combination of technological developments, behavioural changes, and international political forces (such as the liberalization of international trade instigated by the World Trade Organization) has led to the birth of a complex network society characterized by a nodal connectivity structure based on real-time linkages (Castells, 1996). Such a spatial organization of our society at all levels – ranging from local to global – ensures efficient interaction and communication, both in physical and in material terms. This associative structure of a modern network society has laid the foundation for intensive mobility, transport, and communication patterns. This development applies to all sectors of our society – commuting, leisure trips, international trade, and telecommunications.

Seen from this perspective, the modern transport-intensive economy has become a significant contributor to the ongoing growth process in most countries of our world. Statistically, there is a close correlation between gross domestic product per capita and the level of mobility and of transport flows, both domestically and internationally. Our world becomes smaller all the time, and the organization of production and consumption has become a global activity. For example, a standard breakfast in any Western country often has ingredients originating from more than ten different countries; people make more holiday trips, and also over longer distances. It seems plausible that man in the new millennium will operate on various inter-linked geographical scale levels, ranging from local to global.

It goes without saying that the spatial reorganization of human activity patterns has significantly changed the face of earth. In particular, we have observed a widening of urban functions, first reflected in suburbanization and later on in urban sprawl. Attempts to reverse these trends have led to compact city movements, but these have not become very successful. Instead, we observe at present the emergence of a new phenomenon, the so-called edge city, which tends to become a suburban conglomerate of modern high-tech and business service activities, thus stimulating a further erosion of the city centre and more transport flows (Medda *et al.*, 1999). Clearly, spatial dynamics in our mobile society is largely induced by modern transport systems technology and by information and communication technology (ICT). These technologies generate the opportunities for real-time world-wide interaction (the internet, the wired city, the global village and so on) and induce both physical and non-physical interaction.

There is an increasing awareness, however, that a continuation of our mobility-intensive and transport-intensive network society may reach the limits of a sustainable society. The transport flows have become so intensive that the capacity of the networks is becoming insufficient to handle all flows. Capacity does not only refer to physical capacity (such as road congestion), but also to environmental capacity (such as CO_2 levels for example), land-use capacity (such as lack of land for new infrastructure), or safety capacity (such as fatalities). There is apparently a friction between the rational individual motive to be mobile and the interest of society at large. This social dilemma is difficult to solve, as a change in individual behaviour (such as a shift to a different mode) will have a negligible impact on the overall outcome, while a more significant contribution to the solution of the capacity problem (for example a critical mass choosing a different mode) will encourage free ridership. The tension between individual and collective interests is very apparent in the transport sector.

There are several reasons why the negative externalities of transport and traffic often receive such a prominent place in the public debate:

- the transport sector has an important structuring impact on the space-economy;
- transport infrastructure is usually collective in nature and is often regarded as a public good characterized by the non-excludability postulate;
- traffic and transport often have an important strategic – sometimes political and military – role which far exceeds local interest;
- transport infrastructure is often supplied in indivisibilities, so that there is an obvious scope for monopolies;
- mobility and transport generate a variety of unpriced effects which show up as social costs in other segments of society (e.g. noise annoyance).

Altogether, there is a broad-based perception in our society that the position of transport and mobility in the light of broader social and ecological objectives is problematic. It is therefore no surprise that there are increasingly loud voices demanding drastic change to the above mentioned trends. This has culminated in the concept of sustainable transport, which expresses the need that transport be brought in balance with the requirements imposed by the protection of the environment, now and in the future (Frey, 1983; Nijkamp, *et al.*, 1998). This concept does not, however, immediately offer an operational guideline and testable framework for assessing and evaluating environmental, land-use, and transport policies. For this reason, we have developed the concept of decoupling, stating that the annual growth in transport demand should be less than the average growth in gross domestic product (GDP). But one needs to realize that transport is narrowly interwoven with many other activities in our society and that it is therefore largely a derived demand. Thinking in terms of decoupling means paying attention to driving forces for economic behaviour and how these might be changed. Policies on decoupling therefore require a broad portfolio of different initiatives, instruments and regulations.

In this concluding Chapter we make some reflections on the scenario methodology developed in this book, placing it in some of the wider traditions of thinking about the future. We then draw policy conclusions from our research on the strategic decisions facing the EU if they are to take the lead in pursuing a Sustainable Common Transport Policy (S-CTP). Finally, we sketch out some of the continuing challenges which face policy-makers in the new century.

12.2 Innovations in scenario methodology

In scenario building, we are not trying to predict the future, but to describe visions of the future world within a specific framework and under specified assumptions. The real value of the process lies as much in the stimulus to new thinking as in the conclusions. Schwartz (1997) gives a clear comment on the nature and purpose of scenarios, when he says:

> Scenarios are not predictions. It is simply not possible to predict the future with certainty. An old Arab proverb says that 'he who predicts the future lies even if he tells the truth'. Rather scenarios are vehicles for helping people to learn. Unlike traditional business forecasting or market research, they present alternative Images of the Future: they do not merely extrapolate the trends from the present."

The scenario approach used here includes a description of the Images of the Future, designed to compare and examine alternative futures (CEC, 1994). There are different traditions in scenario construction (Becker, 1997), one based in the USA (the American Approach) and the other in the EU (the French Approach).

In the *American Approach*, a distinction is made between context and strategy with the scenarios first being presented as the context within which the system operates and policy-making takes place. Various actors are then asked to choose between alternative strategies and to adapt these – so that 'least regret' strategies can be selected by the user of the scenarios.

In the *French Approach*, a comprehensive picture of the future is presented in terms of the current situation, a description of some future alternatives and a description of a number of events which may connect the present situation with future ones. This is the approach that has been adopted here, but with a particular version of the French Approach – which might be termed the Swedish Approach. A full description of the different scenario building approaches can be found in Rienstra (1998) and Becker (1997).

The *Swedish Approach* has certain clearly distinctive characteristics and they have been mainly used for policy analysis. They are normative in their structure and based on desirable futures or choices. They also use a backcasting approach (rather than forecasting) where an Image of the Future is constructed without taking account of current trends. A path is then constructed on how to move from where one is at present to this desirable future position. The scenarios, the Images and the Policy Paths are all validated at various stages by experts, so that feedback can take place and modification at all stages can be made. The intention is not prescriptive, but illustrative of possible future Paths while at the same time giving an indication of the nature and scale of actions (together with a timetable) of the changes necessary to achieve the scenario targets.

This is the approach used in this research, but the basic backcasting methodology has been modified. The same procedures have been followed in terms of identifying the Images of the Future for sustainable mobility (2020) and the constraints (contextual and strategic) under which Policy Paths can be constructed, but a new approach to policy packaging has been developed. A comprehensive range of policy measures has been investigated and these have then been packaged in imaginative groupings so that implementation can take place through combinations of policies, rather than the more traditional analysis based on individual actions. In addition, the Policy Paths are not just single measures but mixtures of packages and complementary strategies, so that the targets for sustainable mobility can be achieved. It is only through packaging and combining these Packages that targets can be achieved (Chapter 11).

In the *Scenario Building Process* targets have been set to give substance to the Images of the Future. These targets relate to the desire for sustainable mobility, defined as using substantially less non-renewable resources in 2020 than were being used in 1995. The Images themselves are also constrained by contextual elements that do not change and strategic elements which do change over time (Figure 12.1).

- *The Contextual Elements* relate to the level of political intervention, with one Image assuming strong local action and the other Image assuming strong central action;
- *The Strategic Elements* relate to the relative importance given to technological solutions and decoupling policies. Decoupling is a key concept defined as maintaining levels of economic growth, but with lower levels of transport intensity – breaking the historic link between GDP growth (desirable) and traffic growth (undesirable).

Once these contextual and strategic elements have been set, the Images of the Sustainable Future 2020 can be conceptualized, in figures at the EU level (Tables 9.4, 9.6 and 9.8). These Tables summarize in broad terms the changes necessary to achieve the three sets of targets relating to environment, equity and efficiency (Table 8.5). There is a difference of emphasis between the three Images, with one having slightly lower levels of political involvement in the process of change – people are expected to adopt green attitudes and values, with the catalyst for change coming from the 'bottom upwards'. The

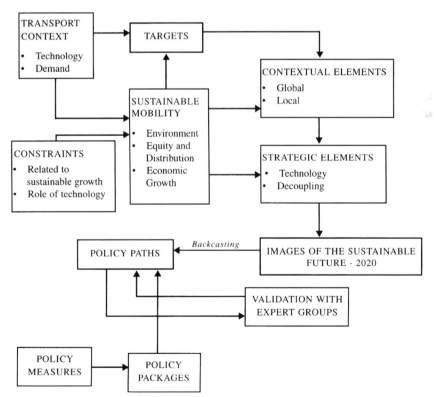

Figure 12.1   The scenario building process

other suggests that political intervention takes place from above ('top down') and that clear action comes from national (and supranational) politicians (Banister *et al.*, 2000).

It is important in the conclusion to reiterate our thinking and to emphasize various key elements in the scenario building process. The concern is not just over visioning the future (desirable and undesirable) based on a series of constraints (such as the role of technology or the expansion of Europe), and driving forces (such as demographic and economic for example). This type of approach is also creative and innovative.

For example, the recent Urban Futures scenarios (Wenban-Smith, 2000, p. 33) identify three possibilities for 2020:

- *Market Quickstep* – describes what might happen if complexity is largely left to manage itself. It is characterized by rapid technological change and international commercial integration; but weak institutions result in weak social cohesion. International institutions fail to develop strongly. Failure of trust in institutions and the imperatives of competitive positioning for survival lead the industrial powers into many differentiated and competing subnational regions and interests. The result is a fragmented world of near city states held together by pervasive webs of commercial value added, by market systems, and by the communications infrastructure.
- *Wise Councils* – by contrast, involves institutional development in support of strategic intervention, whether to manage the knowledge economy, or to mitigate the social consequences of rapid change, or to secure international co-operation towards sustainable development.
- *Atlantic Storm* – is characterized by socio-political backlash against the forces of change, regressive developments in institutions, failure of cohesion amongst the wealthy world and dislocation in developing nations. National politics become skewed to extremist/rejectionist or claimant groups. While the US becomes more market driven, Europe becomes protectionist/collectivist, and the rest of the world experiences instability, ideology and introversion. What is distinctive about this scenario is not the economic driving forces, which still operate, but the political and social response, which is reactionary and negative, reflecting widespread resistance to change, at least outside the US.

These scenarios are some examples of the many that have been developed recently to view the future as a series of possible choices that have to be made. However, the actual scenarios themselves are only part of the story. The modified backcasting approach goes considerably further in that it attempts to 'join up' the future visions with the present (Figure 12.1). It begins to answer the key question that if we know where we would like to go and we know where we are, how can we get from one position to the other (Chapter 11). This is where the policy packaging and Paths have been developed as a key contribution to the scenario building methodologies. To make scenarios a policy tool requires guidance to be given to policy-makers about what actions need to be taken at particular points in time. In the next section, we outline the more general conclusions from this process.

The second major contribution has been the acceptance that it is only through packaging measures and discussion with expert groups, that an understanding of both the scenario building process and the measures/ packages available will be achieved. At each of the three main stages in the scenario building process, discussions have been held with a range of users to present particular elements of the scenarios for comment and discussion. The targets, the Images of the sustainable future, and the Policy Paths were all subject to debate and modification during the analysis stage. This process was one of the most creative parts of the scenario building.

The outcome of the scenario building process is recommendations about what policy decisions need to be taken now in order to reach the assumed targets for sustainable mobility. It is recognized that sustainability is not a definitive end-goal, but it is a direction which policy can head for. Hence the targets used in here (Table 8.5) are intermediate ones. It is a methodology that puts near time decisions in a longer time perspective and based on today's best knowledge. More or less unexpected developments will result in revision of the Images of the Future and the alternative Paths to the Images. This calls for flexibility and adaptability.

Policy options have usually been tested in isolation under restrictive conditions. Although intuitive policy packaging is already a reality in political decision-making, the policy measures have been combined into Policy Packages, and the scenario building process has then put the Policy Packages together as Paths which are likely to lead to the targets and Images set for sustainable mobility (Chapters 8 and 9). The basic argument here is that combinations of policies are more effective in achieving sustainable mobility objectives than individual measures. Although composite policies make it harder to assess the overall impacts, they do allow the direct and indirect effect of individual measures to be assessed. They also permit the advantages and disadvantages of each measure (individually and as part of a package) to be discussed so that compensating actions can be taken. By introducing packages of measures, policies are less seen as restrictive or permissive, but are related to the achievement of particular objectives (such as sustainable mobility).

In summary, the main methodological contributions made by this book are:

♦   to develop further the idea of target setting and backcasting. Putting this concept into operation requires a public discussion on targets and effective monitoring that requires continuous adoption of actions if intermediate targets are not achieved;

- to develop a framework of targets, value orientations, Images, key issues, hot spots, key strategies and policy orientations to facilitate a discussion of these issues;

- to develop an innovative methodology for the construction of the Paths in a backcasting framework;

- to propose a means by which the intuitive packaging of policy measures can be combined with a systematic assessment of these packages in a modified backcasting framework;

- these tools are aimed at supporting a target-oriented management process in transport policy. Such an approach requires a considerable mental, organizational, and behavioural effort compared to conventional incremental policies which have proved to be conflict laden and not particularly effective. Part of the reason is that they often have too short a time perspective. In a longer time perspective, the gains of specific measures will be more clearly visible, and therefore changing the balance between benefits and efforts.

12.3 Policy conclusions

The conclusions reached as a result of the extensive scenario building process outlined in this book are optimistic. We conclude that the targets set (Chapter 8) for sustainable mobility in the EU can be achieved by 2020, but that strong action is required now on both of the main dimensions – decoupling and technology (Figure 12.1).

1 *Decoupling:* Even if the strongest priority is given to technology, this is not sufficient on its own to achieve the targets or Images. This conclusion is based on the notion that transport volumes, both passenger and freight, are expected to continue to grow. Strong decoupling in both the passenger and the freight sectors is therefore also essential to achieve sustainable mobility. This means that a decrease in transport intensity of GDP is needed. The range of measures available and the means to reduce transport intensity have been outlined in Chapter 11.

   - A wide variety of policies is available for decoupling both passenger and freight transport from economic growth. This seems possible without limiting economic growth (further analysis is however needed), but policies would need to accelerate some existing trends of structural change and lifestyle change. However, as decoupling can be regarded as a shift in the transport paradigm, such changes may result in opposition from those who perceive they may lose from these changes. Accelerated decoupling strategies will bring benefits to the overall economy, but may temporarily increase political conflicts.

- To reduce these political conflicts, two important further actions are required. The nature of decoupling and its pivotal role in achieving sustainable mobility needs to be presented to, and discussed among, decision-makers at all levels – an information activity. Secondly, the implications of decoupling have to be discussed with the public and business/industry to think through the necessary actions in terms of travel and activity patterns – a public acceptance activity.

- This conclusion is already generating considerable interest in the EU and is of equal if not greater importance in other parts of the world (particularly in the USA), where energy has been very cheap and the emphasis has been on technological improvement rather than decoupling. The achievement of targets for sustainable mobility requires a fundamental reassessment of the links between transport growth and economic growth.

2   *Technology:* Technology has a key role to play in moving policy in the direction of sustainable mobility, particularly in the longer term. In the shorter term firm action and direction is required at the EU level to promote best practice and to help push particular technological Paths. For example, should research be directed at new technology (hydrogen) or at an intermediate technology (methanol); what should be the role of diesel fuel in urban areas; and how can cleaner technology and fuels be introduced in cities, together with the necessary infrastructure? These actions need to be accompanied by strong decoupling. It may be necessary to protect the market in the short term so that the appropriate conditions for technological innovation are encouraged. In the longer term there should be an open market with pricing and regulation determining which technologies are consistent with sustainable mobility. In some of these areas, industry (for example Ballard Power Systems in conjunction with Daimler-Benz/Chrysler and Ford) has taken a lead in investing in new technology, but there are important institutional and political barriers that need to be overcome before real progress is made on the technological changes necessary to achieve sustainable mobility (Banister, 2000*b*).

3   *Action is needed both within and outside the Common Transport Policy:* The analysis of different aspects of decoupling transport volume growth from economic growth clearly shows that a CTP must be supplemented by measures outside the transport sector (and consequently outside the

CTP). Some of these non-transport policy actions are related to structural changes in society (such as the consequences of IT or increased interest in local-regional markets). Other actions are a matter of more general macro-economic policy intervention (such as a tax shift from labour to resource use). Further, some developments in line with decoupling will be driven without policy interventions (like the rapid growth in the use of information technology). Here actions may be needed to cope with drawbacks, such as increased urban sprawl. Increasingly, the solutions to the problems raised by sustainable transport extend beyond the traditional boundaries of transport analysis.

4   *Dynamics and the Time Element:* The time horizon taken for the scenario building process is 2020, but this is only an intermediate stage in the process towards sustainability. As decoupling is a necessity and those measures often have a long lead-time (particularly with the use of market-based measures), it is important that they start early. Technology will also be important, but measures can be taken stepwise. However, this does not mean that no action should be taken now as clear guidance is required on standards for technology (such as on fuel consumption and emissions), and on whether investment should take place in intermediate technology (such as methanol) or whether encouragement should be given to 'jump' to the ecotechnology (such as hydrogen fuel cells for example). The uncertainty about changes over time should be recognized so that flexibility permits modifications in measures and targets. The issues raised here are crucial to the whole argument relating to sustainability. Actions are required now if the challenging targets are to be achieved, not just within the EU but more generally. Failure to act now means that there is no chance of achieving sustainability by 2020.

5   *The Regional Dimension:* Much of the discussion here (particularly in Chapter 11) has concentrated on the city and urban transport problems. Different problems exist in rural areas and in the peripheral regions of Europe (including the CEEC and CIS countries). The differences in conditions across the EU and wider Europe require different measures, different processes of implementation and phasing. Uniform policies concerning regulations and taxes do not produce optimal results and can create unnecessary conflicts. Ways must be found to adapt measures to local conditions while maintaining overall EU targets and consistency of policies. Differentiated (road) pricing may provide a useful approach to achieve targets with regionally based policies. In the EU, the regional dimension is of key importance as much of the budget is invested in those locations seen as disadvantaged.

6   *The Trans European Networks:* The TENs form an important component in the achievement of cohesion within Europe, but in terms of sustainable mobility their role may be more limited. The main purpose of the TENs in the context of sustainable mobility is to achieve a significant modal shift from road (and air) to rail. If the TENs only increase the supply of transport and encourage more travel overall, then sustainable mobility targets will not be achieved. This means that the TENs must form part of an integrated transport strategy that packages increases in supply of rail with reductions in supply of other modes (see Sections 12.4 and 12.5). The opportunities for the TENs are substantial, particularly if they include the new telecommunications networks which can reduce levels of physical movement. The problems of the TENs extend to the role for freight transfer to rail, and the question of European standardization and harmonization in the freight sector. Consideration should also be given to designing more regional and locally based networks that feed into and are complementary to the TENs. This would allow subsidiarity, with local and regional networks being decided at the appropriate decision level.

7   *Air Travel:* The dramatic increase in passenger and freight travel by air (about 6 per cent growth per annum or doubling every 12 years) is a major constraint on the achievement of sustainable mobility targets, as it is both long distance and energy intensive. Although not central to this research, this growth makes decoupling much harder. The development of new technology with larger aircraft and later hydrogen powered engines may help to reduce energy use and emissions per passenger kilometre. However the effects of H_2O and NO_x emissions at high altitudes is still not clear, but recent scientific evidence (IPCC, 1999) indicates that the greenhouse effect caused by aircraft emissions amounts to 2.5 times that caused by CO_2 alone, as H_2O and NO_x are also produced at cruising altitudes of 10-12km.

The volume growth has also to be addressed. At present the air industry benefits from an advantageous tax situation as there is no tax on kerosene. Equal tax treatment would help raise costs and prices in the air sector, particularly on some goods, but more action is required. The low cost of air travel on shorter European routes may also affect the potential for high speed rail. But, if rail takes over from shorter air routes, it may only release more air space for long distance air travel. Achievement of sustainable mobility objectives requires careful consideration of the future of air transport (Banister, 1999). Elsewhere (in the USA, for example)), this argument must be even more important to the achievement of sustainable transport as there is a much greater dependence on air as a means of travel.

8   *Support for Sustainable Mobility*: Throughout this research, questions have been raised about the nature and scale of change required to achieve sustainable mobility. It is essential to achieve support both for the principles and for the practice of sustainable mobility. Many people are constrained by current value systems and conventions. In the discussion process with the expert groups, it has been found that there is strong support for the principles of sustainable mobility, but equally strong barriers to real change. It has also been found that there are different views from the EU countries and professions, with no clear commonality. One prerequisite for the implementation of the proposed Policy Packages is a gradual shift in attitude towards increasing importance of values in line with sustainable development.

9   *Complementary Actions:* Although the primary elements for the Policy Packages are taken from the transport sector, there are many complementary actions needed in other sectors. These include the important role that land-use and development factors have in reducing transport intensity. It also includes the new technologies within transport (such as telematics), new technologies as they impact on transport (telecommuting for example), and the possibilities of ecological tax reform. In addition, the research has also found that new institutional and organizational structures may be necessary to achieve sustainable mobility. Included here are partnerships between the public and private sectors to facilitate technological innovation, the development of partnerships at all levels to gain support for change (and to inform), new means to encourage and disseminate best practice, and the means by which progress can be monitored over time.

10   *Common Elements:* Whatever the starting point of the scenarios or the path to be followed, there are certain common actions necessary. These include consideration of ecological tax reform (coupled with CO_2 tax, fuel, vehicle and car ownership tax reform), emissions standards (including off-cycle performance, long-term responsibility, automatic monitoring of emissions etc), actions to provide integrated information systems (including the personal communicator), and the promotion of teleactivities. If most (or all) Policy Packages include these common elements, then immediate action on each of them must be a priority.

11   *Lifestyle Changes:* Over the next 20 years, the amount of time available for leisure activities will dramatically increase, particularly within the demographic context of an ageing population, Much of this new leisure time may involve long-distance energy-intensive travel as people wish to

see the world. The question here is whether there is anything that can (or should) be done to reduce this expected growth as it will again severely impact on sustainable mobility. For much of the year people may be 'sustainable' with local travel being undertaken on low energy modes, but once (or twice) a year may travel round the world, thus negating any overall notion of sustainability. This means that changes in lifestyle are essential to meet sustainable mobility objectives, and that actions in the passenger sector may be harder to achieve than those in the freight sector.

12   *Possibilities of Both Strong Decoupling and Technology*: Image I was characterized by co-operation on local and regional levels (mainly bottom-up politics). Image II on the other hand was characterized by a good climate for global co-operation (mainly top-down politics). If both these frame conditions materialize, then Image III is a feasible option (Section 9.6 and 9.7). Originally, it was argued that it may not be possible to combine strong decoupling with strong technological development as the costs would be too high. However, under certain conditions a 'win-win' situation may be possible, with a focus on both strong decoupling and technology (Image IV – Section 9.8.4). In this case, there is a good base for later achieving more far reaching sustainability goals. To reach such an Image requires a high level of commitment and intervention by decision makers across all sectors. The capacity for preparing decisions and implementing them is likely to be a bottleneck in realizing this Image. Transport policy at the EU level is only one of many competing areas of action.

13   *Choosing Initial Measures*: If national governments and the EU commit themselves to the long-term goal of sustainable mobility in Europe, then a consistent policy should be developed. This policy will have to evolve and be adapted to contextual factors that are more or less impossible to predict and control. We have suggested a few guiding principles for choice of *initial measures* to be included in a start-up package (more details were given in Section 10.4):

   ◆   the measure should not be too controversial today (*principle of acceptability*);
   ◆   measures that are essential to goal fulfilment but will have a delayed effect should be implemented early (*principle of inertia or long lead-times*);
   ◆   measures that will set dynamic processes in motion should be implemented early (*principle of positive dynamic effects*);

◆   measures that tend to retain freedom of action in the future are usually
    to be preferred to measures leading to lock-in solutions (*principle of
    adaptability*).

Only the first point is (close to) a necessary condition. Perhaps these
necessary and other conditions need to be discussed in the different national
and international contexts.

In some areas the system dynamics governing development are only roughly
understood. The predictability is low, at least in the longer term. For
example, this is true for the interdependence between travel behaviour,
infrastructure development and spatial patterns of production and residential
areas. The same can be said for the development and dissemination of new
technology, such as cleaner and more energy efficient vehicles. Economic
incentives, city planning, and supply of good public transport certainly will
have an impact on trips by private cars in urban areas, although it is hard to
say how much. Also, there may be unpredictable and unwelcome side effects
of the policy actions.

The dimensions of uncertainty and potential impact can be combined to
form a framework for discussing political strategy. Several issues concerning
sustainable mobility can be characterized by large potential impact of policy
and large uncertainties. A testing and learning strategy is then required. A
Common Transport Policy should accept this lack of predictability and
proceed in small steps and have frequent follow-up activities. It is also
preferable to try several solutions in order to gain experience and learn. The
role of public policy is then to promote variety and to set targets that play the
role of selection mechanisms.

In the past, transport has mainly been seen as having a serving function for
the economy and leisure activities. Where sustainable mobility is a major
policy objective, transport cannot fulfil these demands in an unlimited way.
Transport has to be integrated with other policy. Transport is at a turning
point, and it is clear that transport interventions alone will not move policy in
the direction of sustainability. The role of transport policy among other
policies must be given a stronger emphasis, together with different policy
strategies that are required. More emphasis has to be placed in influencing
economic, structural, agriculture, tourism, and other policies to find the
means to decouple transport growth from economic development (Banister
and Berechman, 2000).

12.4 The complex force-field of mobility in space and time

This essentially optimistic set of conclusions on sustainable transport in
Europe must be tempered by the current underlying realism of the growth in

unsustainable patterns of mobility. Bridging distances – physically or virtually – is a sign of economic progress and a modern way of life. Spatial interaction and geographical mobility contribute to efficient economic development and offer the actors involved a strong competitive position in an open and increasingly global society. The economic and social benefits of our mobile way of life are tremendous and are partly responsible for the current level of economic welfare. It is also increasingly recognized, however, that a mobile society incurs high social costs and causes a host of negative externalities of various kinds: traffic congestion, accidents and fatalities, pollution, noise, annoyance, destruction of visual beauty and landscapes and so on. Such costs are, in general, not charged to the user of transport, so that an over-use of the good 'mobility' takes place. Relatively cheap fossil fuel, ongoing economic growth, and the fluid lifestyles in a modern society cause a situation where the '*homo mobilis*' has become the dominant pattern of life.

One may argue that the extension of the geographical coverage of human activity patterns is a major factor in the above problems, but it seems plausible that the need to minimize travel time – or to maximize travel distances – is a more important factor. It is therefore conceivable that, in recent years, speed reduction is frequently mentioned as an effective measure for diminishing the environmental burden of transport; the goal of 'sustainable transport' would be at odds with a high travel speed or with fast modes of transport. The current debate on this issue seems to prompt important analytical questions such as: Can speed reduction be seen in isolation from general time management choices? Can a critical mass of 'slow travellers' be identified, and if so, what are their motives? (Nijkamp and Baaijens, 1999).

It is noteworthy that in conventional economic choice theory much attention has been given to the analysis of time consumption of economic actors in relation to their personal utility levels, in which time has its indigenous shadow value in a scarcity context. This economic view of time is reflected in many time allocation and time budget studies and, in particular in value-of-time studies in transport research. In general, there appears to be a high willingness-to-pay of actors in order to gain extra (discretionary) time (a phenomenon also reflected, for example, in speed limit violations and related penalties). But a general analysis of travel time preferences against the background of social costs is still missing. This applies also to travel behaviour: travelling consumes valuable time that cannot be spent otherwise. Consequently, it has generally been accepted in our modern world that travelling – as a deliberate spatial movement – has to take place in the shortest time possible. This close connection between overcoming distance and consuming time has been extensively analysed in the framework of space-time geography as developed in particular by the Swedish school of geography. In a reflective article, the leading geographer Hägerstrand (1987) notes that time pressure is at the heart of spatial behaviour and has dramatic implications for the spatial organization and spatial interaction patterns of a modern society. Clearly, the worldwide trend towards high mobility has adverse, disadvantageous consequences for environmental sustainability and safety of the modern transport sector. However, despite the social costs of fast modes of travel, a major performance criterion of a transport system in our society is still speed. Even though speed reduction can be shown to have demonstrable financial and environmental benefits, the drive towards increasingly higher speeds in transport seems to be irresistible. Some authors have even formulated the so-called 'law of a constant travel time budget', which suggests that, on average, the total daily travel time of an individual in the course of history is remarkably stable. This appears to hold in particular for trips in metropolitan areas. As a consequence, higher speeds will not even lead to time savings on travelling, as these savings will immediately be used to make new or longer trips (Lay, 1992; Nijkamp and Baaijens, 1999).

Fluidity is thus the sales label of a modern developed economy and one may wonder whether a return to 'slow motion' would ever be feasible and acceptable, even though the awareness is growing that a continuation of current trends may have devastating environmental impacts. Clearly, several environmentalists make a plea for a forced speed limit for cars, trains, and aeroplanes, but it is an open question whether a return to a 'snail society' would, at present, receive broad social support. Hörning *et al.* (1995) develop the concept of a 'time pioneer' and they have empirically investigated it. In contrast to a restless society characterized by permanent hurry, these authors propose a new lifestyle that is not only based on material welfare, but also on 'time welfare'. They define time pioneers as economic actors who deliberately resist the fast motion culture and who are prepared to exchange part of their income for more time, without immediately having a new economic purpose for this new discretionary time. Time-pioneering behaviour may relate to all economic activities and implies a substitution between the quantity of hours of productive, paid work and freely available leisure hours.

At the individual level, the acceptance of lower speed travel modes would imply reduced time efficiency in economic life and hence lower opportunities in someone's career pattern. It is noteworthy, however, that the recent literature mentions notable and illustrative examples of the phenomenon of *downshifters* – people who deliberately and voluntarily accept a lower position on the job ladder in exchange for more leisure time or a more relaxed lifestyle, including lower transport speed (Schor, 1992). Although this group of time pioneers is, for the time being, likely to be relatively small, it certainly makes sense to address the phenomenon of time pioneers in order to examine the feasibility of a 'slow motion' policy, based on the goal of a sustainable development of the transport system.

In the modern age of telecommunications and virtual reality, many people have lost their 'sense of place' and replaced it by a 'sense of flow' (Castells, 1996). Modern activity patterns presuppose a synchronic management of time and space (Carlstein *et al.*, 1978). For many people the world as a whole has become the 'place of action' connected by various types of network (Urry, 1995; Waters, 1995). The various modes of transport in the age of globalization and mobility are partly complementary, partly competitive. This applies to both physical transport modes and telecommunication modes. Mobility has ultimately become an intrinsic feature and driving force of a modern economy.

Against this background we have to interpret the popular ideas on 'slow motion' characterized by the old Roman wisdom of *festina lente* (hasten slowly). The environmental and socio-psychological stress of present-time behaviour in a modern society has – in the eyes of many authors – become unbearably high (more hurry, less speed), even to the extent that 'to hasten slowly' is sometimes advocated as a new mode of economic and social behaviour (Rifkin, 1987; Zoll, 1988).

In the framework of transport behaviour, time pioneers would not regard travel time as a cost component that might prevent them from making more money (or from increasing the economic opportunities) in their professional life. Rather, they would attach an intrinsic value to a relaxed way of travelling and hence be prepared (or even seek) to use slower and more relaxing modes of transport, even if this would negatively affect their income or job possibilities. Thus, time pioneers derive their utility from an extension of their choice spectrum regarding the additional free time. Consequently, more flexible time behaviour (such as flexihours for the departure time of trip-makers) is not the typical feature of time pioneers. This would imply that time pioneers might be prepared to accept slower modes of transport and also longer travel times, as a relaxed travel time contributes to their well-being. There is clearly a need for a more thorough behavioural investigation into the opportunities of slow motion for sustainable transport. We may conclude here that human activity patterns are extremely complex and need a thorough examination at the interface of time and space. Since space-time decisions are induced by a variety of motives, it will be difficult to influence directly travel decisions of individuals. But the current pattern of high and increasing mobility is not unchangeable.

12.5 Transport as an integrating force

The movement patterns of people and goods display an amazing complexity. The simple view that the supply of transport technology and infrastructure would be a steering mechanism cannot be maintained as it neglects the interrelationship with behaviour or attitude and with policy and regulation. In contrast to the past, where scientific research has mainly focused on engineering aspects, we observe now the need for an interdisciplinary approach by rigorously including concepts from the social sciences and the humanities, while there is also a need to address issues of policy implementation and process management. Transport cannot properly be analysed while isolated from its context; on the contrary, the driving forces in mobility and communication are a direct offspring of broader social, economic, technological, and policy development. Figure 12.2 demonstrates an integrative approach by including in a comprehensive way major direct and indirect influences on transport and communication from driving forces in the economic and social system, and policy frameworks. The figure equally underlines the interaction of the spatial organization of society, transport infrastructure and industry, and new transport technology with transport and communication.

Furthermore, it makes explicit reference to the natural and built environment, which is strongly influenced by land use, transport and

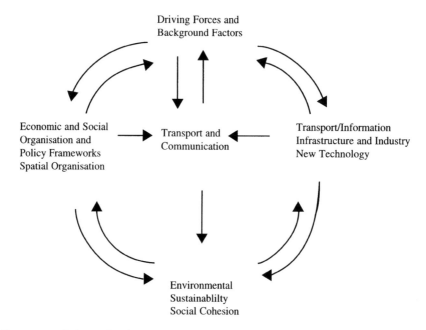

Figure 12.2   An integrative view on transport

transport infrastructure, and new technology solutions, but has only weak reverse impacts. The same position is true for social cohesion (exclusion) on various geographical scales (Van Doren, 1991). It is evident that transport and communications contribute, both to trends for the spread and differentiation between groups and to co-operation. Clearly, the global network society induces new forms of co-operation, communication, interaction, and mobility.

12.6 The policy scene for sustainable mobility

Our industrial world is in a state of flux. Industrial linkages have in the past decades increasingly assumed the form of internationally operating industrial networks, exerting a profound impact on the volume and structure of international trade (containerization and outsourcing are two examples) and service delivery. In addition to such external network developments, the transaction costs for intermediate deliveries made up an additional important motive for such changes. Transport and trade is not an autonomous force in this complex network configuration, but is influenced by both local and global drivers.

The twenty-first century will see a variety of new social and technological trends that will influence the way in which transport is supplied and utilized. At present a wide range of social phenomena, including rising incomes, increased leisure time, new communication technologies, an ageing population, and a declining role for the traditional family, are changing the nature of the demands we place on transport. In response to new techniques of production, shipping, and the growth of markets, economic activities are also changing. Institutional reforms such as privatization and deregulation have changed transport in ways that are not yet well understood. At the same time increasing use of petroleum resources for travel and transport has raised concerns about the eventual depletion of fossil fuels as well as its contribution to global warming and decreases in urban air quality. Europe and the United States are the world's major energy consumers and transport users. However, the long-term sustainability of current transport systems is increasingly being questioned as levels of motor vehicle fatalities and injuries as well as congestion continue to rise. These trends raise questions of whether our current transport systems are sustainable beyond the next half century.

It should be added that transport is not only a 'breaker' but also a 'maker' of society (Clark, 1958). Transport can open up large numbers of new opportunities for living, working, leisure, shopping, and social activities. The positive externalities of transport are to be seen as major anchor points for creative spatial economic policy in the years to come.

Transport research can be viewed as a prime example of a field where the promotion of an interdisciplinary research approach is needed. Traditionally, transport research is seen as an applied field dominated by engineering and logistics research approaches. There is, however, a need to highlight the contribution of the social, economic, and behavioural sciences to the theoretical and methodological development of research in the transport field, in particular with a view to the achievement of sustainable mobility. It is sometimes argued that recent regulatory changes do not encourage a move towards sustainable development in the transport sector.

It should be noted that there is a clear trend in current transport policies towards liberalizing European and global markets. This is caused by an increasing attention to market incentives in general, in order to improve the competitive position *vis à vis* other countries. Devolution trends seem to dominate governmental policies. There are clear trends towards privatization, deregulation, and governments 'stepping back'. Market forces seem to become more dominant in all regulated sectors. One of the well-known examples in transport is the policies to make railway companies more independent from governments; in some countries railways have been privatized (as in the United Kingdom). It may be concluded also that governments are increasingly subject to market forces and are increasingly rationalized on the basis of efficiency principles (Self, 1993).

At the same time, individualism has become a key trend in society. Individuals seem to act more and more as 'calculating citizens', who are oriented towards monetary gains and their own societal position. The influence of societal organizations (such as churches, labour unions and others) has diminished. As a result, it seems that altruistic behaviour has decreased too, which is also reflected in public policies tending to abolish subsidies for social support, and subsidies for housing of lower income groups. A consequence is that it becomes more difficult for governments to steer individuals towards forms of sustainable behaviour, while (financial) incentives and market-based interventions are becoming increasingly more important.

Traditional welfare theory argues that social welfare can be maximized through market transactions based on free exchange in perfectly operating markets. In this idealized environment, government intervention would negatively affect the Pareto-optimal outcome of a freely operating market (Coase, 1988). In practice, there is a clear role for the government in all market economies, but this influence is usually oriented towards various specific economic sectors or the fulfilment of specific socio-economic objectives (Fokkema and Nijkamp, 1994). It is often argued that the transport sector is one of those sectors which cannot be left entirely to the competence of the private sector because of the large number of externalities involved and because of equity reasons (Marcou, 1993).

In public choice theory, it is assumed that politicians are in the first place focused on re-election (Frey, 1983). Only when this is more or less secured, ideologies and altruism may come into play. Certainly in the present time, when voters seem to shift very easily from one party to another, the re-election issue receives more emphasis than in the past. This reduces the possibilities for politicians to act in an altruistic way, for example, in order to stimulate a sustainable transport policy stronger than that desired by the voters. As a consequence, it may be expected that politicians will carefully monitor and follow the opinions of their voters, who are in general not in favour of strict transport policy measures focused on sustainable mobility (Rienstra *et al.*, 1996).

At the same time, one should be aware of the large shifts in opinion of voters. As observed by Rietveld (1997), the priorities of voters may change drastically, depending on general economic conditions, unexpected disasters or threats, or other reasons. For example, in the Dutch elections in 1989 environmental issues seemed to receive less attention, and so the focus on transport policies may then also shift over time from environmental to other priorities (accessibility issues for example).

Therefore, particularly important in this respect is the voting behaviour. During election periods people may vote for parties which promise to care for social and environmental issues. However, when measures are introduced which influence the life of the voter, these measures are often strongly opposed. As a result, politicians may act in a different way during election times than after the elections. One of the basic assumptions may therefore be that 'political parties formulate policies in order to win the elections, rather than winning elections in order to formulate policies' (Downs, 1957). A result of this observation is that politicians often remain vague during election times, promise too much (credibility is also important, but only to a limited extent), and try to bind the median voters.

Another important observation is that voters may choose a party because of many relevant subjects involved. It is likely that one party is preferred for a given subject (such as financial/budgetary policy), while another party is preferred for other reasons (environment for example). A voter has to make a trade-off, and will vote for the party with the optimal mixture. A result, however, may be that the preferences of all voters are not consistent, as is witnessed by the Arrow paradox (A > B, B > C, A > C; see also Downs, 1957). This provides a politician with considerable degrees of freedom, which may be used for personal gains.

An important feature of many transport problems is the long-term impacts and the wide range of solutions that are necessary (such as infrastructure projects to solve congestion and climate change levies). Because of the short term in which elections take place, such long-term problems tend to be more or less neglected by politicians. The main reason is that it is not possible for politicians to present results of their policies before the next elections, while at the same time there are many negative impacts for their voters (restrictions on car use for example). This trend may be reinforced by the increasing impact of the media in past decades. Because individuals can be reached and informed more easily, the degrees of freedom for politicians are decreasing even more.

Also in this respect the policy cycle presented by Van Dijk (1991) is relevant. This cycle applied to transport may be as follows:

+ sustainable transport becomes a political issue (because of a disaster or new information for example);

+ the issue is taken over by politicians and it becomes an electoral issue, therefore many policy measures are promised;

+ after the elections concrete targets and instruments are proposed as an 'information battle' starts, in which lobby groups inform the policy-maker;

+ new decisions are taken; however, in the previous stage many possibilities are not regarded as acceptable, while later the issue may no longer be very relevant politically; therefore, strong measures are (often) not introduced.

The picture presented above suggests a rather weak administration that is not able to impose long-term strategies in order to solve transport problems. This may have serious consequences for policy strategies focusing sustainable mobility. Transport policy is indeed part of a complex force field.

12.7 The final word

The transport sector is a source of concern all over the world. Not only is car ownership increasing, but so is car use for a large number of purposes. The main causes of the stress on urban space as a result of the rise in transport are: the geographical structure of modern cities with their suburbs and interurban network configurations, the use of the private car as a relatively cheap and convenient vehicle for multi-purpose trips, the steady rise in welfare of consumers and households inducing new spatial movements, and the status symbolized by the car (freedom, prosperity, speed and so on). From an economic perspective, the causes of the problem may be found in the fact that the social costs of individualized forms of transport are not borne by the users (at least not sufficiently). Unfortunately, the results of intervention measures are not very impressive. More road capacity or better traffic management appears to generate more traffic. More and more cities (including Bangkok, Rome, Athens, Mexico City, Paris and Jakarta) are facing a grid-lock situation, with negative impacts on their accessibility, efficiency, quality of life, and image. Policies have thus far not led to promising achievements (ECMT, 1997). Engineers believe in the technology paradigm ('the death of distance'), economists believe in market-based financial instruments ('make them pay'), and social scientists at large believe in behavioural adjustments (social engineering). But even restrictive traffic measures cannot boost a high degree of success (let alone a high degree of public support).

The structural relationship between mobility and land use calls for new and creative polices, which may sometimes adopt the form of creative utopias. Such utopias do not only refer to the use of public transport or of bicycles, but also to subterranean forms of transport or new airships such as zeppelins. Even more interesting concepts are to be found in the use of the 'third dimension' in modern urban architecture and design, in car-free cites, and quality neighbourhoods (Banister, 1997). All such modern concepts aim to ensure a sustainable city where economic interests are brought into harmony with social and ecological interests (Capello *et al.*, 1999). Transport problems in the city are not a conflict between the mobility-rich and the mobility-poor, but essentially the outgrowth of a conflict of interest between prevailing multifaceted values of the urban inhabitants. The above observation will make it difficult to change the travel patterns of modern man, as these movements mirror their socio-economic and cultural values. Consequently, sustainable transport policy should not only be concerned with travel in a strict sense, but increasingly with lifestyles, time management of people, social interaction, and perhaps with cyberspace.

For the time being, there is hardly any successful example of sustainable transport policy. New – more sustainable – transport alternatives may be adopted by travellers but this does not necessarily mean that less sustainable forms of transport will be used less. Thus, it seems that the drive for mobility is so strong that new – more environment-friendly – options are not acting as a substitute for older forms of transport, but merely as an addition. This paradox poses formidable policy challenges, some of which we have tried to address in this book with novel methodologies and new means to package innovative policy options.

More and more, the view is growing that environmentally-benign forms of transport in the city require a portfolio of Policy Packages, based on economic incentives and disincentives, effective traffic management, ICT, upgrading of public transport, and – most of all – sustainable forms of urban land-use planning. But, underlying all the measures, the packaging and the importance of the issue, is the necessity for all participants to accept the need for change. This means all stakeholders must accept that need and be prepared to act in a more sustainable manner – this is the challenge. The alternative is also clear, namely to accept that transport is unsustainable and that there is nothing that can or should be done about it. We would strongly argue against that alternative as transport is central to sustainable development and must be seen as an integral and leading partner in change. We have also presented the means by which it is possible to move towards sustainable mobility without excessive pain. It is now up to the politicians to accept the responsibility and to respond positively to the challenge.

Note

1   Some of the material in Sections 12.1, 12.4, 12.5, 12.6 and 12.7 is adapted from Nijkamp (1998).

Abbati, C. degli (1986) Transport and European Integration. Commission of the European Communities *European Perspectives*. Brussels: The Commission.

Acutt, M. and Dodgson, J. (1996) The impact of economic policy instruments on greenhouse gas emissions from the transport sector, in Hensher, D.A. and King, J. (eds.) *World Transport Research. Proceedings of the World Conference on Transportation Research*, Vol. 2. Amsterdam: Elsevier.

Anderson, V. (1991) *Alternative Economic Indicators*. London: Routledge.

Andersson, A.E. and Strömqvist, U. (1989) The emerging C-society, in Batten, D.F. and Thord, R. (eds.) *Transportation for the Future*. Berlin: Springer, pp. 64-82.

Appleyard, D. and Lintell, M. (1969) The environmental quality of city streets: the resident perspective. *Journal of the American Planning Association*, 35, pp. 84-101.

Arthur, B. (1990) Positive feedbacks in the economy. *Scientific American*, 262(2), pp. 80-85

Arthur, B. (1996) Increasing returns and the New World of Business. *Harvard Business Review*, 74(4), pp. 100-109.

Axelrod, R. (1984) *The Evolution of Cooperation*. New York: Basic Books.

Banister, D. (1994) *Transport Planning*. London: Spon.

Banister, D. (1995) Transport and the environment. *Town Planning Review*, 66(4), pp. 453-458.

Banister, D. (1997) Reducing the need to travel. *Environment and Planning B*, 24(4), pp. 437-449.

Banister, D. (1998) Introduction: transport policy and the environment, in Banister, D. (ed.) *Transport Policy and the Environment*. London: E and FN Spon, pp. 1-16.

Banister, D. (1999) Some thoughts on a walk in the woods. *Built Environment*, 25(2), pp. 162-167.

Banister, D. (2000*a*) Sustainable urban development and transport – a Eurovision for 2020. *Transport Reviews*, **20**(1), pp. 113-130.

Banister, D. (2000*b*) The Future of Transport. Paper prepared for the RICS Research Foundation, London, January, p. 35.

Banister, D., Anderson, B. and Barrett, S. (1995) Private sector investment in transport infrastructure in Europe, in Banister, D., Capello, R. and Nijkamp, P. (eds.) *European Transport and Communications Networks – Policy Evolution and Change*. Chichester: John Wiley, pp. 191-220.

Banister, D. and Banister, C. (1995) Energy consumption in transport in Great Britain: macro level estimates. *Transportation Research A*, **29A**(1), pp. 21-32.

Banister, D. and Berechman, J. (eds.) (1993) *Transport in a Unified Europe: Policies and Challenges*. Amsterdam: Elsevier.

Banister, D. and Berechman, J. (2000) *Transport Investment and Economic Development*. London: UCL Press.

Banister, D., Dreborg, K.H., Hedberg, L., Hunhammer, S., Steen, P. and Åkerman, J. (2000) Transport policy scenarios for the EU: 2020 Images of the Future. *Innovation*, **13**(1), pp. 27-45.

Banister, D. and Marshall, S. (2000) *Encouraging Transport Alternatives: Good Practice in Reducing Travel*. London: The Stationery Office.

Barde, J-P. and Button, K. (1990) Introduction, in Barde, J-P. and Button, K. (eds.) *Transport Policy and the Environment. Six Case Studies*. London: Earthscan, pp. 1-18.

Becker, H (1997) *Social Impact Assessment*. London: UCL Press.

Bovy, P. (1995) Informatietechnologie en benutting van infrastructuur, in *Verkeerschaos en verkeershonges, perspectief op mobiliteit*. Amsterdam: SMO Informatief.

Breheny, M. (1996) Counterurbanisation and sustainable urban forms, in Brotchie, J., Batty, M., Hall, P. and Newton, P. (eds.) *Cities in Competition: The Emergence of Productive and Sustainable Cities for the 21st Century*. Melbourne: Longman Cheshire, pp. 402-429.

Bruinsma, F., Nijkamp, P. and Rietveld, P. (1991) Infrastructure and metropolitan development in an international perspective, in Vickerman, R. (ed.) *Infrastructure and Regional Development*. London: Pion, pp. 189-205.

Bruinsma, F. and Rietveld, P. (1998) *Is Transport Infrastructure Effective? Transport Infrastructure Accessibility and the Space Economy.* Berlin: Springer-Verlag.

Capello, R., Nijkamp, P. and Pepping, G. (1999) *Sustainable Cities and Energy Policies.* Berlin: Springer-Verlag.

Carlstein, T., Parkes, D. and Thrift, N. (eds.) (1978) *Timing Space and Spacing Time.* London: Edward Arnold.

Castells, M. (1996) *The Rise of the Network Society.* Oxford: Oxford University Press.

Cecchini, P. (ed.) (1989) *The European Challenge, 1992.* Aldershot: Gower.

Central Statistical Office (1997) *Annual Abstract of Statistics.* London: The Stationery Office.

Clark, C. (1958) Transport – the maker and breaker of cities. *Town Planning Review*, 28(4), pp 237-250.

Coase, R.H. (1988) *The Firm, the Market and the Law.* Chicago: The University of Chicago Press.

Commission of the European Communities (CEC) (1985) *Official Journal of the European Communities*, C 144, June 13.

Commission of the European Communities (1992a) *The Impact of Transport on the Environment: A Community Strategy for Sustainable Development.* Green Paper, DGVII. Brussels: CEC.

Commission of the European Communities (1992b) *The Future Development of the Common Transport Policy: A Global Approach to the Construction of a Community Framework for Sustainable Mobility.* Com (92) 494. Brussels: CEC.

Commission of the European Communities (1992c) *Transport and the Environment.* Luxembourg: Office for Official Publications of the European Communities.

Commission of the European Communities (1993) *Towards Sustainability. A European Community Programme of Policy and Action in Relation to the Environment and Sustainable Development (Fifth Environmental Action Plan).* Brussels: CEC.

Commission of the European Communities (1994) *Strategic Transport Glossary.* Brussels: CEC.

Commission of the European Communities (1995*a*) *The Common Transport Policy Action Programme 1995-2000*. Communication from the Commission, COM (95) 302. Brussels: CEC.

Commission of the European Communities (1995*b*) *Towards Fair and Efficient Pricing in Europe. Policy Options for Internalising the External Costs of Transport in the European Union*. Luxembourg: Office for Official Publications of the European Communities.

Commission of the European Communities (1996) *European Sustainable Cities. Report of the Expert Group on the Urban Environment*. Luxembourg: Office for Official Publications of the European Communities.

Commission for the European Communities (1997) *Intermodality and Intermodal Freight Transport in the European Union*. COM (97) 243. Brussels: CEC.

Commission of the European Communities (1998*a*) *The Common Transport Policy – Sustainable Mobility: Perspectives for the Future*. Communication from the Commission to the Council, the European Parliament, the Economic and Social Committee and the Committee of the Regions, Brussels, December, COM (98) 716 Final. Brussels: CEC.

Commission of the European Communities (1998*b*) *Communication from the Commission on Transport and CO_2 – Developing a Community Approach*. Luxembourg: Office for Official Publications of the European Communities.

Commission of the European Communities (1999) For details about the Fifth Framework Programme, including information about 'Sustainable Mobility and Intermodality' Key Action, see http://www.cordis.lu/ growth.

Commission for the European Communities (2000) *Labour Force Survey*. Luxembourg: Office for Official Publications of the European Communities/EUROSTAT.

Committee on the Medical Effects of Air Pollutants (1998) *The Quantification of the Effects of Air Pollution on Health in the United Kingdom*. London: The Stationery Office.

Daly, H. and Cobb, J. (1990) *For the Common Good – Redirecting the Economy towards Community, the Environment, and a Sustainable Future*. London: Green Print.

Department of the Environment (1996) *Indicators of Sustainable Development for the United Kingdom*. London: HMSO.

Department of the Environment, Transport and the Regions (DETR) (1997*a*) *Land Use Change in England No.12*. London: DETR.

Department of the Environment, Transport and the Regions (1997*b*) *Transport Statistics Great Britain 1997*. London: The Stationery Office.

Department of the Environment, Transport and the Regions (1997*c*) *Digest of Environmental Statistics 1997*. London: The Stationery Office.

Department of the Environment, Transport and the Regions (1997*d*) *Air Quality and Traffic Management* [LAQM. G3(97)]. London: The Stationery Office.

Department of the Environment, Transport and the Regions (1998) *A New Deal for Transport – Better for Everyone*. London: The Stationery Office.

Department of Trade and Industry (1997) *Digest of UK Energy Statistics*. London: The Stationery Office.

Downs, A. (1957) *An Economic Theory of Democracy*. New York: Harper and Row.

Dreborg, K.H. (1996) Essence of backcasting. *Futures*, **28**(9), pp. 813-828.

Dreborg, K.H., Eriksson, A. and Wouters, A. (1997) *External Scenarios for the STEEDS Decision Support System*. STEEDS Project Deliverable D2. FOA (Sweden) and AEA Technology plc. Harwell (UK). Available from http://fms.ecology.su.se.

Elvik, R. (1993) Quantified road safety targets. *Accident Analysis and Prevention*, **25**(5), pp. 569-583.

Enquete-Kommission Klima (1994) *Mobilität und Klima*. Bonn: Economica Verlag.

Eriksson, A. (1992) Strategi för att begränsa vägtrafikens koldioxidutsläpp. (Stragegies for Limiting Emissions of CO_2 from Road Traffic). TFB – Rapport 1992:29. Stockholm.

European Conference of Ministers of Transport (ECMT) (1997) *Trends in the Transport Sector*. Paris: ECMT.

European Environment Agency (1999) *EMEP/CORINAIR Atmospheric Emission Inventory Guidebook*, 2nd ed. Copenhagen: EEA.

European Investment Bank (EIB) (1991) *Briefing Series: Communications*. Luxembourg: EIB.

European Parliament (1991) *Community Policy on Transport Infrastructures.* European Parliament. Research and Development Papers, Series on Regional Policy and Transport 16. Luxembourg: European Parliament.

European Round Table of Industrialists (ERTI) (1988) *Need for Renewing Transport Infrastructure in Europe, Proposals for Improving the Decision Making Process.* Brussels: ERTI.

European Round Table of Industrialists (1990) *Missing Networks in Europe. Proposals for the Renewal of Europe's Infrastructure.* Brussels: ERTI.

EUROSTAT (1997) *EU Transports in Figures – Statistical Pocketbook.* Luxembourg: Office for Official Publications of the European Communities

Fokkema, T. and Nijkamp, P. (1994) The Changing Role of Governments: The End of Planning History? *International Journal of Transport Economics,* 21(2), pp. 127-145.

Frey, B.S. (1983) *Democratic Economic Policy: A Theoretical Introduction.* Oxford: Basil Blackwell.

Gérardin, B. (1989) *Possibilities for, and Costs of, Private and Public Investment in Transport.* European Conference of Ministers of Transport, Round Table 83. Paris: ECMT.

Gérardin, B. and Viegas, J. (1992) European Transport Infrastructure and Networks: Current Policies and Trends. Paper Presented at the NECTAR International Symposium, Amsterdam, March.

Gordon, I. (1997) Densities, urban form and travel behaviour. *Town and Country Planning,* 65(9), pp. 239-241.

Gorissen, N. (1995) Massnahmenplan Umwelt und Verkehr. Konzept für ein nachhaltig umweltverträgliches Verkehrsgeschehen im Deutschland. Vortag anlässlich der Düsseldorfer Umweltkonferenz ENVITEC, am 20 und 21 June. Berlin.

Group Transport 2000 Plus (1990) Transport in a Fast Changing Europe. Paper Commissioned by the Transport Commissioner of the European Commission (Karel van Miert), December.

Grubb, M., Vrolijk, C. and Brack, D. (1999) *The Kyoto Protocol: A Guide and Assessment.* London: Royal Institute of International Affairs/Earthscan.

Grübler, A. (1992) *The Rise and Fall of Infrastructures.* Heidelberg: Springer-Verlag.

Grübler, A. and Nakicenovic, N. (1991) *Evolution of Transport Systems: Past and Future.* Laxenburg: IIASA.

Hägerstrand, T. (1987) Human interaction and spatial mobility: retrospect and prospect, in Nijkamp, P. and Reichman, S. (eds.) *Transport Planning in a Changing World.* Aldershot: Avebury, pp. 11-28.

Hall, J.V. (1995) The role of transport control measures in jointly reducing congestion and air pollution. *Journal of Transport Economics and Policy,* **29**(1), pp. 93-103.

Hardin, G. (1968) The tragedy of the commons. *Science,* **162**, pp. 1243-1248.

Hardin, G. (1982) *Collective Action.* Baltimore: Johns Hopkins University Press.

Hart, T. (1994) Transport choices and sustainability: a review of changing trends and policies, *Urban Studies,* **31**, pp. 705-727.

Harvey, D. (1967) Models of the evolution of spatial patterns in human geography, in Chorley, J. and Haggett, P. (eds.) *Models in Geography.* London: Methuen, pp. 549-608.

Hey, C. (1996) The Incorporation of the Environmental Dimension into the Transport Policies of the EU. *EURES Discussion Paper No 50,* Freiburg.

Hey, C., Nijkamp, P, Rienstra, S.A. and Rothenberger, D. (1999) Assessing scenarios on European transport policies by means of multicriteria analysis, in Beuthe, M. and Nijkamp, P. (eds.) *New Contributions to Transportation Analysis in Europe.* Aldershot: Ashgate, pp. 171-192.

Hillman, M., Adams, J. and Whitelegg, J. (1990) *One False Move: a Study of Children's Independent Mobility.* London: Policy Studies Institute.

Himanen, V., Kasanen, P. and Lehto, M. (1996) Information transfer saves time and trouble: reduction of energy use for work related passenger transport. LINKKI Publication 10/1996, Helsinki University (in Finnish with English summary).

Hofbauer, J. and Siegmund, K. (1988) *The Theory of Evolution and Dynamical Systems.* Cambridge: Cambridge University Press.

Hörning, K.H., Gerhard, A. and Michailow, M. (1995) *Time Pioneers. Flexible Working Time and New Life Styles.* London: Polity Press.

Howard, D. (1990) Looking beyond the technical fix. *Town and Country Planning,* **59**(12), pp. 343-345.

Hunhammar, S. (1997) The Possum Dictionary. Possum WP 09/01 – 97/ESRG 11.1. Available from http://fms.ecology.su.se.

Intergovernmental Panel on Climate Change (IPCC) (1996) Technical summary in *Climate Change 1995. The Science of Climate Change.* Cambridge: IPCC.

Intergovernmental Panel on Climate Change (IPCC) (1999) *Aviation and the Global Atmosphere.* Special Report of the Intergovernmental Panel on Climate Change, Geneva. p. 12.

International Union of Railways (2000) *The Way to Sustainable Mobility – Cutting the External Costs of Transport.* Paris: UIC.

Jackson, T. and Marks, N. (1994) *Measuring Sustainable Economic Welfare – A Pilot Index: 1950-1990.* Stockholm: Stockholm Environment Institute.

Jacobs, M. (1993) *Sense and Sustainability.* London: Council for the Protection of Rural England.

Johansson, T.B., Steen, P., Fredriksson, R., and Borgen, E. (1983) Sweden beyond oil: the efficient use of energy. *Science,* **219,** pp. 355-361.

Jones, D.M. (1990) Noise, stress and human behaviour. *Environmental Health,* 98(8), pp. 206-208.

Kitamura, R., Mokhtarian, P. and Laidet, L. (1997) A micro-analysis of land use and travel in five neighbourhoods in the San Francisco Bay Area. *Transportation,* 24(2), pp. 125-158.

Kunzmann, K.R. and Wegener, M. (1991) The pattern of urbanisation in Western Europe. *Ekistics,* **350/351,** pp.282-291.

Lagendijk, A. (1994) *Internationalisation of the Automobile Industry in Spain.* Amsterdam: Thesis Publishers

Lay, M.G. (1992) *Ways of the World.* New Brunswick, NJ : Rutgers University Press.

Lönnroth, M., Johansson, T.B. and Steen, P. (1980) Sweden beyond oil: nuclear commitments and solar options. *Science,* **208,** pp. 557-563.

Lichtenthäler, D. and Pastowski, A. (1995) Least Cost Transportation Planning. Wuppertal Institute Working Paper 47. Available from www.wupperinst. org.

Maclaren, V. (1996) Urban sustainability reporting. *Journal of American Planning,* 62(2), pp. 184-202.

Maddison, D., Pearce, D., Johansson, O., Calthrop, E., Litman, T. and Verhoef, E. (1995) *Blueprint 5. The True Costs of Road Transport.* London: Earthscan.

Maggi, R., Masser, I. and Nijkamp, P. (1992) Missing networks in European transport and communications. *Transport Reviews* 12(4), pp. 311-321.

Marcou, G. (1993) Public and private sectors in the delivery of public infrastructure. *Environment and Planning C*, 11(1), pp. 1-18.

Maritime and Coastguard Agency (1997) *The Sea Empress Incident: Summary Report.* Southampton: Maritime and Coastguard Agency.

Masser, I. Svidén, O. and Wegener, M. (1992) *The Geography of Europe's Future.* London: Belhaven.

Medda, F., Nijkamp, P. and Rietveld, P. (1999) Urban industrial relocation: the theory of edge cities. *Environment & Planning B*, 26(5), pp. 751-761.

Michaelis, L. and Davidson, O. (1996) GHG mitigation in the transport sector. *Energy Policy*, 24(10/11) pp. 969-984.

Mitchell, G., May, A. and McDonald, A. (1995) PICABUE: a methodological framework for the development of indicators of sustainable develop-ment. *International Journal of Sustainable Development and World Ecology*, 2, pp. 104-123.

Moon, D. and Brand, C. (1999) *Scenario-based Framework for Modelling Transport Technology Deployment: Energy-Environment Decision Support (STEEDS).* Final Report. Harwell: AEA Technology.

Newman, P.W.G. and Kenworthy, J.F. (1989) Gasoline consumption and cities: a comparison of U.S. cities with a global survey. *Journal of the American Planning Association*, 55, pp. 24-37.

Nijkamp, P. (1994) Roads toward environmentally sustainable transport. *Transportation Research*, 28A, pp.261-271.

Nijkamp, P. (1999) Sustainable transport: new research and policy change for the next millennium. *European Review* 7(4), pp 555-567.

Nijkamp, P. and Baaijens, S. (1999) Time pioneers and travel behaviour. *Growth and Change*, 30(2), pp. 237-263.

Nijkamp, P. and Blaas, E. (1993) *Impact Analysis and Decision Support in Transportation Planning.* Boston: Kluwer.

Nijkamp, P. and Blaas, E. (1994) *Impact Assessment and Evaluation in Transportation Planning.* Dordrecht: Kluwer.

Nijkamp, P. and Rienstra, S.A. (1995) Private sector involvement in financing and operating transport infrastructure. *Annals of Regional Science,* **29**(2), pp. 221-235.

Nijkamp, P. and Rienstra, S.A. (1996) Sustainable transport in a compact city, in Jenks, M., Burton, E. and Williams, K. (eds.) *The Compact City; A Sustainable Urban Form?* London: E and FN Spon, pp. 190-199.

Nijkamp, P. and van Geenhuizen, M. (1997) European transport: challenges and opportunities. *Journal of Transport Geography,* **4**(1), pp. 3-11.

Nijkamp, P., Pepping, G. and Banister, D. (1996) *Telematics and Transport Behaviour.* Berlin: Springer Verlag.

Nijkamp, P., Reichmann, S. and Wegener, M. (eds.) (1991) *Euromobile.* Aldershot: Gower.

Nijkamp, P., Rienstra S.A. and Vleugel, J. (1998) *Transportation Planning and the Future.* Chichester: John Wiley.

Nijkamp, P., Vleugel, J.M., Maggi, R. and Masser, I. (1994) *Missing Transport Networks in Europe.* Aldershot: Avebury.

Olson, M. (1971) *The Logic of Collective Action: Public Goods and the Theory of Groups.* Cambridge, MA: Harvard University Press.

Organisation for Economic Cooperation and Development (OECD) (1988) *Transport and the Environment.* Paris: OECD.

Organisation for Economic Cooperation and Development (1991) *The State of the Environment.* Paris: OECD.

Organisation for Economic Cooperation and Development (1992) *Energy Balances of OECD Countries, 1989-1990.* Paris: OECD.

Organisation for Economic Cooperation and Development (1993) *Indicators for the Integration of Environmental Concerns into Transport Policies.* Environment Monograph No. 80. Paris: OECD.

Organisation for Economic Cooperation and Development (1997) *Energy Balances of OECD Countries, 1995-1996.* Paris: OECD.

Organisation for Economic Cooperation and Development (1998) *Environmentally Sustainable Transport - Report on Phase II of the OECD EST Project.* Volume 1. Paris: OECD.

Organisation for Economic Cooperation and Development/European Conference of Ministers of Transport (OECD/ECMT) (1995) *Urban Travel and Sustainable Development.* Paris: OECD/ECMT.

Ostrom, E. (1990) *Governing the Commons: The Evolution of Institutions for Collective Actions*. Cambridge: Cambridge University Press.

Peake, S. (1994) *Transport in Transition*. London: Earthscan.

Peake, S. and Hope, C. (1994) Sustainable mobility in context – three transport scenarios for the UK. *Transport Policy*, 1(3), pp. 195-207.

Pearce, D. (1993) *Blueprint 3: Measuring Sustainable Development*. London: Earthscan.

Pharoah, T. and Apel, D. (1996) *Transport Concepts in European Cities*. Aldershot.: Avebury.

Quinet, E. (1994) The social costs of transport: evaluation and links with internalisation policies, in OECD, *Internalising the Social Costs of Transport*. Paris: OECD, pp. 31-76.

Rienstra, S.A. (1998) *Options and Barriers for Sustainable Transport Policies: A Scenario Approach*. Rotterdam: Netherlands Economic Institute.

Rienstra, S.A., Vleugel, J.M. and Nijkamp, P. (1996) Options for sustainable transport; an assessment of policy choices. *Transportation Planning and Technology*, 19, pp. 221-233.

Rienstra, S.A., Rietveld, P. and Verhoef, E.T. (1996) The Social Support for Policy Measures in Passenger Transport: A Statistical Analysis for the Netherlands. Discussion paper TI96-117/5. Tinbergen Instituut, Amsterdam.

Rietveld, P. (1997) Political economy issues of environmentally friendly transport policies. *International Journal of Environment and Technology*, 7(3), pp. 398-416.

Rifkin, J. (1987) *Time Wars*. New York: Henry Holt.

Robinson, J.B. (1982) Energy backcasting: a proposed method of policy analysis. *Energy Policy*, 10(4), pp. 337-344.

Robinson, J.B. (1990) Futures under glass – a recipe for people who hate to predict. *Futures*, 22(8), pp. 820-842.

Ross, J.F.L. (1998) *Linking Europe – Transport Policies and Politics in the European Union*. Westport: Praeger.

Royal Commission on Environmental Pollution (RCEP) (1994) *Eighteenth Report. Transport and the Environment*. London: HMSO.

Saloman, I., Bovy, P. and Orfeuil, J.P. (eds.) (1993) *A Billion Trips a Day – Tradition and Transition in European Travel Patterns*. Dordrecht: Kluwer Academic.

Schleicher-Tappeser, R., Hey, C. and Steen, P. (1998) Policy approaches for decoupling freight transport from economic growth. *Proceedings of the Eighth World Conference on Transport Research*, Antwerp, July.

Scholl, L. Schipper, L. and Kiang, N. (1996) CO_2 emissions from passenger transport – a comparison of international trends from 1973 to 1992. *Energy Policy*, **24**(1) pp. 17-30.

Schor, J.B. (1992) *The Overworked American*. New York: Basic Books.

Schumpeter, J.A. (1934) *The Theory of Economic Development*. Oxford: Oxford University Press.

Schwartz, P. (1997) *The Art of the Long View*. Chichester: John Wiley.

Self, P. (1993) *Government by the Market; The Politics of Public Choice*. Basingstoke: Macmillan.

Standing Advisory Committee on Trunk Road Assessment (SACTRA) (1999) *Transport and the Economy*. London: The Stationery Office.

Stead, D. (1997) Environmental targets in land-use planning, in Farthing, S. (ed.) *Evaluating Local Environmental Policy*. Aldershot: Avebury, pp. 65-77.

Stead, D. (1999) Planning for Less Travel – Identifying Land Use Characteristics Associated with more Sustainable Travel Patterns. Unpublished PhD Thesis, Bartlett School of Planning, University College London, London.

Stead, D. (2000) Unsustainable Settlements, in Barton, H. (ed.) *Sustainable Communities. The Potential for Eco-Neighbourhoods*. London: Earthscan, pp. 29-45.

Stead, D. (2001) Transport intensity in Europe – indicators and trends. *Transport Policy* (forthcoming).

Steen, P., Dreborg, K.H., Henriksson, G., Hunhammar, S., Höjer, M., Rignér, J. and Åkerman, J. (1998) A Sustainable Transport System for Sweden in 2040. Paper presented at the World Conference on Transport Research, Antwerp.

Svidén, O., *Scenarios; on Expert Generated Scenarios for Long Range Infra-Structure Planning of Transportation and Energy Systems*, Linköping

Studies in Management and Economics, Dissertation No. 19, Linköping. (Available from the author).

Taylor, S.M. and Watkins, P.A. (1987) *Health Effects from Transportation Noise Reference Book*. London: Butterworth.

UK House of Lords (1995) *Report from the Select Committee on Sustainable Development*, Vol. 1. London: HMSO.

United Nations Conference on Environment and Development (1992) *The Rio-Declaration*. New York: United Nations.

Urry, J. (1995) *Consuming Places*. London: Routledge.

US Environmental Protection Agency Office of Policy, Planning and Evaluation (USEPA) (1996) *Indicators of the Environmental Impact of Transportation*. Washington: USEPA.

Van Dijk, F. (1991) Decision making about the environment: the role of information, in Kraan, D.J. and in't Veld, R.J. (eds.) *Environmental Protection: Public or Private Choice*. Dordrecht: Kluwer, pp 71-87.

Van Doren, C. (1991) *The History of Knowledge*. New York: Ballantine.

Van Geenhuizen, M., Nijkamp, P. and Black, W.R. (1999) Social Change and Sustainable Transport. Paper presented at SCAST Conference, Berkeley, March (mimeographed).

Verhoef, E.T. (1996) *The Economics of Regulating Road Transport*. Cheltenham: Edward Elgar.

Vickerman, R. (1991) Transport infrastructure in the European Community: new developments, regional implications and evaluation, in Vickerman, R.W. (ed.) *Infrastructure and Regional Development. European Research in Regional Development*, Vol.1. London: Pion, pp. 251-269.

Vickerman, R., Spiekermann, K. and Wegener, M. (1999) Accessibility and economic development in Europe. *Regional Studies*, 3(1) pp. 1-15.

Vlek, C. and Michon, J.A. (1992) Why we should and how we could decrease the use of motor vehicles in the near future? *IATTS-Research*, 15, pp. 82-93.

von Weizsäcker, E.U. and Jessinghaus, J. (1992) *Ecological Tax Reform: A Policy Proposal for Sustainable Development*. London: Zed Books.

von Weizsäcker, E.U., Lovins, A.B. and Lovins, L.H. (1997) *Factor Four: Doubling Wealth, Halving Resource Use*. London: Earthscan.

Waters, M. (1995) *Globalisation*. London: Routledge.

Wenban-Smith, H. (2000) *Urban Futures: Report of the Cities and Transport Group of the Chatham House Forum.* London: The Royal Institution of International Affairs.

Whitelegg, J. (1997) *Critical Mass. Transport, Environment and Society in the Twenty-First Century.* London: Pluto Press.

Wissenschaftlicher Berat für Globale Umweltfragen (WBGU) (1996) *Welt im Wanderk – Wege zur Lösung Globaler Umwelprobleme, Jahresgutachten.* Berlin/Heidelberg: Springer-Verlag.

World Bank (1995) The Use of Sectoral and Project Performance Indicators in Bank-financed Transport Operations. Report TWU21. Transportation, Water and Development Department, World Bank, Washington DC.

World Bank (1996) *Sustainable Transport – Priorities for Policy Reform.* Washington DC: The World Bank.

World Bank (1998) *World Development Indicators* (CD-ROM). New York: World Bank.

Zoll, R. (1988) *Zerstörung und Wiederaneignung von Zeit.* Frankfurt: Suhrkamp.